Like a Rushing Mighty Wind

Gordon Williams

by

Rev. Gordon Williams

with

Diane Roblin Lee

ISBN 1-896213-26-X

1st printing 1999
2nd printing 2002

PUBLISHED IN CANADA
By Praise Productions
R.R. #2, Woodville, Ontario, Canada K0M 2T0

PRINTED IN CANADA
By Gorden & Gordon Associates, Inc.

COVER DESIGN — Diane Roblin Lee
LOGO DESIGN — Rick and Sharon Janzen

Dedication

This book is dedicated to the Person about Whom it is written, Who has been sent to be our Counsellor by Jesus Christ and our Heavenly Father, and Who equips us with His gifts and His fruit: the Holy Spirit.

It is also dedicated to those who have faithfully encouraged me over the years in my ministry: to my wife, Ruth Williams, and children: Geoffrey, Margaret, Douglas, and Karl; to Dr. Connie den Bok; to my Board of Directors, all men of great faith: Arthur Kelly, Donald Railton, and Wayne Sproule; and to all those who have faithfully supported our ministry.

Contents

Foreword

When I think of Gordon, I think first of his most hearty laughter and I smile at the memories. Then I think of his amazing boldness for the Gospel of his Saviour and Lord, Jesus Christ, and I rejoice in the memories.

But memories speak of the past and Gordon is out there for Christ in the present. This special servant of the Lord continues to bless people everywhere, as he blessed us and the people of Canada during his seven years as a regular on the daily "100 Huntley Street" telecast.

As evidence of God's blessing through Gordon, I have in front of me a letter from Dr. Derek Duvall, B.Sc., D.D.S., of Peace River, Alberta, from whom I requested confirmation of the remarkable miracle that God gave to the little girl mentioned in the Preface of this book. Dr. Duvall, the little girl's dentist, writes, *"I hereby verify the portion of Gordon Williams' Preface to be correct regarding the changes in the girl's dentition. You may use my name with this book if needed."*

Having witnessed the transformation in his young patient, Dr. Duvall met with Gordon and shared that he, personally, had a bad back and had been in serious pain for many years. Gordon suggested that the doctor should attend one of his meetings, and so he did — that night. The doctor's back was healed, and he has run the "Iron Man Marathon" every year since! Hallelujah!

That's a tiny bit about Gordon and his Lord and Master. I recommend that you read this book and attend an event where Gordon Williams is ministering.

Rev. David Mainse,
Regular Host "100 Huntley Street" Television,
President, Crossroads Christian Communications Inc.

Excerpt From a Letter Written by Dr. Derek Duvall, B.Sc., D.D.S., dated May 1, 1981:

"I have an interesting story for you. During our lunch *(with Gordon Williams)* at the Old House Restaurant, I expressed my astonishment at faith healing. Anyhow, after considerable thought, I went ahead and asked Jesus for healing of my fifteen year lower back problem. That night, my back hurt like .... and after praying, there was no pain.

The next morning, I arose from my bed carefully. Again, no pain, although the lower back muscles were very tense. Since I run 5–10 miles every day, I would come home hurting if I ran more than 1 hour per day. I now run 25 miles with no pain, and I am entering a couple of marathon races. Not only that, but I run relatively fast (for me). How about that ... me — a member of the health profession, being healed by prayer!"

Preface

"Do you want to see what Jesus did for me?"

I looked down at the eleven-year-old freckled face smiling broadly up into my own. The face looked vaguely familiar, and I began to remember praying for the child in the previous night's prayer line.

And then it hit me. This little girl's top lip had protruded badly with very pronounced buck teeth — and here she was, just one night later, with perfectly aligned, beautiful teeth!

"He fixed them," she announced with shy pride.

The rushing, mighty wind of the Holy Spirit is blowing throughout the world today with all God's wonderful gifts of revelation, power, and utterance, enabling those who will receive Him to live and minister the abundant life that Jesus came to give!

Abundant life means full, overflowing, bountiful life. Sometimes when I let loose in a booming laugh, I see heads turn quizzically towards me with stern eyes peering over lowered glasses. However, the stifling atmosphere of a mortuary is not the intended atmosphere of a church.

Sadly, just as people usually retreat into their houses when it is windy and raining, unwilling to step out and experience the power of the elements around them, many are unwilling to open up and experience the reality of what God wants to do in their lives today through the power of His Spirit.

In my evangelistic travels throughout the denominational realm, I witness the whole gamut of reactions to the awesome work of the Holy Spirit.

Many Different Reactions to the Work of the Holy Spirit

Many are afraid. Until people have personally experienced the ministry of the Holy Spirit, they are often apprehensive — and rightly so, because the Pentecostal experience of the baptism in the Holy Spirit has occasionally been characterized by wacky antics passing for "the anointing."

Some conclude that the lack of operation of the gifts of the Holy Spirit in one's own church is proof that God no longer distributes the gifts to His people — that they are simply not in use today.

Others flatly reject interest in the gifts, proclaiming their preference for the *fruit* of the Spirit, as though Scripture holds a Chinese menu from which we can select or reject its offerings according to our own wisdom. They don't seem to understand that without the empowerment of the Holy Spirit, the development of the character of Jesus, known as the fruit of the Spirit (Galatians 5:22–23), is an uphill struggle, while it happens effortlessly when one cooperates with Him.

And then there are those who believe that the Holy Spirit was given by Jesus to empower His children to do His work on Earth until His return. Seeing the Lord respond to their desire to be totally immersed in His Person for His service is one of the most thrilling aspects of my ministry.

The Un-familiar Spirit

Amazingly, the majority of churches and pastors I meet are not familiar with the works of the Holy Spirit. To them, He is the "un-familiar Spirit." They place Him firmly and correctly in the 'Doctrine of the Trinity,' but from that point on, understanding is at best vague. With no intended rejection, they unwittingly exclude Him from their personal lives and the life of the church, totally oblivious to the richness of relationship awaiting them.

One problem has been that few teachers of the Bible have any knowledge of Greek as a foundation for really understanding Scripture. With just two or three years of Greek study, concepts that may have seemed difficult become very simple and clear. The Greek of the New Testament is colloquial Greek, which differs somewhat from the classical. Early translators thought that it must be some special form of the language because they were unable to find any other Greek like it. It turned out that it was simply the common dialect of the people of the day. It was how they talked. The Gospel was written so simply.

The Holy Spirit, although generally acknowledged, is most often ignored as a mysterious presence. His ways are perceived as shadowy intangibles. There may be some foggy recognition of Him as the "personality" of God that makes people feel warm, nice, and forgiven. However, there is little expectation of His mighty power to motivate and equip them for what Jesus Christ is calling them to do.

It is not uncommon for the work of the Holy Spirit to be misunderstood and misidentified as the work of the Devil or an evil spirit. It is easier for many to dismiss manifestations of the presence of the Holy Spirit as "just a natural human expression," than to face the challenge of coming to grips with the reality of His operation in lives today. People have been making the same mistake for 2000 years.

Pre-Acts Christians of the 21st Century

Just as the Scribes mistook the work of Jesus as the work of the Devil, *"He is possessed by Beelzebub, and by the prince of demons he casts out demons"* (Mark 3:22), many Christians mistake the work of the Holy Spirit today. They live as though the Holy Spirit had not been sent, in a pre-Acts existence. They strive in the Gospels of Matthew, Mark, Luke, and John, trying their best to follow the life modelled by Jesus.

The result is frustration, deep-seated anxiety concerning one's standing with Jesus Christ, and a prevailing sense that something is missing. It's like trying to swim by standing on the shore, making swimming motions. People need to know that a jump into the Living Water is a normal, healthy part of the Christian life — not something to fear.

Like a Rushing Mighty Wind

When Jesus first sent the Holy Spirit to us, the phenomenon was likened to the coming of a *"rushing mighty wind"* and *"there appeared to them tongues as of fire, distributed and resting on each one of them"* (Acts 2:2–3).

In John 3:8 He said: *"The wind blows wherever it pleases. You hear its sound, but you cannot tell where it comes from or where it is going. So it is with everyone born of the Spirit."*

Other incidents or "gusts" of this wind of the Holy Spirit, further to the initial "coming," are described in Acts 4:31–33, 8:14–17, 9:17, 10:44, and 19:1–7. These are extremely important to study as models for our understanding and verification of manifestations today. We need to know what the parameters were then and therefore are today.

A New Wind?

With increased manifestations of the supernatural in our society, there is tremendous spiritual confusion. People are asking, "Can the Holy Spirit do something new that is not in the Bible?"

No! Absolutely not! Never! One of the most important reasons why God gave the Bible to us was to give us a "covenant" or "contract" describing the kind of things that He will and will not do. Paul warns, *"Do not go beyond what is written. Then you will not take pride in one man over against another"*(1 Corinthians 4:6).

Spiritual pride is running rampant today throughout groups claiming "deeper revelations" and "new things." The dangers are critical at a time when even the elect are vulnerable to deception (Matthew 24:24). Christians must be firm in their understanding of the ways of the Holy Spirit as outlined by Scripture.

The Power of Salvation

The Holy Spirit was sent by Jesus to empower His people — us — to be His witnesses (Acts 1:8). If one ignores the power source of a car, he or she will not go very far. In like manner, if we ignore our God-given Power Source, how effective can our Christian life be?

Jesus' ministry had two purposes. The first was to be both the Saviour of the world and each individual's personal Saviour. John 3:16 says: *"For God so loved the world that He gave His only begotten Son, that whoever believes in Him should not perish but have everlasting life."*

But as John the Baptist explained: *"I baptize you with water for repentance, but He who is coming after me is mightier than I, whose sandals I am not worthy to carry; He will baptize you with the Holy Spirit and fire"* (Matthew 3:11).

That leads us to the second purpose of Jesus' ministry, as Baptizer with the Holy Spirit. He, Himself, said: *"Nevertheless I tell you the truth: it is to your advantage that I go away, for if I do not go away, the Counsellor will not come to you; but if I go, I will send Him to you"* (John 16:7).

How can we neglect so great a baptism any more than we can neglect so great a salvation?

In our ministry, as we have invited His presence to lead and direct us, we have witnessed the manifestation of all the gifts of the Holy Spirit to such a degree that their occasional absence is more remarkable to us than their presence. Operating in the realm of the supernatural is more natural to us than operating in the realm of tangibles. Life lived according to what we see through temporal eyes can be extremely depressing. When hope is based solely on natural expectations, there is often no hope.

Blowing out the Cobwebs

What a difference when the wind of the Holy Spirit is allowed to blow out the cobwebs and replace them with the dynamic, empowering Spirit of God, who replaces hopelessness with hope and victimization with victory!

Once people lay aside skeptical, apprehensive responses to teaching on the Holy Spirit, they usually experience a great hunger to know more.

In the course of my evangelistic and television ministry, I am continually asked:

"How can I receive the Holy Spirit?"

"How can I be baptized in the Holy Spirit?"

"Can you explain the gifts of the Holy Spirit?"

"How are the gifts of the Holy Spirit supposed to be used in my personal life and in my church?"

And so, from the basis of years of study, ministry and personal experience, the following chapters are my attempt to answer the most common questions I receive, not in an intellectual manner, but in a practical way, so that the average Christian can understand and use the "gifts" to grow to maturity in Jesus Christ.

The rushing mighty wind continues to blow — for you — today.

1

Whirlwind in my Life

I was pumped. I had been training for this fight ever since I was a little kid sparring with my dad — Howard "Kid" Williams, Canadian Welterweight Boxing Champion and two time Olympic contestant. Having turned professional following good success in both the Olympics and the Commonwealth Games, Dad was now my trainer. Although he had lost his bid for the World Championship, we knew that I would bring it home. I was his boy — "Sonny Boy Williams."

I had been raised in a gym, cutting my teeth on boxing trophies. From childhood I had never been beaten by any opponent. Every week I travelled somewhere to fight.

For this pre-Olympic trial that would determine who would go into the Canadian championship tournament, I had been in rigorous training. Everyone, including me, expected me to win.

I loved to fight. I loved to hurt people. I figured that now that I had the power of God in my life, combined with my boxing skills, nothing could stop me. I hadn't really known Jesus for very long, but it didn't even occur to me that he wouldn't care about my winning just as much as I did. I was sure that we were an unbeatable team.

In the dressing room, Dad wrapped white gauze tightly around my hands, tending to each individual finger. Despite the pre-fight electricity in the air, he took his time and made sure that the job was done right. The future was in these hands, and they would not be broken.

Massive shoulders hunched over his work, he talked to me as he bandaged. "Win, but don't be dirty," he said. "I want you to beat this guy, but don't hurt him too much." His sleeves were rolled up above his biceps, and his muscles glistened as he worked.

Finally, the gloves went on and he settled the terry robe over my shoulders with a slap on my back. I strode proudly out of the dressing room down the aisle toward the ring. The crowd went mad. I was wearing my dad's colours — purple satin shorts with a gold stripe down the side. I felt good. I was ready.

"Sonny Boy — Sonny Boy — Sonny Boy," they chanted. "Let's go, Boy!" A haze of smoke hung languidly over the tension-charged room.

I was going to beat this guy, and then would come the tournament and the Canadian championship. I could already see Olympic gold.

I jumped up into the ring and a rush of adulation from the crowd pulsed through my veins.

Dad was right behind me in the corner with last minute instructions, reminding me of all the little tricks and skills. He was a ruggedly handsome man, with that "Schwarzenegger" kind of a face. His words were soaked in the heavy aroma of chewing tobacco: "When you get in the clinch, don't forget to twist, turn, and hit." Dad was a master at boxing. He knew things that other boxers didn't know.

The bell rang. "Open up." He shoved my mouth-guard in. "Get out there and win — but don't hurt him any more than you have to." Over the years, two men had died following fights with my Dad. While he was never held responsible, he always carried the sorrow of their deaths.

A swell of anticipation rose from the crowd as my opponent jumped up to meet me in the centre of the ring. Touching gloves, I looked into his face and saw a mirror of my determination. It didn't matter. This guy could be as determined as he wanted to be, but he wasn't going to beat me.

And then the strangest thing happened. Instead of wanting to hit him, I wanted to HUG him!

Obviously, I couldn't do that. Everybody was waiting for me to hit him. My dad — "the Kid" — was watching every breath I took. What could I do?

I danced around, hitting the fellow from every direction, making sure that he didn't get hurt. Jab, dance, hit, dance, jab, twist, dance, duck, hit, dance. I worked just hard enough to assure a winning fight.

Finally, the bell split the primitive sounds of the ring. The referee moved in and held my arm high in victory. The sweat ran in rivulets down my arm and mixed with the blood splattered there from my challenger's nose. Again I felt the elation of triumph. But this time as the crowd gathered around me, slapping me on the back and telling me how great I was, it was different.

There was no eager anticipation for the next event, no feeling that I was on my way to the championship. It was over. My life was going to take a different route than my dad and I had planned.

Smiling in victorious recognition of the hearty approval all around, I made my way through the boisterous crowd; but inside, I knew that what had once been the most important aspect of my life was no longer part of me.

That night, as I went to bed, I stared at the bottom of my brother's bunk above mine. What was happening to me?

My mind turned to our youth group and all the things that had changed with me and with the group since my friend, Bob Webb, had "gotten religion."

....

Our youth group was known all over town as a place to have a good time. We had great dances in the church basement on Saturday nights.

That was until Bob, who had always been a popular guy with everyone who knew him, had gone away one weekend to a Billy Graham Crusade and had come back claiming that he had been "born again." He said that God — Jesus Christ — was now talking to him. It might have been OK if this had been some little nerd, but this was all-round great guy Bob Webb. Guys like Bob Webb weren't supposed to get spiritual. We thought that he had gone crazy.

The group had elected me president, and so everyone had expected me to deal with the influence Bob was suddenly having on the group. The situation had gotten tense.

I remembered that fateful evening when the frustration in the group had exploded in my face.

"Gord! You're our president! You've got to get rid of Bob. It's either him or us. He's too religious. If he continues to do what he's doing, we're going to leave."

As I looked around from face to face, my eyes had been met by angry, challenging stares.

"What are you going to do?" In frustrated agitation, the normally carefree teenagers had surrounded me, shifting from foot to foot, crossing their arms and demanding satisfaction. I knew that unless I acted quickly, I would be the next focus of their scorn.

These were my friends. I had grown up in this church in Kirkland Lake and had been part of this group ever since Wolf Cub membership had required my attendance at Sunday school. While the church had had many fine leaders, they didn't know how to direct young people into a relationship with Jesus.

It was no secret that our youth group didn't have any real "religious" interest. Until that time, our greatest problem had been getting volunteers to "do devotions," which, we had been informed, was a necessary part of our program.

As president, I was sure that I had, however, handled the whole situation brilliantly. I had solved our devotions problem by putting Bob in charge. After all, it had let the rest of us off the hook and seemed to make sense to me. What else was a president supposed to do when someone in a church group suddenly became "religious'

The problem had arisen when devotions à la Bob had become much more than the hasty, superficial lip service to which we had become accustomed.

Each week, Bob would come to our meeting, sit down, and open his Bible. He would wait patiently until we could no longer put off devotions. As soon as I would apprehensively turn the meeting over to him, he would eagerly read a passage to us and then proceed to tell us what he thought it meant. Then, Bible still in hand, he would feel compelled to share what God — Jesus Christ, he called Him — had been talking to him about that week.

For almost three months, every meeting had ended in the same way — with a big argument. That night, however, had been the last straw.

Playing the role, I had told everyone to calm down and assured them that I would handle the situation. Inside, I was asking myself, "Oh yeah, smart guy? What are you gonna do now?" I realized that I was going to have to confront Bob with the problem.

I went to him and suggested that we should go into the church lounge to discuss the obvious problem.

Closing the door, I straightforwardly told him what the others had said and then said, "I'm sorry, Bob, but you're going to have to stop doing the devotions." He listened quietly and then, locking his penetrating blue eyes with mine, stared me squarely in the eyes. Pointing his finger directly in my face, he boldly said, "Gord, if you haven't tried it, don't knock it."

In those days, I liked nothing better than the challenge of proving someone wrong. Figuring that Bob's time had come, I decided to put him to the test and challenged, "Bob, you're the only person I've ever met who claims that God — Jesus Christ — talks to you. How do you get that relationship or friendship with Him?"

He did not hesitate.

"Well, Gord," he responded with rock-solid confidence, "it's very simple. All you have to do is call on the name of Jesus. Even though you cannot see Him, He'll be there."

Now that did not make any sense at all. How can you talk to someone whom you cannot see — someone who might be miles away?

Bob continued. "Just ask Him to forgive you for any sin or wrong that you have done."

Well, at least that sounded reasonable. As I considered the kind of day it had been, I could think of a few things that I had done wrong. Asking forgiveness wouldn't be hard.

The next instruction, however, made no sense at all. "Then invite Him to come into your life and heart."

Now, if there really was a God out there, He would obviously be a lot bigger than I. Would it not make a lot more sense for me to climb inside of Him than for Him to climb inside of me? Nevertheless, I agreed, "OK, what else?"

"Nothing. That's all there is to it," he said.

"Do you mean that a short, small prayer like that is going to get me into a talking relationship with God - I mean with Jesus Christ?"

Bob said, "Gord, you're smarter than the average. You got it right the first time!"

Despite my skepticism, I was willing to give Bob the benefit of the doubt. If I were to disprove him, I would have to do it on his terms. Thus, thinking that I would have to assume some sort of religious position in order to give it a fair chance, I asked, "Do you do this kneeling or standing?"

Grinning, he replied, "You can do it either way."

I said, "Fine, I'll do it sitting."

"Okay," he agreed.

Then, without warning, Bob got all intense and a weird look came into his eyes. (Since then, I've come to recognize "the look." It is the look that a Christian gets when he thinks that he's got somebody on the hook.) "Can I pray with you?" he asked.

"No way," I shook my head. I wasn't going to let any Christian work me into an emotional state and then take advantage of my decision-making process. "If this works," I said, "it will work when I'm alone."

"You're right," he nodded, as he walked out of the lounge. I listened to his retreating footsteps as he made his way towards the outside door. As it clattered closed behind him and the sound echoed through the recesses of the empty building, I knew that I was alone.

I sat down on a chair, feeling profoundly strange and solitary, yet exposed within the four walls. As a person of reasonable integrity, I knew that I had to give this a fair shot, but I felt awkward because I realized that I had never talked to God like this before. Nevertheless, I began to attempt to pray as Bob had instructed.

"Uh ... uh ... Jesus ... ." What was it I was supposed to say? I had to start over again. Collecting myself, I managed to rattle off Bob's suggested formula.

Having prayed "the prayer," I sat and waited, still without any real expectation of response. After almost half an hour of sitting in total silence, I finally decided to get up and leave. I wasn't going to pray again. This was a one-shot deal.

It was then that it happened. Something very warm started at the top of my head and physically filled every cell of my being right through to the soles of my feet.

I know now that what I was experiencing then was the Holy Spirit in accordance with John 3:5–7: *"Jesus answered, 'I tell you the truth, no one can enter the Kingdom of God unless he is born of water and the Spirit. Flesh gives birth to flesh, but the Spirit gives birth to spirit. You should not be surprised at my saying, "You must be born again."'"*

I was "born again" and "baptized in the Holy Spirit" — whoosh — all at once. I knew that Jesus had washed me from the inside out, forgiving me and cleansing me from the guilt of every sin I had ever committed. He made me a brand-new person. (I'll detail this experience in Chapter 6. What I didn't realize, at the time, was that I had been given the gift of interpretation of tongues, so that when a message in tongues would be given by someone else, I would know exactly what was being said.)

What happened next was overwhelming. I discovered that Jesus can talk. The most beautiful voice I have ever heard began to speak to me. Although I could not see Him, I knew it was Jesus talking, telling me that He had some things He wanted me to do. He said He had a plan for my life and He would show it to me. He wanted me to follow Him and do the work He had for me to do. He told me that He wanted to lead me into ministry.

I had no recollection of how I got home that night. I simply remembered having a deep assurance that if I were to die, I would go to Heaven.

I remembered looking in the mirror the next morning. I was physically changed (still as handsome as ever — just happier and healthier looking!). Then I remembered Jesus calling me into ministry, and I began to get nervous. I didn't like that idea at all.

I was going to be a boxer.

The plans for my life had already been made. Ministry had no place in those plans. I told God that I would do anything He wanted me to do. I would be the best layman in the church, but I didn't want to be a minister. I had seen the way people treated ministers and I didn't want any part of it.

Although I continued to be involved in the church and, with Bob, saw many from the youth group accept Jesus as their Saviour, I was determined to be simply the best Christian I could possibly be.

There was no way that I was going to take any steps toward the ministry. When revival broke out in our church under the ministry of a new Scottish pastor, Rev. Ben Morwood, I actively participated as much as any of the others — but no more.

That is not to say I wasn't excited about having the Lord in my life. I was more than enthusiastic. I was downright loud, running around talking to anybody who would listen to me tell about Jesus and what He was doing in the life of our church.

We were in the midst of a revival and it was exciting! As a matter of fact, when one of our well-meaning, mature elders cornered me and warned, "Gordon, I hate to have to tell you this, but, after a few months, maybe a few weeks, well, maybe a few days, you are going to come down and be like the rest of us," I looked at him as though he was from another planet.

I knew that he was wrong. I knew that Christians who continue to witness to others about Jesus and demonstrate the power of the Holy Spirit could never dry up. They would simply get more and more excited.

What I didn't understand at the time was that many Christians who accept Jesus as their Saviour are very excited at first, but they can't sustain that excitement without the baptism in the Holy Spirit to empower them. I didn't realize that my good friend, Bob Webb, was one such Christian. (Years later, Bob showed up at a Full Gospel Business Men's meeting in Timmins, Ontario. Praying for him and seeing the Lord fill him with the Holy Spirit in a powerful renewal was one of the most thrilling experiences in my ministry.)

But for then, I lived the Christian life on my own terms. I loved to witness, to read my Bible, and to pray. I was happy to do anything that fit the way I wanted to live.

Ministry didn't fit.

I'd simply decided to take Jesus on as my sparring partner. I'd let Him make me even stronger than I was before and, hey — with His supernatural ability — we couldn't lose.

Until I got into the ring that day, I didn't know that that wasn't the way God worked.

....

I rolled over in my bunk. What was happening to me? Refusing to face the call on my life, I went to sleep.

In my heart, I knew the score, and I began to run away from God. From that time, I kept running from the ministry for four and a half years.

When I heard about a Christian psychiatrist who specialized in using psychological tools that could help people discover the capacity in which they would be most effective serving the Lord, I determined to go to the retreat centre where he worked. I committed to spending the month required for the testing as a means to get the Lord off of my back. I knew that I had neither the intellect nor the ability to be a minister, and I figured that this test would prove my position to God.

That month at the retreat centre was a remarkable time. Every three hours, a bell would ring calling the residents to prayer. No Christian could dream of an environment more pleasant and conducive to growth in the Lord. At the end of the month, the psychiatrist called me into his office with my results. Among other possibilities, he told me that I was suited for the ministry. Foiled again.

By the time I went home, our non-religious youth group had been transformed into a powerful, dynamic group of young people on fire for Jesus Christ. Most of us were walking, talking miracles. We went to church expecting to meet with God and consequently did not leave disappointed. Lives were changed just as the New Testament describes. We had awesome prayer meetings and Bible studies together.

One night, after our whole youth group had read the entire Book of John out loud to each other, I walked home. It was late, and I walked softly up the creaking steps in order to avoid waking my mother. No matter how soft my footsteps, however, the boards creaked and groaned under my weight. Nevertheless, I managed to undress, turn the light off, and get into bed without making a disturbance.

Just as I was drifting off to sleep, I had an awareness of someone opening our front door. As one of five boys, I foggily assumed that it was one of my brothers coming home. The steps began to creak as he started to come upstairs. My bedroom door opened, and the light came on. I heard someone say my name: "Gordon ... Gordon ... Gordon ... ."

I sat up and, much to my surprise, saw a stranger standing at my bedside. As I looked up, I had a sense of knowing this person, but couldn't place who it was. It was a very ordinary man, wearing ordinary clothes, a thirty-something-year-old stranger who I felt was someone very close to me. Despite the bizarre scenario, I had no sense of fear or apprehension. As He began to talk to me about my life, I realized that Jesus was standing beside me.

He told me that He wanted me to work for Him and to become a fisher of men. He promised that if I would work for Him, He would meet all my needs according to His riches in Glory.

Face to face, I told Jesus that I would be honoured to work for Him.

As He began to leave, He turned and thanked me.

I heard the footsteps retreat down the stairs to the door. The door opened and closed, and He was gone, yet still with me. I sat there on my bed with a peace that I had never before known. My brother woke up and asked me to turn the light off. As I got up to turn it off, I silently thanked Jesus for remembering the "Thomases" of this world who have to see to believe.

In contemplation of the experience in the ensuing years, I know that I have seen that face many times in crowds, often in churches or somewhere where I'm ministering. Curious to know how unique my encounter was, I have quizzed many associates since about how they were called into the ministry and have found many who have had similar experiences but have resisted sharing them for fear of criticism and disbelief.

Every shred of resistance to God's calling on my life was now replaced by a calm yet relentless assurance that the path ahead led directly into ministering God's Word to a waiting world.

The only problem seemed to be the realities that surrounded me.

Although I had graduated from high school with a commercial diploma, I lacked three essential things: the qualifications to get into university, the funding necessary to take me very far, and any confidence in my abilities to succeed.

Enter Miss Hazel Grimmon, high school English teacher and member of our church, whom Jesus used mightily to fulfill His purposes in my life.

Miss Grimmon was a gentle woman who never married. Where others doubted the validity of my calling, she looked at me through the eyes of Jesus and always had a word of encouragement on her tongue. She saw the spiritual and natural potential Jesus had planted in me and was determined to draw it out.

When I returned to school in order to upgrade myself, she spent hours after school tutoring me in English grammar and spelling. No pushover, she demanded excellence, just as she said God did. She was soft-spoken yet strong. Despite the fact that she could cut down the toughest and rudest person with a withering glance and a just-above-a-whisper reprimand, she always seemed to know when a student needed that gentle touch. And, oh, how she loved Jesus Christ!

Next to God, I feared only this little woman who cared for me and who fanned the fire of God in me. From her I learned how to receive Communion. I watched one day while she was eating the bread and drinking the wine and saw her become "aglow in the Spirit." I thought that

Moses must have looked like that when he came down from Mount Sinai. Miss Grimmon was an awesome lady.

She set the goal of an 'A' grade for me (to the howls of laughter of my friends). There were many in our congregation who scorned the idea that Jesus Christ would call a young man like me into full-time ministry. Should they ever voice their opinions in Miss Grimmon's presence, however, they would never dare do it again. More than once I heard how she would give them a list of reasons detailing why God could not do anything else.

With my high school prerequisites and university acceptance finally tucked under my arm, I sold everything and, with proceeds of $150.00 from the sale, I left for university, trusting Jesus to supply my need. Upon graduation, I was debt-free.

I kept in touch with Miss Grimmon throughout university. When I decided to get married, I took Ruth to meet her. Somehow, her approval had come to mean confirmation to me that what I was doing was right in the centre of God's will. This time, I was not surprised at her obvious pleasure with my choice.

Following graduation from Sir Wilfred Laurier University, I was praying about where God wanted me to go to seminary. I had been accepted at several.

On a visit home, I wanted to see my favourite teacher. Of course, with Miss Grimmon, one never just dropped in. A call had to be made and an appointment arranged for Ruth and me to join her for tea. No matter how much I loved Miss Grimmon, I was always nervous in her presence. I remember sitting on the edge of my chair, precariously balancing my teacup and saucer in one hand and my cookie in the other. In spite of the fact that she had suggested that I call her Hazel, I never could summon the courage to assume such informality.

"Well now, Gordon, which seminary will you be attending?" she inquired, penetrating every fibre of my being with her piercing green eyes.

I explained that I had been accepted at several, including Princeton Theological Seminary.

At the name *Princeton*, she sat up straighter than I had ever seen her sit, widened her eyes to their full extent, and exclaimed, "Well, of course, you will go to Princeton!"

"No." I explained that finances would not permit a Princeton education.

"I shall loan you the necessary money, interest-free. You may repay me when you have graduated," she lovingly declared.

My arrival at Princeton with Ruth in 1964 was the first step in a trail of miracles there. Many of the students we met were excited because of something "new" (which wasn't really new at all), something that they called the "charismatic movement of the Holy Spirit." They told us that the Holy Spirit was being poured out into individuals and churches there just as He had been almost 2000 years before, according to the Book of Acts and Paul's Letters to the churches of the New Testament.

That was not news to Ruth and me. Our experiences in Canada with the Holy Spirit and our very presence at Princeton were a living witness to the supernatural reality of God and His vital workings in contemporary life. What was wonderful news to us was that the Family of God was vibrantly alive even here, so far from home. We were filled with eager anticipation at the realization that God had provided a way for us to prepare for His ministry in such a spiritually stimulating environment.

Princeton Seminary was so exciting. It had some of the best teachers available anywhere.

One of my professors, Dr. Bruce Metzger, was the finest Greek scholar in the world. He was behind the translation of the Revised Standard Version of the Bible. Until I understood his teaching method, however, sitting in his class was disappointing. It was like sitting in a Sunday school class where he explained, in terms that any child could understand, what the Scripture was saying. He would tell us, "This is what you have to do, because this is what it said to the people then." We didn't have to uncover layers of religious theology in order to find the essence of truth and reality.

(The most recent head of the Greek Department at Princeton is presently (1999) giving leadership in the translation of the Dead Sea Scrolls. He claims that the Dead Sea Scrolls prove beyond a shadow of a doubt that all the New Testament documents were written before the year 70 A.D. (Until now, the thinking had been that they could have been written anywhere up to the year 300 A.D. Now they know that the entire New Testament was written before the fall of Jerusalem.)

I am not afraid of education, but I am afraid of ignorance.

These were simple men of prayer. One of them used to tell us that the pastor has to be the smartest man in town, because he always has to have a reason ready for what he believes.

Throughout the three years of challenging yet practical seminary study, Ruth and I and our children (one, then two, and then suddenly four with a set of twins!) experienced God's faithfulness over and over again in providing for us in terms of money, health, protection, and the meeting of all our needs according to *"His riches in glory"* (Philippians 4:19) as He promised to do.

At one point, the rent on our seminary apartment began to fall behind. With a growing family, the reality of expenses had exceeded our financial projections. I had taken a position as student pastor in an all-black congregation, Weequahic Presbyterian Church in Newark, New Jersey, and one day, when I was at the church, I ripped my suit pants on a protruding nail. With only one suit to my name and the obvious impossibility of mending it, I felt as though I had surely reached the end of my rope. I knew that the housing office would be calling me and there was no money for anything, much less a new suit. Despite my prayers to God to supply our needs, things appeared to be going from bad to worse.

The next day, the housing office called and told me that I needed to go in to see the administrator. I didn't know what on earth I would ever say to him. I had no money to pay the rent. When I arrived, I was ushered into his office.

Without looking up at me, the administrator continued to work and simply said, "Gordon Williams?"

"Yes," I responded.

"Here's something from someone who wishes to remain anonymous." He handed me a sealed envelope without one word about the delinquent rent.

I thanked him and left, opening the envelope in excited curiosity as I walked out. One hundred dollars!

A million dollars would not have meant one iota more to me in that instant of recognizing God's provision for a new suit.

The dreaded call about the rent simply never came. Several months later, the administrator simply said, "I see you've been having some trouble keeping up with your rent. Don't worry about it. We'll just keep track of what you owe, and then when you're out in ministry, you can pay it back."

Following my first year, when the President of Princeton Theological Seminary, Dr. James McCord, heard that I wasn't going to return because of a lack of finances, he telephoned and said, "You're one of my students and you should return. The Lord will provide."

I said, "You don't understand..."

He said, "No, no, no. You don't understand. I said, 'The Lord *will* provide.'" And He did.

Perhaps even more than my formal studies, the evidence of God's practical workings in our lives through those years prepared us for the supernatural Christian ministry into which we were led.

Shortly after graduation, a gift came in the mail for an amount exactly equal to what was owed for our seminary rent. While God's timing may be different than ours, it is better. Through having to wait, we learned never to give up on God and that He is always faithful to fulfill His promises. Tension and worry are fruitless exercises because God's answer is always somehow on the way. He cares about every detail of our lives.

Following my ordination, I wrote to thank Miss Grimmon and to assure her that at the start of the New Year we would begin to pay back her generous loan. It wasn't long until we received a Christmas card with a cancelled note inside for the full amount of money she had loaned us. The only condition attached was that we would help and encourage others as she had done for us.

Commissioned by both God and Miss Grimmon, our course was set.

2

What's Normal in a Relationship with Jesus?

"All of these must be done for the strengthening of the church."
(1 Corinthians 14:26)

The spiritually stimulating atmosphere of Princeton prepared me well for ministry. The so-called "charismatic movement" I encountered there did not seem strange to me. It was simply an arena within which the Holy Spirit was doing the work that Jesus had said He would do. It was "normal," according to what I read in the Bible. Nothing that I had experienced was anything new in a relationship with Jesus — exciting, supernatural, extraordinary — yes, but new? No, just normal.

I had experienced the "rushing mighty wind" in my own life, and I knew that it was still blowing, just as it had in the Upper Room at Pentecost. I believed that faith in God without expectations of manifestations of His presence would, according to Scripture, be simply, *"a form of godliness denying the power thereof"* (2 Timothy 3:5).

The Quest for a Standard

In the course of my evangelistic travels, one of the most frequently asked questions I hear is, "Gord, what is a 'normal' relationship with Jesus supposed to be like?" People like to feel that they are normal — that what they are doing falls within the range of acceptable behaviour.

Generally, the people who ask this question are people who have known Jesus as their Saviour for some time but are not satisfied with the depth of their relationship with Him. They read the Bible and its accounts of the First Church and are troubled by the differences between the experiences of early believers and what they experience in their own churches. They almost always express a feeling that "something is missing" in their own lives, and they don't know how to tap into the powerful life that is supposed to be available to them as Christians. They want reassurance that they're on the right track and that what they see in the Bible as "normal" is still normal for a relationship with Jesus today.

With so many denominations and divergent expressions of worship vying to be regarded as the standard, the question "what is normal?" is valid. More than that, the question is pivotal, because unless we are willing to receive the standard of what is "normal" from Jesus Himself through Scripture, one's understanding becomes simply a subjective opinion based on experience, culture, and personal biases — a meaningless framework within which to relate to God.

The term "normal," when applied to a relationship with Jesus, therefore, must refer to the range of behaviour acceptable to Jesus, rather than to the opinions of people. Before focusing on what is normal, however, we must first of all understand what is abnormal.

The Abnormal Christian Life

While other religions are built upon humanly devised beliefs constructed to somehow reach God, true

Christianity is simply built on a relationship — a personal relationship with Jesus.

When people accept the general beliefs of Christianity but fail to enter into that intimate, personal relationship with Jesus where they listen for His voice and truly seek to follow Him, what they inevitably experience is abnormal spiritual behaviour.

Many churches are full of people leading dull, boring, so-called "Christian" lives. Rather than looking for opportunities to serve Jesus, these people look for opportunities to avoid Him. Rather than looking forward to exciting services of worship where they can experience the power and presence of God, they look for excuses to do other things. Instead of going to church expecting miracles, they anticipate the tedium of fulfilling their responsibilities of church attendance. Unfortunately, their expectations of boredom are usually met. In sharp contrast to the thrilling accounts of the Early Church, this dead religion has little to do with knowing Jesus. They conclude that going to Heaven is the reward for doing boring things in a church and successfully keeping rules and commandments.

Tragically, multitudes of people reject any interest in Jesus because they want nothing to do with the powerless, tradition-filled organizations which masquerade as Christian churches. Their curiosity is not only unaroused, it is downright squashed by the musty aroma exuded by the various establishments. These people don't understand that what they are seeing is simply a pale, sickly reflection of the powerful reality of the true Christian church. They are witnessing "abnormal" Christianity.

At the other end of the continuum are churches which are permeated by very strange people doing flaky things that were never sanctioned by biblical examples — another example of people manifesting abnormal spirituality. Over and over again, throughout history, true revivals have taken place where God's presence is unquestioned through powerful manifestations of His Holy Spirit. While they are true moves of God, these revivals are invariably accompanied by counterfeit manifestations of power sent by Satan to confuse and deceive Christians.

Non-Christians, often with more common sense than some experience-hungry Christians, shake their heads in disbelief at the crazy contortions not only manifested, but misguidedly encouraged and lauded by many people, who should know better, during times of revival. Anyone with any discernment can sense that what they are seeing is "off the wall." While some of the aspects of early Christianity, like tongues and being "slain in the Spirit'"(which will be addressed in later chapters), may seem strange to many people, we know that they are acceptable because the Bible says they are. The problem arises when spiritually flaky people embrace crazy manifestations of the spirit realm that are not modelled for us in the Bible. Even non-believers know that this is abnormal behaviour. Unfortunately, what most often happens is they throw the "baby out with the bath water," rejecting both a normal and an abnormal relationship with Jesus Christ.

Thankfully, I grew up in a church that experienced a renewal or revival when I was a young teenager. Had I not seen the reality of God's presence in our services, I, too, might have been trapped in a life of boring traditionalism — but I don't think so. Because I am a practical person who enjoys living life to the fullest and because I had other options open to me in life, I was probably less likely to drift into a boring, "religious" lifestyle than someone with a less aggressive, demanding personality. Had I not seen a definite change in Bob Webb's life, I would not have had my curiosity piqued enough to try to disprove him. Without that curiosity in my life, Jesus would not have had the opportunity to reveal Himself to me.

A Normal Relationship with Jesus According to Scripture

A normal relationship with Jesus is the most exciting, profitable life there is. Those who truly allow the Holy Spirit to lead them live lives of great adventure.

For a number of years, I was a regular host and sometime producer of "Nite Lite," a live, two-hour, open-line Christian television talk show.

One night, an anguished listener called in and said, "My name is Bruce Christopher. I was a Christian once. I even went to Bible College. I sinned really bad. I've been running away from the Lord. I became a professional pool player. I'm just about the best there is, but I feel empty. Is there any hope for me? Have I sinned too much to be saved? Have I committed the unpardonable sin?"

As he poured out his story, he told of the success he had achieved in his sport that was far beyond that of most people. He had reached World Champion status and had become known as Bruce "Super Stroke" Christopher. As he talked, it became obvious that he had not achieved all his success on his own. Although he had abandoned Jesus, Jesus had been right beside him, guiding him through his successes and failures, right up to this moment of decision. I assured Bruce that because of the guilt, regret, and pain so alive in his voice, he was certainly not beyond the reach of Jesus Christ. He was what the Bible calls a "prodigal son." I invited him to pray with me in order to rededicate his life to Jesus Christ and get on with God's plan for his life.

He eagerly agreed through tears of repentance. We prayed. Jesus forgave him, and Bruce expressed great relief in finally feeling clean.

I explained to him that all his sins had now been forgiven by Jesus and that every sin he had ever committed had now been removed from his record in Heaven. "God no longer has any record of them," I said. "Whenever you remember something that you did wrong in the past, the memory is not meant to make you feel guilty. It is a reminder for you to say, 'Thank you, Jesus, for reminding me that You have forgiven me for that sin.'" I encouraged him to read his Bible every day, pray, and find a good church where he would fit in. With no knowledge of where it would really lead, I told him that Jesus would now be able to use his skill at pool to save others.

He thanked me as I hung up the phone to take the next caller.

Several months later, I received another call from Bruce. His life was going much better now that he had turned it over to Jesus. "Would you be interested in coming to a $50,000.00 Pool Shoot Out in Toronto at the Royal York Hotel?" he asked. "I'll be shooting against Minnesota Fats." Anyone who has spent some misspent hours in a pool room knows that Minnesota Fats was the best pool player in the world. "Fats is like a father to me," he volunteered.

"I'd love to come," I answered, almost without thinking. I had always wanted to see Minnesota Fats play in person and to meet him if ever possible.

"I'll send you an invitation in the mail. It's a formal dress occasion, so you'll have to wear a tuxedo. I'll have one waiting for you in a hotel room which I'll reserve for your use," Bruce explained.

The night finally arrived. I was a little nervous. As I struggled with the bow tie, the thought crossed my mind that I had never before worn a tuxedo. Finally, I looked in the mirror to assess my transformation. "I was one good looking dude," I thought as I straightened the coat and smiled approvingly at my reflection. This was an evening I would enjoy.

The room was filled with about two hundred and fifty invited guests dressed in tuxedos or brightly coloured formal dresses, both long and cocktail length. There were T.V. cameras and crews scattered around the table that was the focus of everyone's attention. Anxious radio interviewers and newspaper reporters waited like hungry wolves for Super Stroke and Minnesota Fats.

They didn't have to wait long. When the two appeared, the cameras rolled, flashes popped, and microphones were thrust into the faces of the two challengers.

Five mayors of various Ontario towns, including the city of Toronto, made welcoming speeches and gave presentations.

Minnesota Fats was very verbal and he always managed to get the last word. He had a tremendous sense of humour that he had developed over all the years of pool halls and tournaments. I liked him immediately. He and Bruce, dressed in their tuxedos, looked like two polite gentlemen, rather than the two fierce, funny, and deadly serious competitors they were to become with the breaking of the first rack of balls.

It was when the rules of the Shoot Out were announced that I realized that this was not going to be an hour or two of friendly competition. The winner had to win the best of twenty-one games of straight pool. I could see that this was going to be an all-night affair.

They began to shoot. Both were spectacular. Their balls careened off the cushions. Their skill was unequalled. First, Bruce was in the lead. Then Minnesota Fats was in the lead. Back and forth it went. They made every impossible shot that every after-school-would-be-pool-player dreams of making but never does. It was breathtaking to watch.

After an hour of shooting, the play stopped so that the reporters could do more interviewing. It was about that time that I began to talk with Jesus. "Lord," I asked, "what in the world am I doing here?"

The answer was not long in coming. After the Press had finished, Bruce made an announcement to everybody: "Now, before we resume our game, I want to invite a friend of mine from '100 Huntley Street,' Gordon Williams, to come and share with us for a few minutes."

I was momentarily speechless. Then I took my "cue" from the Holy Spirit and stepped up to the pool table.

In the space of about seven minutes, I shared with the two hundred and fifty invited guests about the first night that I invited Jesus to come into my life and how He had been guiding me ever since. I concluded by saying, "Perhaps there may be some of you here tonight who have never invited Jesus Christ to come into your life. You do not have the promise that if you were to die tonight, you would go straight to Heaven. If not, I am going to invite you to pray a simple prayer with me right here while we stand around this pool table. This prayer is similar to the one I prayed that first night so that, like me, you can know Jesus Christ personally as your Saviour and Lord, have the right to go to Heaven, and discover God's plan for your life."

I bowed my head and began to pray, "Dear Lord Jesus..."

People all over that large room followed my lead, saying, "Dear Lord Jesus."

"Please forgive me for any sin or wrong that I have done," I said.

"Please forgive me for any sin or wrong that I have done," they repeated. I heard a gruff voice behind me praying along with the rest. Now I don't generally open my eyes to see who is praying, but I did that night. I turned a bit and saw Minnesota Fats praying the Sinner's Prayer along with me and many others in that room.

"Please come into my heart and my life. Amen." I assured any who had prayed that prayer that they were now saved and had the promise of Heaven.

Then I stepped aside and walked to the back of the room. Minnesota Fats and Super Stroke resumed their play. People began to come to talk to me. One young woman in her mid-twenties approached me from the left side of the room. From the opposite side came a young man in his mid-twenties. They looked at each other, looked at me, and then looked at each other once again. The young woman spoke softly, with tears in her eyes, to the young man. "I just invited Jesus to come into my heart, and He told me that we can no longer live together."

"I know," said the young man as his tears began to well up. "He just told me the same thing."

People from all over that room came to tell me that they had prayed along with me and that Jesus had forgiven them. They had assurance of their salvation.

As far as the game was concerned, it ended in a tie. Some were disappointed, but the two were so evenly matched that there was no other way it could have ended. Bruce called to tell me that when they were driving Minnesota Fats to the airport, he turned to Bruce and said, "Bruce, I just want to tell you one thing. I prayed that prayer with your preacher, and I meant it."

Although Minnesota Fats didn't win the game that night, Jesus won him and many other people for whom He had paid the price in another more serious game on the Cross of Calvary. Minnesota Fats looked forward to Heaven. He often joked, "St. Peter, rack 'em up!" That's how an old, saved pool player lets people know he's become a born again Christian.

That was 1984. Minnesota Fats died and was buried on Saturday, Jan. 20, 1996. He has gone to Heaven. That is so exciting to me!

It was quite an experience to see a man like that receive Jesus as his Saviour and Lord. It will be even more exciting to see him in the Throne Room of Heaven. If there is a pool table somewhere in the New Jerusalem, I'm absolutely certain that you'll hear that gruff voice saying, "St. Peter, rack 'em up."

That was an adventure that I never would have had, had I not listened and been obedient when God opened a door. It was an incredible time when I think of the people who were saved in those most unusual circumstances, and yet it was just part of the normal Christian life — a life of challenges and opportunities with eternal significance.

While salvation is the greatest gift, the normal Christian life is rich in gifts of the Holy Spirit.

Recognition of normalcy with regard to a relationship with Jesus has to be measured by the unchangeable Word of God, rather than by men's traditions or by philosophies of the day. The range of acceptable behaviour has to be defined by God rather than by man, because God is the author of our faith.

A normal walk with Jesus involves experiencing daily, in our lives and churches, what we read about in the New Testament . Orderly, acceptable worship still requires manifestation of the gifts of the Spirit, just as it did in the model established for us in the 14th chapter of 1st Corinthians: *"All of these must be done for the strengthening of the Church"* (vs. 26). It is abnormal to expect anything less.

Throughout the centuries, people have tried to write off important aspects of the normal Christian life, calling the baptism and gifts of the Holy Spirit a "passing phase" or "meaningless emotionalism." Nevertheless, they remain. Without these charismatic elements, people slump back into the boredom and unfaithfulness of the abnormal Christian life.

Thus, the range of normalcy includes anything and everything that happened within the context of the ministry of Jesus and the New Testament apostles, and that includes some very unnatural, even bizarre, behaviour by worldly standards.

Are Denominations "Normal?"

People tend to feel most comfortable when they can put things into boxes. Attempting to categorize Christians as evangelical, charismatic, conservative, fundamentalist, liberal, or whatever serves to clarify the differences between Christians. Taking different corners within the general arena of Christianity — like Presbyterian, United, Baptist, Pentecostal etc. — is a very "natural" thing. However, that doesn't mean it's "normal" for people who have a relationship with Jesus.

Unfortunately, in the Christian realm, what happens is people not only separate themselves into boxes with sides and lids, but they dissect the Christian experience to the extent that they end up with an autopsy and a dead body of Christ. This is totally contrary to the ministry of Jesus.

This so-called "categorization" of Christians disqualifies them all from effective ministry to people who need their help and encouragement. We should not be surprised when people ask, "Why should I want to be a Christian? Those people can't even get along with each other!" When people see disunity in the church, the whole message of the Gospel suffers a loss of credibility.

Paul's example is given as a guide for us. He said, *"I have become all things to all men, that I might by all means save some"* (1 Corinthians 9:22).

People need to see that Christians do not reject those who differ from them in the way they dot their *i's* or cross their *t's*. The body of Christ needs to be seen as a bonding together of individuals who love and respect each other enough to allow each person to grow in Jesus Christ as he or she is led by the Holy Spirit.

True unity happens through the manifestation of the gifts of the Holy Spirit. God's word is confirmed through *"signs that accompany it"* (Mark 16:20). It is interesting to see that wherever dynamic moves of God with signs and wonders take place, denominational barriers break down, and people work in unity through the bond of love.

Denominations confuse the issue for non-believers and cloud the real message of salvation. Jesus decreed, *"This is my commandment, that you love one another as I have loved you"* (John 15:12). To His Father, He prayed, *"I do not pray for these only, but also for those who believe in Me through their word, that they may all be one; even as Thou, Father art in Me, and I in Thee, that they also may be one in Us, so that the world may believe Thou has sent Me. The glory which Thou hast given Me I have given them, that they may be one even as We are One; I in them and Thou in Me, that they may become perfectly one, so that the world may know that Thou hast sent Me and hast loved them even as Thou hast loved Me"* (John 17:20–23).

"What about doctrine?" some growl. "Without denominations, people would have to sacrifice their beliefs for a bowl of hash."

The doctrine of the Holy Spirit is not contrary to any authentic denominational statement of belief. It is simply contrary to the traditions of man, which Jesus warned make void the Word of God (Mark 7:13) and have often befuddled original intents. The doctrine of the Holy Spirit is central to the doctrine of the Trinity, a cornerstone of every major denomination.

We need to be able to say, "Don't worry about the fact that you see a church on every corner. It's natural for people to have differences in the way they approach God. We don't need uniformity to have unity in the Holy Spirit. As long as we agree on the non-negotiables of the faith, the key elements of the Gospel, we can celebrate our diversity in terms of our common foundation. Forget about concentrating on the differences you see. Focus on the message that draws all believers together under the umbrella of the name, *Christianity* — faith in the Bible as God's inerrant, inspired Word; the Trinity; the birth, death, and resurrection of Jesus; the work of the Holy Spirit in our world today; and the redemption of man through faith in Jesus Christ."

It takes the dynamite, miracle power of the Holy Spirit to convince people that there is a God who loves them and who sent His Son to die for them. *"Not by might, nor by power, but by my Spirit, says the Lord of Hosts"* (Zechariah 4:6). Only through cooperation with the Holy Spirit and with each other can we reach this lost, dying, and hurting world for Jesus Christ — the mission of "normal" Christianity.

While Paul addressed the early divisions in the Church in the 3rd. chapter of 1 Corinthians, that doesn't mean that denominations are "normal" to the Church. It simply means that they are "natural" to man. A normal Church is characterized by unity with diversity, rather than division or uniformity.

Christianity as a Gift Designed by God

The ability to have a relationship with Jesus is a gift to us. It was planned, arranged, paid for, and given to us by design. In Greek, the "normal" Christian life is called a *charisma*, which is *"a gift of grace, a gift involving grace on the part of God as the Donor — is used of His free bestowments upon sinners* (Romans 5:15,16; 6:23; 11:29) *and of His endowments upon believers by the operation of the Holy Spirit in the churches* (Romans 12:6; 1 Corinthians 1:7; 12:4,9,28,30,31; 1 Timothy 4:14; 2 Timothy 1:6; 1 Peter 4:10)" (*Vine's Expository Dictionary of Old and New Testament Words,* W.E. Vine, p.147). It cannot be bought or earned. Thus, the whole Christian life is a gift of God.

When I asked Jesus to come into my heart that day in the church lounge, He gave me a gift of His own design, choosing, and dimensions. I had absolutely nothing to do with the nature of the present He bestowed upon me. Although He granted me control over its operation, the characteristics of the gift itself were totally and entirely beyond any scope of my influence. It was He who determined what was "normal" about the gift.

One amazing aspect of God's gift is, as one stays in relationship with God, the relationship broadens and deepens and actually becomes a process of receiving one gift of God after another. We cannot earn these gifts. We can only use them for the purpose of drawing other people, regardless of age, sex, nationality, or lifestyle, into the Kingdom of God.

Is it always "Normal" to Receive the Holy Spirit at the Time of Salvation?

Whenever such questions arise, it is necessary to go straight to Scripture for the answer.

Acts 19:1–6 details an encounter Paul had with some disciples who had received salvation but had not received the Holy Spirit. *"Paul took the road through the interior and arrived at Ephesus. There he found some disciples and asked them, 'Did you receive the Holy Spirit when you believed?'*

"They answered, 'No, we have not even heard that there is a Holy Spirit.'

"So Paul asked, 'Then what baptism did you receive?'

"'John's baptism,' they replied.

"Paul said, 'John's baptism was a baptism of repentance. He told the people to believe in the one coming after him, that is, in Jesus.' On hearing this, they were baptized into the name of the Lord Jesus. When Paul placed his hands on them, the Holy Spirit came on them, and they spoke in tongues and prophesied."

Obviously, salvation does not guarantee the receiving of the Holy Spirit. In this case, it was a second step. The Billy Graham Association has published statistics that show that 80% of the people converted in their meetings fall away from Christianity. While Billy Graham is probably the greatest evangelist that the world has ever known, his message is strictly a salvation message. An invitation to receive the baptism in the Holy Spirit is not part of his ministry.

On the other hand, statistics that I have compiled from my own research on ministries which proclaim Jesus' exhortation to receive the Holy Spirit show that 80% of people who do so concurrent with or following salvation, continue to grow in the Lord.

Until people receive the Holy Spirit, there is almost always a sense of "something missing." When I mentioned this "something missing" in one of my meetings, one woman blurted out, "That's me!" She was so excited to have someone understand the deep longing within her heart that she went on to explain that she had been saved in a Presbyterian church, but had always felt incomplete. Right there and then, I asked her if she would like prayer to receive the baptism in the Holy Spirit. As we prayed, she fell down under the power of God and began to speak in tongues. When she finally got up, she was overwhelmed with thanksgiving to God and claimed that what had been missing was no longer missing. I got a call from her shortly after that, telling me that she had picked up one of my tapes on how to minister the baptism of the Holy Spirit to someone else, and she had prayed for her in-laws to receive. The Gift goes on.

One would think that Pentecostal churches, which preach the baptism in the Holy Spirit, would be full of Holy Spirit-filled people. However, such is not necessarily the case. I had one young woman come to me from a Pentecostal church who asked her pastor about the baptism in the Holy Spirit, and he told her that, to his knowledge, there were only two people in the congregation who were Spirit-filled, and he wasn't one of them. If the leadership in a church has not experienced the fullness of the Holy Spirit, the people will usually either flounder in their efforts to grow or simply stagnate at the level of the leadership.

Obviously, while it is not necessarily "normal" to experience the empowering of the Holy Spirit at the time of salvation, it is important to go on and receive Him in order to have "staying power" in the Kingdom.

The Components of a Normal Relationship with Jesus Christ

The "normal" relationship with Jesus involves a process of receiving and using God's gifts. The most common pattern is the following:

1. Salvation.
2. The gift, baptism, or empowerment of the Holy Spirit.
3. Receiving and using the gifts of the Holy Spirit.
4. The development of a Christ-like character called the "fruit of the Spirit."
5. The development of communication skills with God called "prayer."
6. Witnessing to other people about Jesus Christ.
7. Learning to enjoy worship.
8. The outworking of supernatural signs through our lives as confirmation of our authenticity as Christians.

Let's take a look at each of these eight elements.

1. Salvation

In John 3:3,5–7, Jesus says, *"I tell you the truth, unless a man is born again, he cannot see the Kingdom of God. I tell you the truth, unless a man is born of water and the Spirit, he cannot enter the Kingdom of God. Flesh gives birth to flesh, but the Spirit gives birth to spirit. You should not be surprised at my saying, 'You must be born again.' "*

In this passage, Jesus was explaining the Kingdom of God to his late-night visitor, Nicodemus. Nicodemus had been amazed at the miracles he and the other Pharisees had witnessed in Jesus' ministry. Although he agreed that these were evidence that God was with Him, he was puzzled by the term "born again," as many are today. To Nicodemus, the concept implied the necessity of entering once again into a mother's womb, which, of course, is a physical impossibility. (No wonder the poor fellow was confused!)

Jesus looked this great teacher-theologian squarely in the eyes and explained that spiritual birth is not a natural phenomenon. It is a supernatural change, transporting people out of the kingdom of darkness and giving them residency in the Kingdom of God.

According to Paul, salvation is a "charismatic gift." *"For the wages of sin is death, but the free gift* [charismatic gift] *of God is eternal life in Christ Jesus our Lord"* (Romans 6:23).

Whenever we talk about the necessity of a person being "born again," there are those who react *very* negatively. There are times that, with the vehemence of their postures of offense, one would almost think that they were in danger of harm from the bearer of the Good News. These people argue and attempt to tear down the credibility of the one who is speaking in a frustrated effort to discredit the message. They are spiritually blind. Jesus' desire is to save them from a horrendous fate. Salvation is designed to forgive an individual all his or her wrongdoing, thereby removing barriers that block a relationship with Jesus Christ. It is designed to allow people to participate in the Kingdom of Heaven as joint heirs with Jesus, in right-relationship with their Heavenly Father God.

Salvation is the opening of the doorway to God in our lives, giving Him the right and the opportunity to reveal His plan for each individual.

Jesus made it clear that there is no alternative route to eternal life with God. He said, *"I am the way, and the truth, and the life; no one comes to the Father but by me"* (John 14:6). No matter how many routes other religions claim are available, Jesus declared that there is only one way — salvation through His shed blood.

Salvation is a free gift. There is no age-limit nor sexual preference, no intelligence standards nor financial requirements. It can be neither bought nor earned. It is not guaranteed by church attendance any more than hanging around a garage guarantees that a person will be a car.

So how does one become adopted by God? It is very simple and can happen in a variety of ways. It can come through praying alone, as I did. It can come through praying with some other person who will give encouragement and support. It can come through responding to what is called an "altar call," where an individual walks to the front of a church during a service and prays publicly to invite Jesus Christ to be his or her personal Saviour and Lord.

Although there is no set "formula" for prayer for salvation, it usually goes something like this: "Jesus, please forgive me for any sin or wrong that I have done. Please come into my life and into my heart. Amen."

Recently, Jim Bailey, one of the men in our house meeting, got a call from a fellow I'll call "George,"a man who had once worked for him. George was totally disconsolate and informed Jim that he had just swallowed a bottle of pills because he could not go on living. He said, "I just called to say goodbye to you because you are the only person who ever treated me well," and then he asked, "Will I go to Heaven?"

Jim told him of his need to be born again and very concisely explained the way of salvation to him. When George expressed a desire to be right with God, Jim prayed the Sinner's Prayer with him and then hung up and called the police. Although the man was still alive when the police arrived, he died in the hospital later that night.

At the funeral, Jim told George's common-law wife, Cheryl, how George had accepted Jesus as his Saviour shortly before he died. He tried to comfort her with the fact that George was now in Heaven, free from all his earthly unhappiness. Sensing her isolation and pain, he suggested that she call me and gave her my telephone number. Cheryl didn't call right away. In an attempt to escape her grief, she took her two grandchildren and went away on a vacation. Only halfway through her scheduled time, she became overwhelmed with despair and drove home with the children.

It was then that she called. Sobbing in anguish over the phone, she communicated her inability to handle her grief and expressed a desire to accept Jesus into her heart as George had done. I led her in prayer, and she did just that. The change in the tone of her voice over the phone was remarkable. I sensed a fresh strength and willingness — even excitement — to go on with her life.

When she got off the phone with me, she made arrangements to pick up her grandchildren again. Off they went to finish their vacation. Since then, Cheryl has gone on with the Lord, and her relationship with Him continues to grow.

No matter what the circumstances of the spiritual birth, eternal life with Jesus is the reward. As one woman exclaimed after she had been born again, "It didn't even hurt!"

2. *The Gift, Baptism, or Empowerment of the Holy Spirit*

Untold numbers of people have received salvation through the centuries without ever having gone on with God.

It's as though they were all given beautiful new cars but never went to get gas to put in them. Although they saw others driving around, able to go wonderful places, they themselves either didn't feel worthy to have fuel, were perhaps too lazy to go and get any, or simply didn't know how to find it. It's one thing to have a beautiful car sitting in the driveway. It's quite another thing to get into that car, smell the rich, supple leather, gaze with pride at the streamlined design of the dashboard, turn the key, hear the powerful engine throb under the shiny hood, and drive off toward a determined destination. Without fuel to give the car power, however, it can't function as it was designed to function.

We need the power of the Holy Spirit so that we can do what Jesus wants us to do for him. He gives us the boldness to tell other people about what Jesus has done in our lives so that they, too, can know Him as their personal Saviour and Lord. That is the reason why Jesus said, *"But you shall receive power when the Holy Spirit has come upon you; and you shall be my witnesses in Jerusalem and in all Judea and Samaria and to the ends of the earth"* (Acts 1:8).

There are those who, seeing the supernatural manifestations of power working through Spirit-filled believers, would like to have the power of the Holy Spirit without first being born again. However, receiving the gift of the Holy Spirit is conditional upon first receiving forgiveness of one's sins through the gift of salvation.

When people speak of the "gifts of the Spirit" (which are listed and explained in chapters 7 and 8), they seldom think of the Holy Spirit Himself being a gift. This is what Peter referred to on the first day of Pentecost: *"Repent, and be baptized every one of you in the name of Jesus Christ for the forgiveness of your sins; and you shall receive the gift of the Holy Spirit"* (Acts 2:38).

Jesus came to earth in order to pay for the sins of the world and to minister to the needs of people by healing the sick, casting out demons, feeding the hungry, and baptizing with the Holy Spirit. He had a team ministry with John the Baptist. John explained how their ministries interlocked in Matthew 3:11. He said that while he baptized people who repented of their sins with water, Jesus' work was to baptize people with the Holy Spirit. Even after John the Baptist was killed, Jesus did not baptize anyone with water, although His disciples did (John 4:2).

Unfortunately, many people are afraid of the Holy Spirit, usually because of a lack of understanding. The Holy Spirit is the last person in the world that we need to fear. He is the Spirit of Jesus. He is sent by Jesus to enter into us so that we can have an internal relationship with God. Kathryn Kuhlman, one of the greatest Spirit-filled evangelists in history, used to remind us: "The Holy Spirit is always a gentleman. He will never do anything to embarrass or hurt you."

Jesus prepared the first believers to receive the Holy Spirit after He ascended into Heaven. *"But when the Counsellor comes, whom I shall send to you from the Father, He will bear witness to me"* (John 15:26). The Holy Spirit's job is to be our "legal counsellor," which means our defense attorney — our Heaven-appointed lawyer who can advise us about the things of God. His responsibilities are to convince the world *"concerning sin and righteousness and judgment"* (John 16:8), guide us into all truth, tell us what God wants us to know, declare things that are to come in the future, and glorify Jesus, telling us what He wants us to know (John 15:9–15).

The Holy Spirit is someone we can trust. He and Jesus are inseparable. We need Him in order to be able to serve God. Jesus came to prepare us so that we could welcome Him as a friend and constant companion.

When we are "born again," we allow Jesus to be our Saviour. When we are "baptized in the Holy Spirit," we allow Jesus to be our Lord and God. It's as though we're empty glasses until we're born again, at which time our glasses are filled with water. When we're baptized in the Holy Spirit, those full glasses become immersed in a tub full of water. The Holy Spirit makes the Christian life more exciting than anything else on earth.

3. Receiving the Gifts of the Holy Spirit

Jesus wants us to have and enjoy the gifts of the Holy Spirit.

The gifts of the Spirit are ministry gifts. The condition for receiving them is that a person must be born again and baptized in the Holy Spirit. No one can have any of the gifts without the giver, who is the Holy Spirit. While most people quote 1 Corinthians when listing the gifts, there are actually two lists, the other being found in the book of Romans.

First Corinthians 12:7–11 reads, *"Now to each one the manifestation of the Spirit is given for the common good. To one there is given through the Spirit the message of wisdom, to another the message of knowledge by means of the same Spirit, to another faith by the same Spirit, to another gifts of healing by that one Spirit, to another miraculous powers, to another prophecy, to another distinguishing between spirits, to another speaking in different kinds of tongues, and to still another the interpretation of tongues. All these are the work of one and the same Spirit, and he gives them to each one, just as he determines."*

Thus, the Corinthians list includes:

- the word of wisdom;
- the word of knowledge;
- faith;
- gifts of healing;
- miracles;
- prophecy;
- discerning of spirits;
- tongues;
- the interpretation of tongues.

Romans 12:6–8 says, *"We have different gifts, according to the grace given us. If a man's gift is prophesying, let him use it in proportion to his faith. If it is serving, let him serve; if it is teaching, let him teach; if it is encouraging, let him encourage; if it is contributing to the needs of others, let him give generously; if it is leadership, let him govern diligently; if it is showing mercy, let him do it cheerfully."*

Thus, in list format, the Romans list is as follows:

- prophecy;
- service;
- teaching;
- exhortation;
- contributing aid;
- mercy.

Note that only one of these, the gift of prophecy, is repeated in the two lists.

It is not uncommon for people to see the gifts of the Holy Spirit as a graduation diploma. They wait to manifest one or more of the gifts before they will believe that they have been accepted by God. Others feel that manifestation of the gifts will bring them some sort of spiritual status among believers.

In actual fact, the gifts of the Holy Spirit have little to do with the person who manifests them. The actual recipients of the gifts are those to whom God ministers via the manifestation. For example, when a word of wisdom is spoken, the person speaking the word is simply the instrument God uses. The actual recipient of His ministry gift is the person to whom the word is spoken. Thus, the gifts of the Spirit are given to us so that we can minister to the needs of other people.

The gifts of the Spirit are usually called "charismatic gifts" because they come from a Greek word (*charismata*) that means "gifts of grace" or "grace gifts," which are used for ministry. According to apostle Paul, *"All these* [gifts] *are inspired by one and the same Spirit who apportions to each one individually as he wills"* (1 Corinthians 12:11). The King James version uses the phrase *"dividing to every man severally as he will."* The word *severally* means "individually, separately," according to my dictionary. Although it is true that all the gifts are resident in the Holy Spirit who indwells a Spirit-filled person, it is His choice which gift or gifts will be used through a person for the purposes of ministry.

It is awesome to contemplate the provision of God. Through the manifestation of the gifts of the Holy Spirit, we are actually allowed to participate in the ministry of Jesus. We become a part of the signs and wonders that He continues to work in and through His body, which is called the Church.

We will look at each of the gifts in detail in later chapters.

4. The Development of a Christ-like Character

"There's something different about you," is hopefully the observation of a non-Christian addressing a Christian.

Change is often impossible apart from God. Humans are so trapped by their habits and character flaws that, try as they will, few escape their destructive traits.

How, then, does one become like Jesus? It's a supernatural process, a work of the Holy Spirit in us, accomplished through developing what Paul calls *"the fruit of the Spirit"* (Galatians 5:22–23):

- love;
- joy;
- peace;
- patience;
- kindness
- goodness (meekness);
- faithfulness;
- gentleness;
- self-control: against such there is no law."

The word *fruit* is singular. Because there are nine qualities listed, Paul obviously means that the fruit of the Spirit is composed of all nine characteristics, and thus a fully ripened or mature Christian would be recognized by the presence of all nine.

While this is a process and takes time, changes are apparent right from the beginning.

In my own life, I will never forget the shock I experienced when I realized that I was liking people whom I had once enjoyed hating. I actually liked them! Horrors! My temper disappeared. All the anger that I had carried around for years was suddenly gone. I had a *power* to live according to Jesus' directions.

Basically, Jesus outlined in the Beatitudes the process involved in the development of a Christ-like character. Unfortunately, our translations do not adequately convey His teachings. For instance, when we read, *"Blessed are they who mourn, for they shall receive comfort (be comforted)"* (Matthew 5:4), if we go back to the original Greek, the actual meaning is, *"Blessed are those who mourn over their sins, for they shall receive the Comforter,"* referring to the Holy Spirit, who is called the "Comforter."

Each of the Beatitudes is actually a stage of growth in the Christian life. Through them, we are taken right from salvation through the baptism in the Holy Spirit right to Self-control. The King James Version translates the third Beatitude as,*"Blessed are the meek, for they shall inherit the earth."* The original meaning of the word that was translated as "meek" refers to a person who comes under perfect control of the Holy Spirit, who is teachable in all things and will act on command when directed by the Lord to do something. This obedience results in moulding of the character into conformity with the character of Christ, the embodiment of the fruit of the Spirit. In similar fashion, all the remaining Beatitudes act as a framework for the development of the fruit of the Spirit within the life of a believer.

The greatest change that I discovered in the early days of my own faith was the joy and happiness that replaced my anger. Over and over again, I've been criticized for being phony. People say, "No one is that happy!" and then they proceed to ask my wife Ruth what I'm really like at home.

She just laughs and says, "What you see is what you get!" because this happiness isn't something that can be faked. It's real.

No matter what provision the Lord makes for the transformation of our character, however, He can be successful only with our cooperation. He will never force anything upon us or push us to grow faster than we will permit.

The fruit of the Spirit allows other people to experience the love of Jesus through us and gives credibility to any ministry that we carry out in the name of Jesus. Through the nine characteristics, we become Christ's representatives to others.

There are those who, for whatever reason, have decided that they would rather have the fruit of the Spirit instead of the gifts of the Holy Spirit. The fruit and gifts are not alternatives. They are used in conjunction and cooperation with each other to complement each other. fruit without gifts results in a powerless and boring Gospel. These people end up *"having a form of religion but denying its power"* (2 Timothy 3:5). All they really have to communicate are history lessons from the past combined with moral and ethical teaching for today.

Without the gifts of the Spirit, there would be no empowerment to enthusiastically follow the commandments of Jesus. There would be very little in the way of miracles and healings, which have always been proof of the resurrection of Jesus Christ from the dead.

People who have gifts without the fruit may see signs, wonders, and miracles, but they seldom have stability in their lives, and they lack the love-wielding ability to truly connect and convey the love of Jesus to others, thus short-circuiting His ministry.

The Gospel of Jesus Christ is more than words. It is power — a power that transforms character and carries out the miracle ministry of Jesus Christ. Like apostle Paul, we must be able to say, *"And I was with you in weakness and in much fear and trembling; and my speech and my message were not in plausible words of wisdom, but in demonstration of the Spirit and of power, that your faith might not rest in the wisdom of men but in the power of God"* (1 Corinthians 2:3–5).

The Gospel of Jesus Christ, just like Jesus himself, is the same yesterday, today, and forever.

5. The Development of Communication Skills with God called "Prayer"

We need to learn to pray for everything, as Paul directed. Very few people do this. They have no concept of the real power of prayer for them personally.

For some reason, many seem to need to be taught to reach out to God in conversation with Him. They don't have the confidence to simply approach Him on their own. I am constantly amazed by the number of people who simply don't know how to pray in their own native languages, let alone in their spiritual language called "tongues."

There are surveys that document the degree to which communication skills with God are lacking. Recently, it was discovered that the average born again Christian spends seven minutes in prayer per week. As ludicrous as it may sound, I now believe that that is true. Despite my initial denial of the validity of the survey, after doing a little of my own research, I discovered that Christians really don't pray much. There is so little understanding of how and when to pray.

In one of the house meetings I attended recently, I was speaking on prayer. When I got to 1 Thessalonians 5:17 where we are exhorted to *"pray continually,"* one of the young men interrupted, saying, "Wait a minute - how can you pray so much? I have to go to work, and, with our young family, I don't have an hour to just sit and pray."

"No, no, no!" I corrected him. "You don't understand. You pray as you go."

"What do you mean?" he questioned.

"When I'm driving down the road, I pray," I said.

"When I'm getting dressed, I pray."

"You can't do that," he responded with indignation. "You can't pray as you drive — you'd smash up your car!"

This young man had been so conditioned to thinking that the eyes had to be closed during prayer that it had never occurred to him that he could talk to God with his eyes open!

We take so much for granted with people. I have found that it is futile to instruct the majority to go and pray about something. They don't know how to pray.

People need to know that you can discuss anything with Jesus in a normal conversational attitude any time, every day. So many just take it for granted that nothing they could ever say would have any impact on God. They have to learn that they're wrong. God cares intimately about every aspect of our lives.

So many still have the impression that prayer is something that they memorize or that someone else does for them. Most people do not even know the Lord's Prayer these days. At one time, everyone learned it in school, but that doesn't happen anymore. Even our Sunday schools are not teaching it the way they used to. Consequently, the whole area of prayer needs to be addressed in people's lives. We need to get back to the real basics.

Despite the number of wonderful books written on the subject of prayer, the proportion of Christians who actually read these books and put the information to work in their lives is amazingly low. Those who do read or who do receive teaching on prayer will not profit, unless they talk to Jesus in private and place themselves in situations where they can develop their spiritual communication in public.

Listening to others who may be very articulate in prayer can be intimidating for new Christians. They may get the impression that unless they can come up with fine sounding phrases and deep theological verbiage, they dare not pray in public for fear of sounding adolescent. They need to read Matthew 6:7,8: *"And in praying, do not heap up empty phrases as the Gentiles do; for they think they will be heard for their many words. Do not be like them, for your Father knows what you need before you ask Him."*

People need to have the opportunity to pray in tongues for others. I encourage people to think in their minds about the needs of the one for whom they are praying and to pray in tongues until a peace comes over them. In my experience, the recognition of the peace seems to be God's assurance that He is in control of the situation and He will work it out. The old saints used to call it "praying through." Paul taught in 1 Corinthians 14:14,15: *"If I pray in a tongue, my spirit prays, but my mind is unfruitful. So what shall I do? I will pray with my spirit, but I will also pray with my mind."*

In the 18th verse, he said, *"I thank God that I speak in tongues more than all of you."* In the original Greek, what Paul actually says is, *"I thank God that I speak in tongues more than all of you* ***every day****."* He learned that the key to true communication with Jesus Christ involved speaking not only according to the mind, but in the spirit as well. The more we follow Paul's example, the more direction we will receive for our lives in terms of dealing with our children, making good business decisions, etc. Whatever Paul did should be good enough for us!

No relationship can develop lasting depth and strength without communication. In a good marriage, it's normal to talk and discuss things. In the same way, a normal, healthy relationship with Jesus involves lots of communication.

6. Witnessing to Other People about Jesus

People who really know Jesus have a deep desire for others to know Him as they do. They have no greater joy than sharing their faith with anyone who is open to listen. It's just a normal part of having a personal relationship with Jesus. After all, his Great Commission to us all was to *"go into all the world and preach the good news to all creation."* He warned that, *"Whoever believes and is baptized will be saved, but whoever does not believe will be condemned"* (Mark 16:15,16). Thus, Christians with a "normal" relationship with Jesus have an excitement about sharing something that is going to mean eternal life for anyone who will believe. That excitement, however, is tempered by the awful knowledge of what will happen to anyone who doesn't accept Him. Acts 1:8, *"You will receive power when the Holy Ghost comes on you; and you will be my witnesses in Jerusalem and in all Judea and Samaria, and to the ends of the earth,"* makes it plain that the power to witness comes with the infilling of the Holy Spirit.

Bob Davisson is the owner of the McDonalds Restaurant in Swift Current, Saskatchewan. I first met Bob at a Full Gospel Businessmen's meeting when I was speaking there. Bob had cancerous tumors in his lungs and he was dying. He had been trying to figure out a way to commit suicide and yet make it look like an accident so that his family would still be able to collect his insurance. Friends had brought him to the meeting for prayer.

When I got to him in the prayer line and he told me what his problem was, after assuring him that Doctor Jesus could heal him, I prayed for him for salvation, for the baptism in the Holy Spirit, and for healing. He was slain in the Spirit (he fell to the floor when the Holy Spirit came upon him)[1], and after he got up, he left.

I heard later that he had gone for tests at the hospital in Regina the following week. After the first set of tests, the doctors told him they wanted to do a second battery. Thinking that the cancer had progressed, Bob took the second set of tests with enormous apprehension. Of course the doctors finally met with Bob, shaking their heads with the mystery of the missing tumors. There was no sign of any cancer anywhere!

As soon as the realization of what had happened sunk in, Bob began to tell people what Jesus had done in his life. These days, it doesn't matter where he is: on the street, in his restaurant, behind a pulpit in a church — wherever an opportunity presents itself — Bob tells of the goodness of God. His message is whatever Jesus did for him, He can do for anyone else!

Unfortunately, some Christians seem to think that unless they have a dramatic story of God's intervention in their lives, they can't witness. That's not true. Every Christian testimony, no matter how tame it might sound, has the power to set someone free from Satan's grasp. Revelation 12:11 tells us that the believers overcame *"by the Blood of the Lamb and the word of their testimony."* It's awesome to think that we can thwart the plans and actions of Satan by telling others what God has done in our lives.

When I was working in Toronto as the Area Director for "100 Huntley Street," Canada's first national television ministry, I was in charge of the telephone counselors. An eighteen-year-old girl came in to counsel on the phones. This girl had been raised in a Christian home and had lived a very protected life. She was a lovely young thing with long dark hair and the polished manners of one who had lived with privilege. Several people expressed the opinion that she was too young and inexperienced to go on the phones. I said, "No, let's give her a chance." I sensed an important spiritual maturity in her.

The first call she got was from a hit man with the Mafia. As soon as she found out what she was dealing with, she put her hand over the receiver and in a loud whisper called,"Gordon!" With her huge brown eyes pleading for help, she croaked, "You have to take this call! It's a hit man from the Mafia!"

"Sorry", I smiled. "It's your call."

"But I don't have any testimony!" The poor girl was terrified.

"Listen," I said. "Just tell him what Jesus has done in your life." I turned and walked away just far enough so that I could hear how she handled the fellow.

As she began to speak in the quavering voice of a

nervous young girl, it was obvious that the man had painted a graphic picture of his life to her. She said, "Sir, I'm sorry, but I don't know much about what you've been telling me. I was raised in a Christian home, and I can't remember a time when I didn't know Jesus. I've never smoked a cigarette. I've never tasted alcohol. I've never done drugs and I've never had sex with a man." She went on to list all the things that she didn't do, without knowing that on the other end of the line was a man who was thirstily soaking in everything that he wanted and needed like a dry, hardened, old sponge. When she hesitantly asked, "Sir, would you like to invite Jesus into your heart?", the sin-ravaged, middle-aged hit man began to cry like a baby, and she led him to the Lord.

I had an opportunity to meet this man some time later. He told me that he had worked with his godfather in New York City for 25 years. Following the call to 100 Huntley Street, he had phoned his boss and told him he wanted to talk to him. They arranged a meeting in Toronto. When the time came, our friend took a limousine to the designated place, and the Mafia godfather joined him in the back seat. As they were driven through the streets of the city, the hit man proceeded to tell the godfather what had happened to him.

The godfather lowered his head and thought for a few moments. As he raised his creased forehead, his gaze was penetrating. "You know the rule. Nobody leaves." He continued to stare. "But," he said, "you and me — we've worked together for a long time. If you will promise me that you will never tell one word of what we have done, I'll let you go free." And he did.

That all happened from one little girl who didn't think she had a testimony.

When our children were teenagers, they went to a youth group one time and came home all upset. The kids there had decided that because none of them had a testimony, they were going to go out and "build them." They were going to try drugs and all the things they had heard were ingredients for great testimonies. It's so sad that the understanding of what a testimony really is has become so twisted. A testimony is not about the old life — it is about what Jesus has done for us.

"Normal" Christians can say with John (1 John 1:3), *"We proclaim to you what we have seen and heard, so that you also may have fellowship with us. And our fellowship is with the Father and with His Son, Jesus Christ."*

7. Learning to Enjoy Praise and Worship

There are five Hebrew words for praise. They each have Greek equivalents in the New Testament. Each of these are indicative of particular body movements as well as attitudes of the heart. "Normal" praise, according to God, involves practicing these physical-spiritual exercises. We'll take a look at these five Hebrew words and at the original Hebrew meaning of worship in Chapter Nine.

8. The Outworking of Supernatural Signs through our Lives as Confirmation of our Authenticity as Christians

More and more, people are asking, "How can I identify a real (normal) Christian?"

Of course I take them to Mark 16:17,18, where Jesus, himself, says, *"And these signs will accompany those who believe: in My Name they will drive out demons; they will speak in new tongues; they will pick up snakes with their hands; and when they drink deadly poison, it will not hurt them at all; they will place their hands on sick people and they will get well."*

As bizarre as it may sound to some, according to Scripture, these are the signs Jesus said would identify believers. He does not say that these signs are for some, or for a few, or for a majority or a minority of those who believe in Him, but rather for all believers. The signs are given to us for our assurance and so that other people who do not know Jesus can identify us. All Christians must have authenticating signs as proof that they know Jesus

Christ personally and have been baptized by the Holy Spirit. We must have authority to cast out demons that possess or harass other people. We must speak in "other tongues," or "other languages," supernaturally as a demonstration of Jesus' control of our mouths. We must have His protection as we serve Him and witness to others. We must pray for the sick with the "laying on of hands" so that people will know that Jesus Christ heals people today as their Saviour, Lord, and healer.

The apostle Paul demonstrated what a normal relationship with Jesus is like through his own life. He said,*"When I came to you, brothers, I did not come proclaiming to you the testimony of God in lofty words or wisdom. For I decided to know nothing among you except Jesus Christ and Him crucified. And I was with you in weakness and in much fear and trembling; and my speech and my message were not in plausible words, of wisdom, but in demonstration of the Spirit and of power, that your faith might not rest in the wisdom of men, but in the power of God"* (1 Corinthians 2:1–5.

People have to see authenticating signs. I remember the Pentecostal church in my home town being regarded as a hotbed of holy rollers — yet when people needed a miracle, they went to the Pentecostal church. It must not be forgotten, however, that the Holy Spirit did not take out any special membership in the Pentecostal Church. Almost every orthodox denomination began with a mighty move of God characterized by authenticating signs.

Of course, all these signs must be carried out in an attitude of love — the love of Jesus Christ that is given to us by God and described by Paul. In John 13:35, Jesus gave a further mark of identification. *"By this all men will know that you are my disciples, if you love one another."* Paul warns in the 13th chapter of 1 Corinthians that no matter how great our spiritual gifting may be, if we operate without love, nothing is gained.

3

The Wind Blows Wherever it Pleases

"The wind blows wherever it pleases. You hear its sound but you cannot tell where it comes from or where it is going. So it is with everyone born of the Spirit"
(The words of Jesus in John 3:8).

Although we can't see the wind — neither where it's coming from nor where it's going — anyone who watches the 6 o'clock news can get a rundown on the weather forecast. Details of the current situation, as well as what's ahead for Monday and Tuesday, on through Saturday and Sunday, is routinely blathered forth by either a pretty, young woman wearing size four or a middle-aged man in a plaid sports jacket.

God sent a forecast of the wind of His Holy Spirit through His prophets — weathermen in sackcloth and sandals — in order to prepare people for what He was going to do.

Remember old Noah who warned of a day when no one outside the ark (God's provision) would live? Remember slime-soaked Jonah being discharged from the belly of a nauseated whale in order to warn of God's coming day of wrath on an unrepentant people? Remember John the Baptist, the advance man for Jesus, calling, like a voice crying in the wilderness, for people to prepare their hearts through repentance?

Just before Pentecost, Jesus prepared His followers to receive and welcome the Holy Spirit by forecasting: *"you shall receive power when the Holy Spirit has come upon you, and you shall be my witnesses in Jerusalem and Judea and Samaria, and to the ends of the earth"* (Acts 1:8).

This "coming of the Holy Spirit" had been foretold by the prophet Joel, between six hundred and nine hundred years before the time of Jesus, so that people would have hope and could get ready to receive the mighty Wind. *"And it shall come to pass afterward, that I shall pour out my Spirit upon all flesh. Your sons and your daughters shall prophesy. Your old men shall dream dreams, and your young men shall see visions. Even upon the men servants and maidservants, in those days, I will pour out my Spirit"* (Joel 2:28–29).

Until Pentecost, the Holy Spirit had been given to only a few people of faith, usually patriarchs, judges, kings, queens, or priests who were specially chosen for a particular work of God. "Whosoever" became eligible for the empowerment only after the resurrection of Jesus. Now all His children have been "specially chosen" for a particular role in the Kingdom. However, just as God tailor-designed each empowerment of the Holy Spirit for His purposes before Pentecost, He continues to work uniquely among us today.

God's surprises are about the "how" and the "when" — not the "what." We know *what* God will do, because He tells us in the Bible. We just don't know *how* or *when* it will happen. The concrete promise of the Holy Spirit is packaged in freedom and life. We can't orchestrate God.

I had a United Church minister friend who asked me to pray for the baptism in the Holy Spirit for him. He specified that he wanted to be prayed for at his church. When I arrived, he appeared in long flowing robes and proceeded to advise me of his plan. He wanted to stand before the communion table in his robes and begin to speak in tongues as he received the Holy Spirit.

Despite my misgivings, I agreed to his plan and began to pray. However, almost before I began, the Holy Spirit spoke to me and said, "No. I will not be orchestrated."

I said, "I'm sorry, it's not going to work."

"What do you mean, 'it's not going to work'?" my friend asked with surprise.

"The Holy Spirit just told me that He would not be orchestrated." Because this man was a musician who understood orchestration, he accepted my words. I continued, "You're going to have to go to an altar, just like everybody else." That's what he did, and the Holy Spirit met him there.

Why did the Holy Spirit Come at Pentecost "Like a Rushing, Mighty Wind?"

The Holy Spirit brings with Him a power — *dunamis*. This is the Greek word from which we get the word *"dynamite."* Because sin has a death grip on man, it requires this explosive, supernatural power of God not only to set people free, but also to keep them free.

Without hurricane or tornado warnings, people become victims of the surprises of nature. Moves of God are not spontaneous bursts of some sort of divine impulse, but are carefully orchestrated happenings, foretold in His Word and perfectly designed for the furtherance of His Kingdom.

How Does the Wind Reach us Today?

My theology professor, George F. Hendry, used to remind us that God knows that we need more than a one-dimensional relationship with Him. It has to be three-dimensional. That is why He revealed Himself to us as Father, Son, and Holy Spirit. He is the Father who is over us, or above us in Heaven. He is the Son who came to Earth and who walks alongside of us as a brother and a friend. He is the One who comes to us in the form of the Holy Spirit, who comes inside of us to live and guide as a friend and counsellor.

But, before He will come inside of us, we have to be willing to give Him permission to do so. He will not force His way in like an intruder, an enemy or an unwelcome guest. He is sent by the One who waits for an invitation. *"Behold, I stand at the door and knock; if anyone hears My voice and opens the door, I will come in to him and eat with him, and he with Me"* (Revelation 3:20).

Just as with salvation, the Holy Spirit must be invited to come into our lives with His power. That is why Jesus told us: *"And I tell you, ask, and it will be given you; seek, and you will find; knock, and it will be opened to you. For everyone who asks receives, and he who seeks finds, and to him who knocks it will be opened. What father among you, if his son asks for a fish, will give him a serpent; or if he asks for an egg, will give him a scorpion? If you then, know how to give good gifts to your children, how much more will the Heavenly Father give the Holy Spirit to those who ask Him!!"* (Luke 11:9–13).

The Six "Days" of Pentecost

A weatherman might say, "We're in for some stormy weather: On Monday, we'll have hurricane-force winds. Tuesday, the winds won't be as powerful, but we'll receive eight inches of rain. On Wednesday, we can look forward to gentle breezes and sunny skies ..." in order to foretell the differences in the manifestations of the coming wind. There are extreme variations in the ways that it may come in scattered parts of the globe.

In the same way, the wind of the Holy Spirit comes upon different people in different ways.

I don't know why God works differently in each life. I don't know why there is no set formula for receiving the baptism in the Holy Spirit. Some are baptized in the Holy Spirit at the same time as they are saved. Some must have the laying on of hands in order to receive the Holy Spirit. I only know that we serve a very flexible God who cares enough to tailor each situation to be most meaningful to each individual.

While He doesn't provide us with calendars of His agenda, God gives us warnings, guideposts, and models (examples) of His work so that those with the wisdom to listen can prepare for what He has planned.

To demonstrate the absolute individuality of the way the Holy Spirit comes upon each life, we're going to look at the ways that people were baptized in the Holy Spirit as described in the Book of Acts. As we examine the Scriptures, notice that the outpourings of the Holy Spirit are not described in emotional, experiential terms, but rather, in objective terms. Thus, each person is free to react or respond emotionally, or not have an emotional reaction at all. There is not any one "correct" response. Each experience is unique.

The six models we have been given for the ways that the Holy Spirit meets individuals will be referred to as "days."

Although Pentecost was originally a great pilgrimage feast of Judaism, which began annually on the third day after the Passover, its significance for Christians is the anniversary of the coming of the Holy Spirit. Because the first outpouring was followed by five more specific instances where people were baptized in the Holy Spirit in totally original ways, we will refer to these six models as "days" of Pentecost.

1) The First "Day" of Pentecost — Model #1
A sovereign act of God upon all individuals gathered in one place.

The first "day" of Pentecost happened on a Sunday. On Saturday, one hundred and twenty people who had followed Jesus were waiting in the Upper Room in Jerusalem for what Jesus had called *"the promise of the Father."* He had told them, *"Do not leave Jerusalem, but wait for the gift My Father promised, which you have heard Me speak about. For John baptized with water, but before many days, you shall be baptized with the Holy Spirit"* (Acts 1:4–5).

One word, in particular, had caught their attention — *wait.*

They stayed all night. About nine o'clock on the morning of Pentecost, they suddenly heard the sound of a rushing, mighty wind that filled the room in which they were waiting. Amid the howling of the wind, flames like tongues of fire appeared to come through the ceiling and then to separate, coming to rest on each of them. Not one person was hurt, but a monumental landmark in the history of the world happened. *"And they were all filled with the Holy Spirit and began to speak in other tongues, as the Spirit gave them utterance"* (Acts 2:4). Every person in that room was filled with the Holy Spirit.

They *all* spoke in legitimate languages that they had not learned — a totally supernatural phenomenon. They ran out into the streets where they drew a large crowd of people who had come from many different countries around the world to Jerusalem to celebrate Pentecost.

The crowd, a mishmash of different nationalities, heard them speaking about the great and mighty works of God in different languages. Most were impressed, to say the least.

But some were not. In fact, they thought that these people who were talking about God in languages other than their own had been out on an all-night party and were returning home drunk. Perhaps another reason they were not impressed was because the people spoke with a Galilean accent. This must have been true because, despite the fact that all were strangers, these people were recognized as Galileans. Galilee was considered to be an uneducated, backwater fishing area. The Galilean accent was so strong that the Sanhedrin, the ruling council of Jerusalem, had passed a law which said that no person with a Galilean accent was to be allowed to read the Torah in public because the sound of the accent was considered to be an abomination to God. Besides this, there was the female factor. Some of the believers were women, and they, too, were speaking in tongues. Orthodox Jews of the day did not believe that women could be used of God other than in exceptional circumstances.

In spite of the skepticism of the onlookers, these people were no abomination to God. They were His chosen people. They were His First Church. They were going about the work that they had been empowered by Jesus to do.

Peter stood up to explain what was happening to the crowd that had gathered. With a thunderous Gospel message that has resounded through 2000 years, he reminded them that what they were experiencing was exactly what the prophet Joel had prophesied and that his prophecy had included both men and women.

In response to the words of this once shy fisherman, the listeners were *"cut to the heart"* (Acts 2:37).

Convinced of their need, they asked, *"Brethren, what shall we do?"*

"Repent, and be baptized every one of you in the Name of Jesus Christ for the forgiveness of your sins; and you shall receive the gift of the Holy Spirit" (Acts 2:38), came the reply. What an altar call! Three thousand people were added to the church that day!

The same thing that happened to the people in the Upper Room happens to individuals who are baptized in the Holy Spirit today. The Spirit of God comes inside of him or her to live and to stay. He then exercises the Lordship of Jesus over that individual life. He gives the person the right to say *no* to sin, wrong-doing, and law breaking, and to say *yes* to God's plan.

In the same way that the early Christians were so transformed by the infilling of the Holy Spirit that they rushed right out to tell others what God had done, Spirit-filled believers, today, have a burning passion to witness or tell other people about Jesus so that they, too, can come into a personal relationship with Him. Any who have lost this desire to share Christ need a fresh infilling. The original Greek text of Ephesians 5:18 implies the need for a continuous filling of the Holy Spirit, rather than a one-time memory.

When I was first saved and baptized in the Holy Spirit, I was probably every pagan's worst nightmare. I was enthusiastic, loud, and rambunctious about my wonderful new life. I ran around talking about Jesus and what He was doing in my life and in the life of our church to anyone who would listen. We were in the midst of a revival, and it was so exciting to see God's power being demonstrated in the lives of our people!

One of our well-meaning, seasoned Christians took me aside. In his most *I-am-a-mature-Christian* voice, He carefully explained to me, "Gordon, I hate to have to tell you this, but after a few months, maybe a few weeks, well, maybe a few days, you are going to 'come down' and be like the rest of us."

I looked at him, stunned. I said, "You've got to be kidding me. If that is true, then I've been lied to. I've been conned."

He was wrong. People who witness to others about Jesus, demonstrating the power of the Holy Spirit, will never be bored. In fact, the Christian life will get more and more exciting.

The pastor of a church where I was once speaking made a comment about a man in his church who had recently become a Christian and had been baptized in the Holy Spirit. "He needs to be locked up for about six months until he calms down."

"No! No! No!" I objected. "Let him loose. He will accomplish more for Jesus Christ in the next six months than in the rest of his life. If we silence him from witnessing now, someone will, no doubt, get hold of him, throw a wet blanket over his fire and rob him of his joy. He'll end up a dried-up, wizened, old Christian like multitudes of other dead bones."

Newly baptized in the Spirit believers should never be harnessed. Let them loose. Don't discourage them — encourage them. Don't stop them — direct them. It is a wise pastor who learns the ways of the Holy Spirit and cooperates with Jesus so that more people than he could ever have imagined will come into the Kingdom of God.

When we are prepared to go out on the street after being baptized in the Holy Spirit, just as happened on the first "day" of Pentecost, we'll see the same kind of dynamic results as they did.

In our church in Englishtown, New Jersey, we experienced a similar phenomenon, a modern day likeness of that first "day" of Pentecost.

I was a young pastor and had never given an altar call. We had been in the church for several months by this time, and, on that particular morning, the church, including the balcony, was full. Shortly after I had begun my sermon I heard a voice, which seemed to come from the choir, instructing me to give an invitation. I turned to my right (where the choir was sitting), to see who was trying to be smart. No one appeared to have said anything.

I turned back to the congregation and continued to preach. A few moments later, the voice came again, this time a little louder. "Give an invitation." I looked again to see who it was. Again, no apparent source.

By this time, I was getting a few strange looks from people who were wondering what was going on!

As I continued to preach, I remembered the story in the Old Testament about Samuel in the temple with Eli. God had called him in an audible voice. I started to sweat. I thought, "No!" The voice came a third time. "Give an invitation!"

Quickly, I ended my message and invited people to come forward to invite Jesus into their hearts or, for those who had already done that, to recommit their lives to Him.

With no experience in such things and no idea of what to expect, while the congregation was singing the closing hymn, I began to pray in silence, negotiating with God, saying, "Lord, if two or three people come forward, it would be fantastic." (I didn't even know what I would do with them!) I began to hear wind blowing in the church. Then I heard a rustle in the pews. When I opened my eyes, to my utter astonishment, I saw that the whole church, with the exception of one man, had come forward! That one man had a full-length cast on his leg and was unable to walk. God moved in an incredible way. When those people left the church, they began to witness to others on the streets. They went home and got on their phones, and all over the community people were spreading the good news of what God had done in their lives.

Our church had to expand from one service to two, and then, in no time, to three services on Sundays. When we prayed for people to be healed, we would see amazing confirmations of God's healing power for today. Alcoholics were set free. People left their cigarette habits at the altar. Deliverances from all kinds of bondages became routine. We prayed with bad-tempered people and they became nice! It was incredible!

Our Sunday school exploded.

We began a coffeehouse ministry. By that time, the drug trade was really heavy in New Jersey, but we saw teenagers saved every week. When we prayed for addicts, they would get saved, baptized in the Holy Spirit, and released from their addictions with no withdrawal symptoms.

We channeled many young people through Teen Challenge, but we had a real problem dealing with all the drugs we confiscated from the kids. At first, I was burning almost a full garbage can of marijuana every week, but, with concerns about turning the whole town on with the fumes, I began to hand it over to Teen Challenge for disposal. One would think that we could simply have flushed some of the drugs down the toilet; however, anyone who has tried that knows that it doesn't work because pills float! Consequently, I had to start taking the pills to Teen Challenge as well. Every week, I would have boxes of drugs to cope with. My trunk would be full of them!

A crisis arose when a friend of mine, Dennis Baker, who was a youth pastor in Philadelphia, got arrested. I had been taking the drugs to him for disposal at the Teen Challenge in Philadelphia, simply because it was more convenient for us at the time than sending them to New York. The problem began when my friend got sidetracked with some pressing ministry and stored the drugs in his garage, meaning to take them to Teen Challenge later.

One night, some kids broke in and got into the drugs. When the police picked them up and heard their story, they arrested my friend! He, of course, gave my number to the chief of detectives at the police department in Philadelphia. The chief phoned me and said, "I've got a case on my hands that involves drug pushing, and I've got a fellow here by the name of Dennis Baker who claims that you gave these drugs to him because some teenagers turned them over to you. I've heard every story in the book, but I just had to check this one out."

"Sir," I said, "That's true."

"What?!", he exploded. "Don't you know that you've been breaking the law by transporting illegal drugs across state borders? Where are you getting all this stuff?"

When I told him about our ministry, he said, "Well, that's great. I'm going to let you off this time, but, from now on, get rid of them in New Jersey — please!"

The Key to Church Growth

People who are interested in church growth need to look at how it was carried out on the first "day" of Pentecost. There are pastors who have travelled all over the world in order to attend church-growth seminars, trying to find the key to revival and to building successful churches. Unfortunately, most have overlooked the key that is found right in the Book of Acts.

The key is not only to duplicate the experience of being baptized in the Holy Spirit, but then also to do what the first believers did. They went out into the streets speaking in tongues, glorifying and praising God. The listeners heard languages being spoken supernaturally by ordinary people who had never learned to speak them. The results were fantastic.

Unfortunately, today, we are too smart and sophisticated to do that. We're afraid of being called fanatics. We all know that people are not supposed to speak in tongues in public.

The Bible, however, does not say that! In fact, Paul tells us that *"tongues are a sign not for believers but for unbelievers"* (1 Corinthians 14:22) when combined with the interpretation of tongues.

Because of the fanatical devotion and willingness to witness to other people, the Early Church grew to a membership of 5000 in its first week of existence. Those people had the key to revival, or renewal.

This is what I believe Jesus Christ was trying to get the church in Ephesus to go back and do again. He rebuked them and, I believe, us, too: *"But I have this against you, that you have abandoned (lost) the love that you had at first. Remember then from what you have fallen, repent and do the works you did at first"* (Revelation 2:4,5).

The apostle Paul told us,*"And I was with you in weakness and in much fear and trembling; and my speech and my message were not in plausible words of wisdom, but in demonstration of the Spirit and of power, that your faith might not rest in the wisdom of men but in the power of God"* (1 Corinthians 2:3–5). Whenever tongues are spoken, something supernatural occurs in the heart and mind of an unbeliever and it creates a desire to know Jesus Christ as Saviour, Lord, and God.

People need a demonstration of the reality of God and His work. They need to see how the Holy Spirit operates. It relieves anxiety and eliminates fear, giving people the calm assurance that God is not out to hurt or punish them, but to rescue, help, save, and love them.

I know a young woman who has grasped the importance of this truth in such a profound way that she boldly demonstrates the supernatural presence of the Holy Spirit in her life when she witnesses. After she has told people about the time when she invited Jesus Christ into her life as her Saviour, she tells them about the evening when she was baptized in the Holy Spirit. She usually concludes with something like, "Then I was baptized in the Holy Spirit and began to speak in tongues. Would you like to hear what my tongues sound like?"

Because she is so excited and enthusiastic, people don't get offended. In fact, most are attracted. They usually say, "Sure, why not?" After the little demonstration, she offers to pray with the person to invite Jesus Christ into his or her life. Many, having been struck by the reality and joy in her life, have prayed with her and have found Jesus as their Saviour and Lord.

Waiting in the 21st Century

The outpouring of the Holy Spirit on the first "day" of Pentecost came in response to the obedience of Jesus' followers as they *waited* according to His instructions. *Wait* is a word that needs to grab our attention as it did theirs.

Wait? Come on. We don't have time to wait these days. Early believers didn't have televisions, twenty-mile drives to church, lineups to beat at the local chicken emporium, day-timers, fax machines, computers, and cell phones. Our schedules run our lives. They don't allow for *waiting.*

Our restlessness is reflected in our worship services. One hour is tolerated, but less is preferable. We arrive late. We leave early. We consider it a "good service," a "good message," a "good prayer," a "good song service," a "good prayer meeting," if it is short. And then, we proceed to the next slot of our daily schedules.

Christian Celebrities and Trendy Rituals vs. Peter and the Upper Room

In the majority of churches, worship services have become trendy religious rituals that leave us empty — a far cry from the *fire* of the Upper Room.

We have become followers of popular preachers, like fans of movie stars. We follow popular Christian television and radio personalities, regardless of whether they are God's men and women of vision or not. Success is measured by the world's yardstick of numbers and dollars. The Templeton Prize is never awarded to some faithful preacher who has cooperated with the Holy Spirit over years of faithful preaching and ministering, in the power of the Holy Spirit, to some small congregation numbering under 200.

Having been involved in television ministry, I know that it can be an immensely important vehicle for imparting the Gospel and doing the work of the Holy Spirit, but we have to get our priorities straight and keep them straight. There can be only one celebrity in our lives — Jesus Christ. It is only He who sends the Holy Spirit to occupy our lives until His return.

Sadly, so-called "Christian television" has attracted many whose greatest desire is personal glory, power and earthly gain. They know who they are and will have a hard time giving an account of their work and motives on that final day.

Truly Godly preachers and Christian teachers in high profile positions despise the celebrity status accorded them by their followers. They tremble at the thought of becoming false gods in people's lives or having glory rest on them, when they long to give all glory, honour and praise to the Father to Whom it belongs.

Godly Teachers Must also be Spiritual Teachers

I was talking to a friend in Western Canada who has almost become a professional student. We were discussing the baptism in the Holy Spirit and he said, "You know, Gordon, not everyone agrees that speaking in tongues is for everyone. I've studied under some very Godly men who claim they are not."

Something clicked inside and I suddenly understood something that had bothered me. I said, "They might be Godly men — but they're not *Spirit*ual men."

My friend looked at me quizzically and asked, "What do you mean by that?"

"They're Godly in that they've had their sins forgiven, but they are not spiritual in terms of what Paul describes as being filled with the Holy Spirit. He makes a definite distinction between "fleshly" and "spiritual." The fleshly person is a person who does not have the Holy Spirit, but is nevertheless a Christian.

"Do you realize the implication of what you just said?" my friend asked.

"It's pretty frightening, isn't it," I nodded. "It means that a lot of Godly people are teaching wrong things, because they're not being guided by the Holy Spirit. They deny that many of the things described in the Bible such as: healing and the other gifts of the Holy Spirit are for us today. They cannot understand the Scripture because they're spiritually discerned (1 Corinthians 2:14) and if a person doesn't have the Holy Spirit, he or she cannot discern things. That was the message that Paul was trying to convey."

Thus the first "day" of Pentecost (our first model) was characterized by waiting for the promise, coming into agreement with God, and then receiving, speaking in tongues, witnessing and teaching. It is important to note that as "believers," every person who was in the Upper Room had already received salvation. Like many today, however, they were saved but had not yet received the baptism in the Holy Spirit, which was a separate and distinct experience for them, as it is for us today.

2) The Second "Day" of Pentecost — Model #2
As people met together for prayer, they were all baptized in the Holy Spirit.

Acts 4:23–33 tells the story of an amazing prayer meeting in Jerusalem. Just after Peter and John were released from custody for healing the lame beggar, at the Beautiful Gate of the Temple, they went back to the group of believers, where they reported all that had happened. The whole group took the matter to the Lord in prayer. They prayed that, despite the threats of the rulers, the servants of the Lord would be strengthened with boldness to speak the Gospel, and that God would continue to confirm His Word, by stretching forth His hand with healing and signs of His supernatural power.

Suddenly, the place where they had gathered was shaken and everyone there was filled with the Holy Spirit. This was the second outpouring of the Holy Spirit. In the same way that it had happened in the Upper Room, all who were present began to speak the Word of God with boldness. This was a fulfillment of Jesus' promise, *"But you shall receive power when the Holy Spirit has come upon you; and you shall be My witnesses in Jerusalem, and in all Judea and Samaria, and to the end of the earth"* (Acts 1:8).

The fact that the Spirit was poured out on every one of those present reconfirms the fact that God's promise is for all — without favouritism. All who are willing can receive.

Over and over again, I have been in meetings where, in the midst of prayer, the Holy Spirit has baptized believers and they have begun to shake and tremble and speak in tongues, which, according to the first outpouring, was a sure sign that they truly were baptized in the Holy Spirit.

One Sunday night in Dresden, Ontario, I was ministering at the altar when an amazing phenomenon began to occur. As people stood in the prayer line talking to God as they waited for me to reach them, one by one, the Spirit began to move on them sovereignly, baptizing them all in the Holy Spirit. One teenage girl who had come to pray for a friend became breathless and asked, "What is happening to me?" She said, "I haven't asked for the baptism in the Holy Spirit. I just came to pray for my friend." With that, she began to speak in tongues, as the Holy Spirit moved on her life.

Is Speaking in Tongues a Necessary Sign of the Baptism?

The question for many, is whether or not speaking in tongues is the only definitive sign of the baptism.

The majority of pastors and church leaders attempt to disregard the necessity of speaking in tongues and try to explain the baptism of the Holy Spirit in emotional terms. Although emotions are usually involved, just as they are in every major change in our lives, from the taking of marriage vows to the changing of jobs, the experience of speaking in tongues is not any more of an emotional experience than speaking in any language that we normally speak. The only emotion evoked by the experience of speaking in tongues is, particularly initially, the wonder of speaking words never learned through the intellect.

Those who were baptized in this second outpouring were, without a doubt, some, if not all, of the 5,000 Jewish believers who *"heard the Word and believed"* (Acts 4:4) in response to Peter's message at Pentecost. Although we are not specifically told that these people spoke in tongues, I believe that we can make some educated assumptions.

Because the only experience these people had had with the baptism in the Holy Spirit was the incredible outpouring at Pentecost, when everyone began to speak in tongues, and because they credited this second event as being the same kind of happening, I believe that we can assume that these people spoke in tongues as well. It was the only criteria they had to establish what was normal to the phenomenon. They no doubt spoke in a fulfillment of the prophesy, *"With stammering lips and another tongue will He speak to this people"* (Isaiah 28:11) which is no doubt the verse to which Paul referred when he said, *"In the law it is written, with men of other tongues and other lips will I speak unto this people, and yet for all that will they not hear me, saith the Lord"* (1 Corinthians 14:21).

Joel prophesied the outpouring of the Spirit *"upon all flesh."* If the first fulfillment of that prophesy included speaking in tongues, surely it must be an integral aspect of the manifestation. It's an obvious sign that one has received the baptism of the Holy Spirit.

In trying to decide how to integrate the new Gentile (non-Jewish) believers into the church, the early church leaders concluded that these people must be acceptable to God because they had all received tongues on the first "day" of Pentecost.

While tongues are available to everyone who receives, not all Spirit-baptized people actually speak in other languages right away. I didn't and neither did my wife, Ruth. Although there was no question that I had received the baptism at the time, I had such an intellectual block against tongues that it stopped my freedom. When Ruth received the baptism, she was so aware of my disapproval of tongues that I believe it stopped her freedom as well. It wasn't until the Lord set me free from that mental block, that we were both able to flow fully in the Spirit.

The wonderful thing about tongues is that it is a sign not only to onlookers, but also to the individual that he or she truly has received the baptism. It acts as a continuous sign and assurance. Whenever one needs to be reassured that he or she truly has been baptized in the Holy Spirit, all the person needs to do is begin to speak in tongues. This can happen as an act of the will. There does not have to be any emotional or spiritual trigger to begin.

Tongues is always available to be used in prayer, praise or worship. It is a constant reminder that He never leaves us nor forsakes us, as promised in Hebrews 13:5.

Thus, the second "day" of Pentecost (our second model) was characterized by people who were all baptized in the Holy Spirit in a sovereign act of God, as they met together for prayer.

3) The Third "Day" of Pentecost' — Model #3 People received the baptism in the Holy Spirit following the laying on of hands of a Spirit-baptized person.

The third "day' of Pentecost happened outside of Israel in Samaria (Acts 8:4–7; 14–17) as a result of Philip's ministry.

Persecution had started up in Jerusalem, in protest against the thousands of people who were becoming Christians. Fearing for their lives, the believers scattered throughout the countryside.

Philip escaped into Samaria. He was not as smart as many of us would have been. If we were escaping from a persecution that could result in our imprisonment and death, the logical thing to do would be to keep our mouths shut about Jesus Christ and save ourselves (so that we could be of use to God later). But Philip was not that kind of a person. He loved Jesus and knew that he was called to preach the Gospel and tell others about Him, no matter what the consequences.

The result was that some of the Samaritans became Christian believers. Fearlessly, Philip took them down to the nearest river and openly baptized them in water. When the apostles in Jerusalem heard about Philip's success, they sent Peter and John to Samaria to make certain that everything was being done correctly. They wanted to help this "Revival in Samaria" succeed.

When Peter and John arrived, they discovered that these new believers had not yet received the Holy Spirit. *"For He had not fallen on any of them but they had only been baptized in the Name of Jesus Christ"* (Acts 8:16). Without hesitation, Peter and John *"laid their hands on them and they received the Holy Spirit"* (Acts 8:17).

For many people, the experience of salvation (being born again, saved, converted or justified) is a separate and distinct experience from the baptism in the Holy Spirit. For others, like myself, the two happen in one awesome experience of concurrent rebirth and baptism in the Holy Spirit.

Because it was all one experience for me, I initially made the mistake of assuming that it happened in one experience for everybody else. I could not understand why Christians would come to me and say there was something missing in their spiritual lives. Upon examination, I had no question that these were saved people who loved Jesus Christ and were trying their best to serve Him. Their dilemmas puzzled me.

One day, a woman, who was the best Christian that I had ever known, came to me and asked me to pray with her to be baptized in the Holy Spirit. This woman loved to attend worship services, Bible studies, and prayer meetings. She genuinely showed the love of Jesus Christ to other people and her family. She would help anyone who needed help. As far as I could tell, she had been baptized in the Holy Spirit. I told her so and dismissed her concern. Unconvinced, she came to me from time to time, over the period of several months, saying, "There is something missing in my life. I think that I need to be baptized in the Holy Spirit. Will you please pray for me?"

I kept putting her off, saying, "Ruth, you got it all when you got saved!"

One day, she came to me and said, "If you won't pray with me to be baptized in the Holy Spirit, then I'll go to another minister and ask him to do it!" Such a threat from my own wife quickly clued me in to the fact that I had better do something about it.

More to prove Ruth wrong than anything, I prayed for her. Much to my amazement, I was the one proven wrong. She was baptized in the Holy Spirit! Despite the fact that she did not speak in tongues until some time later, she knew that it had happened. The grass was greener. The skies were bluer. She no longer felt that she was missing anything.

I went to the Book of Acts for an explanation. Suddenly it was clear to me. When I approached the Bible with a truly seeking mind, free of my own preconceptions, I discovered that the experience of salvation and the baptism of the Holy Spirit truly can be separate experiences.

The one condition that invariably runs constant throughout Scripture and my experience, is that while salvation usually precedes the baptism of the Holy Spirit, the baptism in the Holy Spirit never precedes salvation.

One time at "100 Huntley Street" (Canada's Daily Christian Television Program) following the daily telecast, I escorted the members of the studio audience who wanted to have prayer for their various needs into the prayer room. I gave a simple invitation for anyone who would like to have prayer to please come forward for salvation, healing, rededication to Jesus Christ or to receive the baptism of the Holy Spirit.

A woman whom I did not know approached me. She bluntly asked, "Where does it say in the Bible that a person can be a saved Christian believer but yet not be baptized in the Holy Spirit?"

"Well," I said "in Acts, Chapter 8."

"Will you show me where it says that?" she asked, puzzled.

"Certainly. I'll get my Bible." I reached for one on the lectern.

"What version do you use?" she queried.

"I use four versions of the Bible: the King James Version, the Revised Standard Version, the New International Version and the Good News For Modern Man," I quipped back. "Which one would you like?"

"I use the Revised Standard Version," she replied cautiously.

"Good, I'll get mine," I said as I reached for it.

"No! No! Show me in mine," she protested as she handed me her Bible.

"Sure thing. Ah! Here it is!" I said, as I opened her Bible to the page. Her eyes followed my finger as I underlined the verses. *"Now when the apostles at Jerusalem heard that Samaria had received the Word of God, they sent to them Peter and John, who came down and prayed for them that they might receive the Holy Spirit; for it had not yet fallen on any of them, but they had only been baptized in the Name of Jesus. Then they laid their hands on them and they received the Holy Spirit"* (Acts 8:14-17).

"How come I never saw that before?" she questioned, shaking her head.

"I don't know, but is there anything to prevent you from being baptized in the Holy Spirit now?" I asked cautiously.

"No, I don't think so." She smiled like a little girl who had been caught with her hand in the cookie jar.

"Now, I'm just going to do what Peter and John did. I'm going to lay hands on you." I led her in prayer and asked Jesus to baptize her in the Holy Spirit. As she prayed, her face relaxed as the Holy Spirit came upon her and she gently fell to the floor under His power. Her head fell between the feet of a woman who was sitting in the front row of seats. I knelt and began to pray for her. Her lips moved, and quivered as she began to speak in tongues.

I looked up at the woman between whose feet the other's head lay. She was biting her nails and saying, "Oh dear, oh dear, oh dear!"

"Is there something wrong?" I asked.

"Oh, yes! There is. That's my minister's wife and she doesn't believe in this sort of thing!" she exclaimed.

"Well, she does now," I smiled.

Thus, the third "day" of Pentecost (our third model) was characterized by Christians, people who were already saved and baptized with water, who received the baptism in the Holy Spirit as a "second blessing" in response to the laying on of hands by a Spirit-filled believer.

4) The Fourth "Day" of Pentecost — Model #4
A sovereign act of Jesus, reaching out to a chosen individual in a unique experience.

A friend, whom I met in university, had spent some time in jail before I met him. He had been a very angry young man before his transformation. When in jail, a chaplain visited him and gave him a Bible. In his fury, my friend took it and tore it to shreds, throwing the pieces on the floor. Sitting on his bed with his head buried between his arms and his knees drawn up, his eyes fell on a torn page that littered the floor. It was a passage from James that said, *"No man can tame the tongue. It is a restless evil, full of deadly poison"* (James 3:8).

"That's me!" he thought. He heard what he assumed was a guard walk over to the bars. The man called him by name.

It was Jesus. My friend fell to his knees in repentance and allowed the oil of forgiveness to flow over him. "I want you to become a pastor," Jesus said.

"I'll do whatever You want Lord." At that point, he was totally cleansed of all the anger and sins of his past.

When he tried to tell his chaplain what had happened, the chaplain peered at him with eyes of seasoned cynicism and said, "Oh yeah, another one of those guys. You figure if you get some religion we'll give you a break and let you out early."

"No, I don't want a break," my friend countered. "I'm guilty and I want to serve my time." When his sentence was up, he walked out of prison committed to serving God and immediately enrolled in university so that he could become a pastor.

The fourth "day" of Pentecost is characterized by Jesus Christ acting in His own behalf to reach out to meet a person who is fighting against Him. He still does this today, whenever He knows that it is necessary. It happened to me.

The fourth "day" of Pentecost is revealed to us in the 26th Chapter of Acts through one man's experience. The man was Saul and he was a Jew. Saul was a very religious man, a quality that does not always make a person right. By his own admission, he was super-spiritual. He was a Pharisee who did everything that he could to destroy the Church of Jesus Christ.

Saul heard that there were some Christian believers living in the city of Damascus. He got the proper authorization to arrest them. As he was travelling on the road to that city, he was suddenly confronted by a bright light from Heaven. He heard a voice speaking to him in Hebrew, *"Saul, Saul, why do you persecute me? It hurts you to kick against the goads."*

Suddenly blinded, Saul was shocked. *"Who are you, Lord?"*

The surprising reply must have stunned him. *"I am Jesus whom you are persecuting."* It must have just about blown Saul's mind. He had staked his whole life on his belief that Jesus was dead and gone forever. Yet here He was, brighter than life. Jesus then gave him some instructions and told him to go and wait in Damascus. He would be contacted later. Saul was led into the city like a helpless child. There he waited for three days that must have seemed like an eternity.

Many people tell me that they would like to have what they call "a Damascus Road experience," similar to what Saul experienced. Not me! I want what happened three days later.

In Damascus, there was a Christian man by the name of Ananias, who was doing what most of us do at the start of each day. He was praying and asking God what He wanted him to do that day. Ananias, like many of us, didn't really expect that day to be much different than the day before. But it was.

Jesus appeared to Ananias in a vision. He told him that He had something special for him to do that day. Ananias was to go to a certain address, where he would find a man named Saul from Tarsus who has, *"seen a man named Ananias come in and lay his hands on him so that he might regain his sight"* (Acts 9:12).

Ananias immediately recognized the name. To paraphrase his response, Ananias said, "Lord, I don't want to presume to tell You Your business, but that guy is here to arrest me."

Nevertheless, the Lord instructed him, *"Go, for he is a chosen instrument of mine to carry My Name before the Gentiles and kings and the sons of Israel; for I Myself will show him how much he must suffer for the sake of My Name"* (Acts 9:15–16).

Ananias went. If he was anything like me, he went with great apprehension and a good measure of skepticism, wondering if he was going to survive. There are some people, we know without any doubt, who Jesus can save and transform; and then, there are those certain people who we are not really sure can be saved. For Ananias, Saul was in the latter category.

I picture Ananias nervously knocking on the door of Saul's room in fear and trepidation. Upon hearing the former persecutor's voice telling him to come in, he gingerly lifts the latch and, once in, he breathlessly blurts, *"Brother Saul, the Lord Jesus who appeared to you on the road by which you came, has sent me that you may regain your sight and be filled with the Holy Spirit"* (Acts 9:17). Stuffing his fear below his faith, he remembers his mantle of authority, places his hands on Saul's head, and prays. Immediately, Saul is baptized in the Holy Spirit and his eyesight is restored.

We are not told whether or not Saul spoke in tongues at that point. However, we know that his name was changed to Paul, signifying a complete change of identity. At some point, whether immediately or not, we know that he began to speak in tongues because later on, while trying to encourage the rest of us to use our spiritual gifts, he said, *"I thank God that I speak in tongues more than all of you"* (1 Corinthians 14:18).

In the story of this fourth "day" of Pentecost it is clear that even the worst enemy of Jesus Christ is not beyond being reached and even being converted into a leader in the Church.

Also clear is the fact that no matter what religion a person follows, religion cannot save anyone. Saul was a very religious Jew, but it didn't do him any good. It is possible for a person to be so religious that other people can be turned against Jesus Christ by mistaking religion for Christian faith. Many try various forms of religion, only to be so disappointed that they reject any concept of relationship with God and thus miss finding the real thing. They don't realize that religion is simply man's way of trying (ineffectively) to reach God. Christianity is God's way of reaching man.

In the strictest sense, the Christian faith is not a religion. It is a personal relationship with the living Jesus Christ.

One cannot earn favour with God by conducting contrived rituals, repeating formulated prayers or obeying man-made traditions and rules. The Christian Life is a gift of Eternal Life with Jesus, starting here in this lifetime and extending beyond death.

Following his baptism in the Holy Spirit, Paul spent time getting to really know Jesus Christ personally (Galatians 1:17–18) before taking his place in the Church. That is what Jesus wants us to do as well: be saved, be baptized in the Holy Spirit, get to know Him personally and then take our place in His Church.

Thus, the fourth "day" of Pentecost (our fourth model) was characterized by a sovereign act of Jesus, reaching out to a chosen individual with salvation and then sending a Christian to pray with him in order to receive the power of the Holy Spirit and healing, all in one unique experience. It demonstrates the fact that no one, not even our worst enemy, is beyond the reach of Jesus Christ. However, just as He required Ananias' obedience in order to reach an anti-Christian person, Jesus requires our cooperation. If Saul, the ultimate enemy of the Church, responsible for the first recorded death of a Christian (Acts 7:58-8:1) can be saved and filled with the Holy Spirit, no one is immune to the call of God.

5) The Fifth "Day" of Pentecost — Model #5
The Holy Spirit fills people as they receive His Word.

Some time ago, I spoke in a Baptist church near St. Thomas, Ontario, in response to one of the strangest invitations of my ministry.

The church was pastored by a lady with an intriguing story of her divine appointment with God.

She told me that she had been reading her Bible one night in Acts, Chapter 2, and she asked the Lord Jesus if what she was reading about could happen to her. He simply said, "Yes."

As He moved on her heart, she gently received the baptism in the Holy Spirit and began to speak in tongues right there in her own home. She was overwhelmed with the magnitude of the experience but had no idea how the Lord wanted her to proceed with her life and ministry from that point. She asked, "Lord, what do I do with this?"

The Lord replied, "Phone Gordon Williams."

"Who's he?" she asked.

This woman did not know any one by that name. She didn't watch "100 Huntley Street" and she knew absolutely nothing about me. The next day, she began to ask people in her church if any of them knew a man by the name of Gordon Williams. Someone remembered me from a crusade I had conducted there about 10 years before. This person thought that I worked at "100 Huntley Street."

When she called, they gave her my number and she relayed the amazing story to me. "What do I do with this?" she asked.

I showed her how her experience was entirely scriptural and counselled her on the baptism in the Holy Spirit and how to cooperate with Him.

She invited me to speak in her church. On the first night there, when I gave the altar call, I realized that I didn't have any catchers. I called the Pastor's husband over and asked him to stand behind people as I prayed for them so that he could catch anyone who fell down under the power of the Holy Spirit. He did that for the entire three services. Following the prayer time after the final service, I began to leave to go for coffee. The husband said, "Wait a minute. I need prayer too."

"What do you need?" I asked.

"Well, I guess I need it all," he said. As soon as I began to pray for him, he went down under the power of God and began to speak in tongues.

I left him there, knowing that he was in Good Hands and I went to the refreshment table to have a coffee. The pastor came to me and asked, "Have you seen my husband?"

"He's in the sanctuary," I said.

She went into the sanctuary and then returned with a puzzled look on her face. "He's not there."

"Oh," I said, "he's on the floor, speaking in tongues."

"But he's against this," she protested.

"Not any more!" I smiled.

The fifth "day" of Pentecost is demonstrated in Scripture through the story of a Gentile (a non-Jew), who was considered to be an enemy of the Jewish state because he was a Roman soldier and an officer or Centurion. He was part of the occupying army that controlled Israel. His name was Cornelius (Acts 10:1–41).

Cornelius was an unusual Roman. He was a man who sought after the God of Israel. Romans were generally known for worshipping a pantheon of so-called gods. Cornelius, however, wanted to know the one and only God. He sought Him diligently in every way he knew. He was *"a devout man who feared God with all his household, gave alms liberally to the people, and prayed constantly to God"* (Acts 10:2).

The condition of Cornelius' heart caught God's attention. Although one cannot buy a place in heaven with money, the use of one's money in God's service can be an effective indication of where the heart is. The combination of prayer and giving reflects a person's desire to know God. Thus, God sent an angel to Cornelius with a message: *"Your prayers and your alms have ascended as a memorial before God. Now send men to Joppa to bring back a man named Simon who is called Peter. He is staying with Simon the Tanner, whose house is by the sea"* (Acts 10:4,5).

Many people would like to catch God's attention, and so, they try to follow Cornelius' example. However, many fall down in not understanding what God expects from them financially. They get tithes, offerings and alms confused. "Alms" is a financial contribution for poor and needy people, people who have financial problems. However, before alms-giving is acceptable, a person has to be willing to pay his or her tithe, which means giving 10 percent of the income to the local church. *"'Bring the whole tithe into the storehouse, that there may be food in My house. Test Me in this', says the Lord Almighty, 'and see if I will not throw open the floodgates of Heaven and pour out so much blessing that you will not have room enough for it'"* (Malachi 3:10).

After tithing, God expects us to give offerings to support his various ministries, as recorded in Philippians 4:15–19, where Paul thanks the Philippians for their support of his ministry. Finally, God expects us to give our alms to help people in need.

Too many people cheat God by not paying tithes. *"But you ask, 'How do we rob You?' In tithes and offerings. You are under a curse — the whole nation of you — because you are robbing Me"* (Malachi 3:8,9). They give neither offerings nor alms. These people catch God's attention alright, but not in the way they hope. They prevent God from meeting all of their needs and requirements. Paul tells us that, *"God loves a cheerful giver"* (2 Corinthians 9:7). After all, we are made in the image of God, and if we are going to reflect Him in our lives, part of that is reflecting the fact that God Himself is a cheerful giver.

The other thing that caught God's attention about Cornelius was that he lived a *"devout"* life. That means that he was faithful to God without complaining. The desire of his heart was to know, love and serve God with all of his heart, mind, and soul.

Although the angel had told Cornelius to send for Simon Peter, God had to prepare Peter for his Gentile visitors.

According to the law, Jews did not visit with Gentiles or else they would be spiritually "unclean." As a conscientious Jew, Peter would have been very mindful of this stipulation. Thus it was, that God gave Peter a vision to show him that His grace was now available to all, regardless of race. *"What God has cleansed, you must not call unclean"* (Acts 10:15).

By the time the three messengers from Cornelius arrived, Peter's heart had been prepared to receive them and accept the invitation.

What an awesome time it must have been. Having received such unquestionable direction from God, Peter must have gone to Cornelius' house in eager anticipation to see what the Lord was going to do. He must have felt like dancing all the way there. When he arrived, the house was full of Cornelius' friends and relatives. He was eager for all of his loved ones to share in whatever it was that God was going to do. As Peter began to share the Gospel with those assembled, *"the Holy Spirit fell upon all who heard the message"* (Acts 10:44). They began speaking in tongues and praising God.

This must have been an amazing experience for Peter. The Jewish believers who had accompanied Peter were astonished that the gift of the Holy Spirit had been poured out even on the Gentiles. There was no laying on of hands and, in reverse to the normal procedure, these new believers were first baptized in the Holy Spirit and then baptized in water.

Thus, the fifth "day" of Pentecost (our fifth model) was characterized by people being sovereignly filled with the Holy Spirit as they heard the Gospel. This is the way that most people would like to be baptized in the Holy Spirit — sitting listening to a preacher as the Holy Spirit comes upon them, almost unnoticed. They seem to think this is more spiritual than if it happens through the laying on of hands. They want to know that man has nothing to do with their experience with God.

However, Jesus custom designs each experience for each individual, dealing with each one according to His higher knowledge of their needs.

6) The Sixth "Day" of Pentecost — Model #6
Believers received by the laying on of hands.

The story of the sixth "day" of Pentecost' happened in the city of Ephesus where Paul found some *"disciples,"* meaning that they were already believers in Jesus Christ (Acts 19:1–7). They were probably Jews, since they had been baptized by John. However, that wouldn't have mattered, just as it makes no difference today. *"There is neither Jew nor Greek, there is neither slave nor free, there is neither male nor female; for you are all one in Christ Jesus"* (Galatians 3:28). He asked them, *"Did you receive the Holy Spirit when you believed?"*

Their answer is similar to what many believers would say today: *"No, we have never even heard that there is a Holy Spirit"* (Acts 19:2).

These people had been baptized by John the Baptist and so they had been saved through their repentance. When Paul told them that John the Baptist had told them to believe in the One who was to follow him, they were baptized in water in the name of the Lord Jesus. Paul then laid his hands upon them and the Holy Spirit came upon them and they were baptized in the Holy Spirit. All twelve of them spoke in tongues and prophesied.

Sometimes, people think that they might have received the Holy Spirit, but they are not sure. They mistake the clean feeling of the experience of salvation for the "power-peaceful" experience of the Holy Spirit. When a person has been baptized in the Holy Spirit, he or she knows that it has happened. There is no guessing or speculating. It's like falling in love. When you are really in love, there is no question — you know you are. All the wondering about whether you are or not is gone.

When I was speaking in Western Canada a couple of years ago, a man came for prayer and he said, "I've been to some of the best of 'em. I've been to Oral Roberts and Rex Humbard and several others. I've been trying to get baptized in the Holy Spirit for a long time."

"Well," I said, "you've come to the worst of 'em!" We had a good laugh together and then I asked, "Have you had the laying on of hands?"

"No, I don't think so," he said.

"Well, tonight you're going to be baptized in the Holy Spirit." I laid hands on him and sure enough, the Holy Spirit met him and filled him. He began to speak in tongues right away.

When people come to me, as this man did, saying that they've been seeking the baptism of the Holy Spirit for a long time, I go through my check list with them, asking what they have done to that point. If they've never had the laying on of hands, that experience will allow them to receive the baptism of the Holy Spirit.

I don't know what significance the laying on of hands has. I simply do it out of obedience to the Bible and trust Jesus for the rest. For some reason the Holy Spirit moves in when we cooperate by doing that.

In some circles, the New Age Movement has begun to infect Christian thinking with pagan philosophy. Rather than laying hands on people, when they pray they keep their hands a few inches away from the person's body going all around it with the hands, but never touching it. Sometimes they use scooping motions with their hands towards people as though to splash them with air. The idea is that some sort of an energy force field is transmitted to bring healing or somehow empower the person. If a church allows people to use New Age techniques in its meetings, it will have problems, whether the people know what they're doing or not.

Our instructions from Jesus are to lay hands on the sick and lay hands on those seeking to receive the Holy Spirit. The occult people always tell us to do something other than what Jesus tells us to do.

Thus, the sixth "day" of Pentecost (our sixth model) was characterized by believers who received the baptism in the Holy Spirit and spoke in tongues through the laying on of hands.

Other Examples of Individual "Days" of Pentecost

The Holy Spirit is not limited to particular buildings or places or times. Any time is the right time. Any place is the right place. He is more flexible than we are. It is Jesus' desire to save all people and to baptize them in the Holy Spirit so that He can guide their lives.

Every person needs to have his or her own "day" of Pentecost. People can be prayed for almost anywhere — on the telephone, in a living room, in a Bible study, at a prayer meeting, or wherever. My wife Ruth and I have prayed with people in a car in a McDonald's Restaurant parking lot, in offices, at sporting events, in people's homes, at camp meetings and in churches. I have prayed with people in hall ways, on street corners, at universities, in garages, and on beaches. Any place where people are willing to pray, Jesus is willing to send the Holy Spirit.

Some time ago, I was visiting my home town of Kirkland Lake, Ontario, Canada, in order to transact some business for my father. While there, I remembered that a friend, who worked in the Christian book store located on the main street, was grieving the loss of her 17 year-old daughter, who had been murdered. I went into the store to see how she and her family were handling the situation. She had just begun to share with me how, through the terrible experience, Jesus had comforted and helped them, when suddenly, the front door of the book store opened. A young man walked in and said, "Gordon Williams!"

"Yes," I replied.

He walked over to me, took my hand, which I had extended toward him in greeting, and placed it on his head. He said, "I need the Spirit."

Startled, I quickly responded, "Oh, you mean that you want to be baptized in the Holy Spirit?"

"You've got it," he answered with a pleasant smile, still holding my hand firmly on the top of his head.

He prayed along with me as we asked Jesus to forgive him and to baptize him with the Holy Spirit. While we were praying, I felt his body going limp. He fell to the floor under the power of the Holy Spirit. I got down on my knees beside him and he began to speak in tongues. It turned out that he was an old friend who I had known some 30 years ago. Imagine that! He received the Holy Spirit in the book store!

The beautiful thing is, that like salvation, there is no age limit, either upwards or downwards. The youngest child that I can remember praying with to be baptized in the Holy Spirit was three years old. As we prayed, she began to speak in tongues. Her mother was so excited about it that she brought her eight-year-old daughter for prayer the next night. Both mother and daughter were baptized in the Holy Spirit and spoke in tongues.

The oldest person that I have prayed with one-on-one was a 98 year-old man. As he left the worship service where he had just become a born again, Spirit-filled, tongue-talking Christian, he told me that he knew that if he had died previous to that night, he would have gone to Hell. "I was hanging on by the skin of my teeth, Gordon. And, if you look closely, you will see that they are false teeth." He smiled with a twinkle in his eye.

Intelligence levels or IQs have nothing to do with receiving the Holy Spirit. I have prayed with university professors and students to be baptized in the Holy Spirit and they have received with tongues. I have prayed with mentally-challenged children and adults and they too were saved and baptized in the Holy Spirit.

One 13 year-old boy with Down's Syndrome came forward for prayer at a camp meeting in Saskatchewan, Canada. He was baptized in the Holy Spirit and spoke in tongues. I then prayed for six brothers and sisters and his mother, who was the camp cook, to receive as well. They were all baptized in the Holy Spirit and spoke in tongues before the camp meeting was finished. There is no such thing as a retarded spirit. Everyone's spirit can respond to Jesus Christ.

Nor is a physical handicap a barrier to becoming a born again, Spirit-filled Christian. We have prayed with deaf people, people with congenital deformities, and almost every kind of physically handicapped person. They, too, have been saved and baptized in the Holy Spirit and spoken in tongues. There is no such thing as a handicapped spirit.

There are times, however, when only the protection of the Lord prevents preachers themselves from becoming handicapped!

I was preaching at the Carrick Camp Meetings near Walkerton, Ontario, when I learned the truth of that statement. When I gave the invitation for prayer and ministry at the conclusion of my message, I began to pray with people and they were being "slain in the Spirit" (when the Holy Spirit came upon them, they would fall down).

There was a professional wrestler in the audience who was critical of what was happening at the altar. He had never before seen the Holy Spirit at work in such a way. I guess he thought that I was pushing people down. This huge man, almost seven feet tall, decided that he would come to the front, put a wrestling hold on the preacher and throw him to the ground.

He came marching down towards me. Of course, I had no idea what was on his mind, but as he got close to me, I reached out my hand to shake his and welcome him. Immediately, the Holy Spirit came upon him and he was floored. While on his back, he was saved, baptized in the Holy Spirit and began to speak in tongues.

Sometimes a person is all alone, when she or he is baptized in the Holy Spirit.

While I was the senior minister at St. Paul's United Church in Brampton, Ontario, Canada, I conducted a retreat weekend at "Friendly Acres" retreat centre near Alton, Ontario. As I taught about the Holy Spirit, one lady became offended, because she thought that she heard me say that she was not baptized in the Holy Spirit. She was so angry that she spent most of the weekend in her room. When she went home, she complained to a young girl who was staying with her, "I know that I received the Holy Spirit when I believed in Jesus Christ."

The young girl told her that since she was a new Christian, she didn't know about it and suggested that she go and pray about it.

Irene did. She went into her bedroom and prayed, "Lord Jesus, I know that I received the Holy Spirit when I believed in you. But, if I didn't, would you please send Him now."

A tremendous wind came into her bedroom with such force that the dresser mirror came off the wall and her door slammed shut. She was filled with the Holy Spirit and some time later spoke in tongues.

A young man who was an attendant at a service station was watching the "100 Huntley Street" daily Christian television program between customers at the gas pumps.

At the conclusion of that particular program, I invited anyone who was watching and would like to be baptized in the Holy Spirit to pray along with me. He did.

The bell rang for the next customer. He opened his mouth to ask how much gas the person wanted and instead of his normal English, tongues came out of his mouth. The customer said, "Fill 'er up."

For the next three days, every time the gas attendant opened his mouth in order to ask a customer how much gas he or she wanted, all he could do was to speak in tongues. The answer was always the same: "Fill 'er up!"

Jesus wants to fill each one of us up with the Holy Spirit.

Is it Necessary to Have a "Catcher" When Praying for Someone?

People who stand behind those who are receiving prayer in order to catch them if the Holy Spirit causes them to fall to the floor, are usually referred to as "catchers." Many pastors refuse to use them because they feel that having backup security may encourage people to fall for attention, rather than for any truly spiritual reason. They say that if God is going to put someone who is seeking Him on the floor, He certainly isn't going to allow that person to be harmed in the process. Many actually scoff at the use of catchers.

I use them more for the sake of the people watching, rather than for the sake of those who fall. People sitting in their pews, particularly those unaccustomed to seeing the Holy Spirit move, often have concern when they see people fall over without support. They sometimes get very indignant when they see the apparent lack of concern Christians show for someone on the floor. Some get frightened that someone is going to get hurt or perhaps that someone has had a heart attack. They don't realize that this is a very normal aspect of the working of the Spirit.

There are times when I do use a catcher for the sake

of the person for whom I am praying. Those who have never been "slain in the Spirit" or "fallen under the Power" may fear falling on the floor. If they have never experienced the gentle way that Jesus lays people down for His ministry, they may be nervous. In such cases, I simply tell them that they won't necessarily fall, but if they do, there will be someone behind them to assist.

I was ministering in Owen Sound, Ontario some time ago when a large, portly woman and her husband responded to the altar call.

I prayed for the husband first and he immediately fell under the power of the Spirit. I then turned to his wife. Her elegant attire and obviously schooled mannerisms bespoke a person of some breeding. Someone told me later that she was an opera singer. "What would you like prayer for?" I asked.

"I do not wish to fall down," she intoned in a British accent.

"It's not a requirement," I said. "The Holy Spirit is a Gentleman. He won't do anything to embarrass or hurt you. He understands your needs."

"Fine," she nodded. "Let it be so."

"What would you like prayer for?" I asked again.

"I," she paused, "would like to be baptized in the Holy Spirit."

I took her hands and explained that this would technically suffice for the laying on of hands and I began to pray for her. Right away, I sensed the power of God fall on her and she fell to the floor where she lay, speaking in tongues, until the end of the meeting. When she began to get up, I went over to her and asked how she felt.

"It wasn't too bad after all," she conceded and smiled with somewhat less starch than in our initial dialogue!

I have never seen anyone get hurt without a catcher, but I have seen injury when catchers have not been paying attention to what they were doing. I've seen people bump into or be misdirected by catchers with unfortunate consequences. That's why I instruct catchers to pay strict attention to what is happening around them.

I've seen people fall into pews and chairs with no harm whatsoever. One evening, at a meeting in Toronto at West Ellesmere United Church, I had finished praying for everyone and went to get my Bible off of the pulpit, thinking that everyone had left. Just then, the organist, who was a huge man, approached me, saying that he would like prayer to receive the Holy Spirit.

I said, "Fine," not thinking at all about him falling. As soon as I led him in a prayer for the baptism, he fell back, crashing into the pews and hitting his head hard before jamming his body between the pews. "Oh no," I thought, "Lord, you've killed him!" I crawled down under the pew and I could see his lips moving. I thought that he was trying to ask for help — and then I heard the most beautiful language proceeding from his mouth. I left him there for awhile until he began to try to get up.

"How do you feel?" I asked, pulling him out from under the pew.

"I feel wonderful," he grinned.

Ordinarily, he should have had a massive concussion at the very least. "Are you sure you're OK?"

"Yes, I feel incredible," he reassured me with a new softness in his voice.

Some time later, I was invited to do some teaching on the gifts of the Spirit in that area. The organist was at the meeting. I went to him and asked him how he was feeling. "Why do you keep asking me that?" he laughed.

"I don't know whether you realize it or not, but the night that you received the baptism, you really gave your head a crack when you fell into the pews. Under normal circumstances, you should have been black and blue all over!"

"Well, I wasn't!" he smiled.

The Wind Blows Wherever it Pleases.

"The wind blows wherever it pleases. You hear its sound but you cannot tell where it comes from or where it is going. So it is with everyone born of the Spirit"(The words of Jesus in John 3:8).

I have been accused of making the baptism of the Holy Spirit too easy for people to receive. I am not the person who determines who is going to be baptized in/with/by the Holy Spirit. Jesus is the person who makes that decision. All we can do is ask. If a person's attitude is wrong, or there is sin and unforgiveness in a person's life, or they want to receive the baptism of the Holy Spirit for the wrong reasons, then Jesus will not baptize them.

The main problem with many people, pastors included, is that they try to decide who is worthy or acceptable. We all need to learn the lesson that God showed Peter through his vision. *"Truly, I perceive that God shows no partiality, but in every nation anyone who fears him and does what is right is acceptable to Him"* (Acts 10:34,35).

We must always keep in mind that Jesus died on the Cross of Calvary in order to pay for our salvation. That gave Him the right to equip believers for His service and exercise His Lordship over their lives by baptizing them with His Holy Spirit.

4

Prayer and the Gifts of the Holy Spirit

"Praise the Lord, O my soul, and forget not all His benefits" (Psalm 103:2).

Suppose a car owner were to choose to use gas in his car, but refused to use oil because he didn't like the smell of it. The owner of another vehicle decided to use oil in his car, but refused to use gas because he had heard somewhere that it was a highly flammable substance. How far would those cars go? Obviously, cars are designed with the need for both gas and oil. Without either one, they may look fine on the surface, but in actual fact be useless space fillers.

One of the most counterproductive influences on the "normal" Christian life is the ever present attempt by well meaning people to choose between the different components of the Christian life. They don't understand that God gave all of the elements to be used in complementary conjunction with each other.

By assuming that we have the option of choice and then taking the liberty of arbitrarily eliminating important elements, we are left weak and unable to carry out the ministry to which Jesus has called us.

In travelling from church to church, I have witnessed the continuation of this troubling phenomena. Most distressingly, many Christians are still choosing between prayer and gifts of the Holy Spirit.

In some churches, the leadership and people have decided to pray for people's needs, but not to use the gifts of the Holy Spirit to minister to those needs. These churches downplay the importance of the gifts, to the detriment of their people's spiritual growth. They place them in danger of losing, not only their personal relationship with the Holy Spirit, but also the help that Jesus sent Him to give us.

On the other hand, I have preached in churches where the leadership discourages people from having prayer for their needs. Instead, they direct them to someone with a particular gift of the Holy Spirit, according to the specific need involved. In downplaying prayer, these churches place their people in danger of losing their personal communication with Jesus Christ.

It is never a question of prayer or gifts of the Holy Spirit, just as it is never a question of fruit of the Holy Spirit or gifts of the Holy Spirit. Both are needed for the equipping of the saints for ministry.

Prayer is our communication system with God. Gifts of the Holy Spirit function through prayer. The gifts of the Holy Spirit are like guided missiles and prayer is the guidance system by which they operate.

The Arrogance of Choice

Because God answers prayer, some Christians don't think that they need the gifts of the Holy Spirit. They see God moving in response to their prayers with healing or whatever and therefore think that, through prayer, they can receive the same thing that the gifts of the Holy Spirit will bring. While this may be true in some regard, there are other considerations.

God designed both prayer and the gifts to be effective in particular situations, but never with the thought that either is to be considered adequate to the exclusion of the other. In other words, it is spiritual arrogance that sets aside either prayer or gifts of the Holy Spirit. God gave both, so that people can receive the benefits of their salvation through the ministry of others. We don't have the right to decide not to use one or the other. Our responsibility is to pray and allow those who have particular gifts to use them, in order to minister to the needs of people as the Holy Spirit directs.

The Dangers of Short-Circuiting the Power of God

Any Christian, whether in leadership or not, who arbitrarily selects elements of the faith to the exclusion of other God-given components, is vulnerable to the attacks of the Devil; through sin, unhappy circumstances or sickness. Expecting other Christian believers within his or her sphere of influence to make the same choices, actually counsels rejection of God's protection. Such choices are dangerous. Those who dare to select only those elements which fit his or her personal theology serve God either ineffectively or not at all.

Whenever we try to deny the importance of God's equipping or gifting, we get confused about what Jesus is doing. We lose the ability to recognize whether or not we are cooperating with the Holy Spirit.

The Bible, with its full outline of all of the components of a normal relationship with Jesus, must be the standard or the measuring stick by which we can determine whether we are living the "normal" Christian life or an "abnormal" Christian life that will leave us disappointed and discouraged.

Many try to ignore the gifts that God has given them. These people end up being very frustrated and unhappy in their lives. In an attempt to justify themselves for not using their gifts, they often go to churches where the gifts are either not encouraged or not allowed, so that they can feel as though they have an excuse for not using what God has given them. However, no matter how far people try to run, they can never escape the gentle urging of the Holy Spirit. They will never find contentment until they become willing to be used.

Answers to Prayer or Gifts of the Holy Spirit?

Sometimes people mistake answers to prayer for gifts of the Holy Spirit.

When we pray and ask Jesus to supply a particular need and He does, that is an answer to prayer. That is not a gift of the Holy Spirit. Prayer is a necessity for every Christian.

A gift of the Holy Spirit is a customized gift of God to be used to meet a specific need. Once given to a person by the Holy Spirit, it is operative all the time. It does not come and go. A person does not have the use of it one day and not the next. *"For God's gifts and His call are irrevocable"* (Romans 11:29).

If someone were to need wisdom in order to solve a problem, he or she could take one of two approaches, but taking both would confirm God's direction. One approach would be to pray for God to meet the need according to James' instructions: *"If any of you lacks wisdom, let him ask God who gives to all men generously and without reproach, and it will be given to him"* (James 1:5). The other approach might involve going to the pastor and finding out if anyone in the church has the gift of "the word of wisdom." That person could then seek and administer the solution to the problem through the use of his or her gift.

The exciting thing about using both prayer and the appropriate gift is that one gets the same answer from God through two different sources, thus assuring confirmation. When a sick person requests prayer for healing, we can follow what Jesus says in Mark 16:18 and *"lay hands on the sick and they shall recover."* When he or she is healed, that is an answer to prayer. On the other hand, the person should be able to call someone in the church who has the "gift of healing," go to that person who can then administer the gift and therefore receive healing. We must be careful not to exclude the use of either prayer or the appropriate gift of the Holy Spirit, or the person may not have the need met.

Like prayer, the gifts of the Holy Spirit are to be used or exercised daily, so that we are not only speaking to God and hearing from Him, but we are also, through the use of the gifts of the Holy Spirit, ministering constantly to other Christians and people who need to know Jesus Christ as their Saviour and Lord.

Holy or Unholy Frustration?

The gifts of the Holy Spirit are given to enable us to cooperate with the Holy Spirit. When He dwells inside, it is very difficult to ignore Him. Those who try to evade His prompting and directions often become irritated, frustrated and even angry, as He prods them to cooperate in carrying out God's plan.

In fact, because most people are unfamiliar with the ways by which the Holy Spirit tries to motivate us, many begin to think that evil spirits are causing their agitation. If they are simply not listening to God's voice, that's probably untrue, regardless of what some misinformed Christians may say. However, if they continue their wilful ways, they will become disobedient, unfaithful, unreliable and uncooperative. The danger of quenching the Holy Spirit (1 Thessalonians 5:19) by constantly ignoring His direction, is a dreadful eventuality. Nothing is worth that risk.

No Refunds — No Returns — No Recalls — No Second-class Citizens

When the Holy Spirit takes up residence in our hearts, He becomes a permanent occupant. In the same way, when He gives us a gift or gifts with which to minister, His gifts are permanent gifts. Paul reminds us that, *"the gifts and calling of God are without repentance"* (Romans 11:29). This means, of course, that the charismatic gifts cannot be revoked, recalled, undone, or taken back.

Anyone who doesn't have a particular gift of the Holy Spirit can pray for it. Anyone who does have one, needs to pray and use it continuously. People who complain and bury their gifts in the ground or neglect prayer are missing the true treasures of life. They need to use what they have and pray for the rest. Thanking and praising Jesus for His love and friendship and for the trust He has demonstrated by allowing us to minister in His Name, gets a lot more mileage than complaints about gifts we may not have.

There are no second-class citizens in the Kingdom of Heaven. The promise is for *"whosoever."*

While the Holy Spirit does not take back the gifts if a person is not living as they should, grave complications can arise through misuse. For instance, I've counselled numerous pastors who have been carrying on sexual affairs, but continue to minister the Gospel. They've said to me, "Well, it really doesn't matter, because look what's happening in my ministry. People are still being healed and delivered."

What has happened in every situation is that everything has fallen apart shortly after our discussions. They may think they can get away with sin for awhile, but they don't for long. The pressure becomes too intense.

Some years ago, I talked with a woman whose husband was a well known evangelist. They had gone to Florida and established a church of over 2000 people and then her husband became involved with the church secretary.

He told his wife, "God is still using me."

His wife pleaded with him to repent, but to no avail. Finally, when everything was exposed and he lost his position, he refused to accept forgiveness and left both his wife and the other woman. His wife went to him one more time and said everything she could to restore him.

She said, "Look, you've counselled hundreds of other people in similar circumstances to simply ask Jesus to forgive them. You know He can do that for you, too."

"I can't do it," he said and committed suicide shortly thereafter.

When I saw his wife, she had three little kids with her and was still very emotional, because she loved him and was having a very difficult time dealing with it all.

A person in such circumstances as this man, who truly repents and gets straight with the Lord, can be restored very quickly .

Joy through Praying with the Mind and Praying in the Spirit

When a person receives the gift of tongues, he or she can speak, pray or sing in tongues at will, whether in a recognized time of need or in simple obedience to the leading of the Holy Spirit. Without the gift of speaking in tongues, through which Paul says we can pray in the Spirit, we can pray with our minds. Both are of the utmost importance.

As Christians, we have a responsibility to pray. However, praying in the Spirit is much more than a dry responsibility. It's fun. It's the source of the abundant life Jesus came to bring.

There's nothing that will turn anyone off faster than a boring, super-spiritual, flaky Christian.

A woman, who had been baptized in the Holy Spirit about three months earlier, came to me for prayer. When she first received, she spoke in tongues, but never used her gift after that initial experience. Part of the problem was that her husband was a very "spiritual" man and she found his attitude so oppressive that she didn't want to participate in anything that would make her life any more dreary than it already was.

I asked her about whether or not she was still praying in tongues and she said, "I can't do it."

"Well of course you can do it," I said. "You've already done it."

"No, no," she said again. "I can't do it."

"Listen," I persisted. "You have grandchildren. What do you say to them when they tell you they can't do something you know they can do?"

"Well, I tell them they can do it."

"That's right and so I'm going to be your grandmother tonight and tell you that you can speak in tongues."

She was still hesitant.

"Wait a minute," I said. "You're afraid of this because you think it won't be fun. Isn't that true?"

"Yeah," she considered for a moment. "That's right."

"Well, I want you to know that it is fun, and it has to be fun or it's not from the Lord."

"Are you sure?" she asked incredulously.

"Yes. That's where the joy comes from. You have to learn that you don't have to be afraid of these gifts, but that you can have a lot of fun with them!"

She still wasn't buying it.

"Let's just try," I continued to encourage her. "You don't have to strain your voice or do weird things like your husband does. Just be yourself. You don't have to be like him." We chuckled and then began to pray.

Almost immediately, her tongues began to flow. She continued for about three minutes before she paused.

I said, "Why don't you do it louder? The louder you do it, the more fun it gets!"

Well, she started to pray and pray and it was obvious that she was experiencing a very special time. I said, "See, isn't this fun?"

"Why didn't anyone ever tell me this before?" she asked. "I never knew what it was really like."

Earlier that same day, I prayed with an old acquaintance with a similar problem. He had called initially for marriage counselling, but his wife had told him to see me first and said that she would possibly come with him later on.

"My wife tells me that I don't have the joy of the Lord," he said. "She's right. All of these years, I've never had joy. You seem to have joy, but I don't have it. How do you get that joy?"

"You've been baptized in the holy Spirit, haven't you?" I asked?

"Well, yes," he said.

"Do you speak in tongues?"

"I did in the beginning, but that was 21 years ago."

"Well, that's where the joy comes from," I said.

"What?" he looked shocked.

"That's right," I said. "You've got to pray in the Spirit every day."

We began to pray and by the time he left, he was a different man. As a matter of fact, my wife, Ruth, drove in just as he was leaving. When she came in the house, she asked, "What was with that fellow who left? He went dancing down the driveway and jumped in his car as though he'd just received the best news in the world."

"He did," I smiled.

A Prayerless Life is not Worth Living

Someone once said that a prayerless life is not worth living. Most Christians don't know that. They live their lives by guess and by golly and wonder why they have no power to overcome struggles.

One of the great problems, however, is that many Christians don't know how to pray. We assume that just because someone gets saved, he or she automatically knows how. That's not necessarily true. They need teaching and they're not getting it.

People need teaching not only in what to say, but also in what they're possibly going to experience, such as dry mouths, sleepiness or pounding hearts.

Rosalind Rinker wrote an excellent book about conversational prayer called, *Prayer: Conversing with God,* which is very helpful.

Those who do not spend time walking and talking with Jesus don't really know Him and are vulnerable because they don't know His voice. They don't always recognize the voice of Satan masquerading as God.

Over and over, I hear people saying things like, "God told me not to pray for so-and-so," or "God told me not to help so-and-so." That's not true. God would never say any such thing. He tells us to take all of our needs to Him. A favourite line is, "God told me not to tithe. I don't have to tithe any more." Interesting. It's not long before their lives get into a total mess with financial chaos.

Praying for Healing

We've all known people who have prayed for healing and have subsequently died. However, unless an afflicted person has been told by God that he or she is going to die, we have a responsibility to continue to pray for that person, no matter what we may *feel* about the chances of survival.

If God is not going to heal someone, unless He has given that message Himself to that person, we should continue to pray despite any doubts that Satan tries to plant in our minds (Luke 18). It has been my experience that God speaks directly to the person concerned in such situations, before He speaks to peripheral people.

On one of our trips to Israel, one of the women on our tour had cancer. We prayed and prayed for her but didn't see any results. Some people felt that God was going to heal her and others disagreed. Back and forth it went.

When we returned to Toronto, I visited her in the hospital one day and she asked, "Gordon, do you think the Lord is going to heal me?"

"I don't know," I said. "What is He telling you? You are a Spirit-filled Christian and He will tell you if you ask

Him. Don't take it from anyone else. Some people will have nice opinions for you and others will not. You need to hear from the Lord yourself."

I went to see her another day and she said, "I've been praying. Jesus told me that He's not going to heal me. He's going to take me home."

"How do you feel about that?" I asked.

"I have total peace about it," she smiled.

And that's the difference. When the Lord speaks to a person directly, He prepares them to receive His message.

However, until God speaks, it is vital that the person continue to ask God for healing through every avenue He presents. That means going wherever necessary for prayer and not to stop going until either healing comes, or God's word that He has a different plan comes.

When I had my heart problem and the doctor gave me two years to live, I became a nuisance. If I was sitting beside someone and I began to get a pain, I'd grab his or her hands, place them on my heart and say, "Pray for me." People get tired of that, and we get tired of asking. But that's what we have to do. The Lord eventually healed me completely!

One time a minister asked me, "Gordon, what is the percentage of people who get healed when they receive prayer?"

I thought about it for a moment, because I had never compiled any statistics on the results of prayer. It suddenly occurred to me that, despite the fact that we don't have statistics, we do know this one thing: if we don't pray for anyone, then nobody gets healed, but if we do pray, then many are healed.

When I was working at "100 Huntley Street,"after the program one day, I gave an invitation in the chapel for anyone who would like to receive salvation or healing to come forward for prayer. One of the women stormed out in very apparent agitation. Her friend approached me a little later and told me that the woman was very angry with me. She asked me to talk with her.

When I approached the woman, she accused, "You said that God heals everyone if you pray for them."

"I didn't say that," I replied. "I said that if Jesus is not going to heal someone that He will tell them and He will tell them why."

"That's exactly true!" she exclaimed. "My seven-year-old boy had cancer last year. There were all kinds of supposed prophesies over him claiming that he was going to be healed and that this was, "not unto death;" but after praying for awhile one day, I asked, "Lord, are You not going to heal my boy?"

The Lord said, "No. I'm not going to heal your boy, because I want to prepare you to minister to dying children."

"Is that what you're doing now?", I asked.

"Yes", she said. "I go to the Hamilton hospital every week to minister to dying children."

That's why we have to hear from the Lord ourselves. It's such a personal thing. We can't trust that others will hear correctly from God in critical situations. Although people, such as this woman's friends, are usually very well meaning, they have not been taught to listen to God properly.

One-Way vs. Two-Way Prayer

How often do we think we are praying when we talk to God, but don't really experience communication, in terms of hearing from Him as well as talking to Him? How often do we wait to listen to what He has to say to us? How often do we wander about, complaining that, "God never answers my prayers," when in fact, we stonewall His answers?

If we are to grow in relationship with Jesus Christ, we need to learn to recognize His voice so that, when He calls to us, as He did with Samuel in the Temple, we can say, *"Speak, Lord, for your servant is listening"* (I Samuel 3:9–10).

A woman came to me one day and said, "You claim to hear the Holy Spirit talking to you. How do you hear Him?"

"Do you want to learn how to hear Him?" I asked.

"Yes," she said.

"Get yourself a notebook and a pen," I said. "Each day when you pray, tell Him everything that is on your heart and then sit and listen. Tell Him, "Lord, I'm listening." Then sit and write down everything you suspect He might be saying to you. It will take about a month before you really tune in to all that He is trying to say to you."

That's what I generally find it takes for people — 30 days of diligent listening and recording — before they learn to hear the voice of God.

Time — the Essential Factor in Relationship

Unfortunately, the majority of people do not spend enough time in prayer to be able to distinguish the voice of the Holy Spirit from that of Satan. With the average Christian spending only seven minutes per week in prayer, the problem is compounded by the fact that they do not know the Bible well enough to confirm whether what they are hearing when they pray is truly from God.

Therefore, despite the fact that the Holy Spirit will never direct us to do anything that is not according to Scripture, the average Christian is more vulnerable than he or she can imagine. Ignorance of the content of the Bible and an inability to recognize the voice of Jesus, place people in dangerous positions.

The Key to the "Normal" Christian Life

Prayer in cooperation with the Holy Spirit is the key to the "normal" Christian life.

Prayer in line with the will of Jesus opens access to all of the promises of God. Praying in unity with the Holy Spirit, to facilitate the use of His gifts, is always fruitful, because it is totally in line with the will of God. Such prayer will demonstrate that no one is beyond the reach of God and that nothing is impossible with Him. It changes not only other people's lives, but our own.

We need to pray for and encourage one another so that we can all share in the "normal" Christian life. *"Let love be genuine; hate what is evil, hold fast to what is good; love one another with brotherly affection; outdo one another in showing honour. Never flag in zeal, be aglow with the Spirit. Serve the Lord. Rejoice in your hope, be patient in tribulation, be constant in prayer. Contribute to the needs of the saints, practice hospitality... . Live in harmony with one another; do not be haughty, but associate with the lowly; never be conceited"* (Romans 12:9–13,16).

The Holy Spirit constantly urges us, to the point of irritation, to use the gift or gifts that we have received. When we do, as individuals and as the church, we grow and mature, as people receive ministry and have their needs met.

Having a gift or gifts of the Holy Spirit does not excuse us from prayer or give us the right to live a prayerless life. The opposite is true. Having gifts of the Holy Spirit makes us even more responsible to *"Pray without ceasing,"* (1 Thessalonians 5:17) so that we can be sure of using our gifts at His direction, rather than to focus attention on ourselves. Jesus must be the only one who receives the glory.

5
The Jigsaw Puzzle Church

"For just as the body is one and has many members, and all the members of one body, though many, are one body, so it is with Christ. For by one Spirit we were all baptized into one body — Jews or Greeks, slaves or free — and all were meant to drink of one Spirit. For the body does not consist of one member but many"
(1 Corinthians 12:12–14).

Any young mom, cleaning up after her little ones, knows that one tiny, seemingly insignificant piece of a jigsaw puzzle, lying forgotten under a bed, is precious. If she were to carelessly throw it into the trash, the whole puzzle would be ruined. Never again could someone enjoy the intense satisfaction of pressing that last, elusive shape into place. It wouldn't matter whether the piece was a nondescript section of blue sky or a key piece of lettering, every piece is equally vital to the whole. As she picks up the odd little shape, she does so carefully, for she knows that if she were to bend or break it, the whole picture would suffer damage.

To me, church congregations are like jigsaw puzzles. Every member represents a piece. On Sunday mornings when I look out at the congregation in worship, the puzzle all comes together.

From where I stand, I have a clear picture of what Jesus Christ is calling us to do — and what a picture it is! I see men and women, young and old, who love Jesus Christ and have been spiritually gifted for His service, being deepened in their relationship with the Master. When I see the fantastic potential that the body of Christ has, I get so excited that I just have to shout, "Praise You, Jesus Christ! Thank You for equipping this church with so many people who have spiritual gifts, so that we can accomplish the vision that you have given us for this church!"

On the other hand, I have often felt sorry for the people who sit in the pews. When they focus on the pulpit, all they see is one piece of the jigsaw puzzle: that's me. Unless they look around, they miss the big picture.

One Body — Many Parts

Jesus compared His church to a human body which, like a puzzle, consists of many different parts, organs, or members, each vital to the welfare and good health of the whole body. If one part is sick, or hurting, then the whole organism hurts. In the same way, every person is important to the body of Christ. Every one has a specific function, without which the rest would be incomplete.

Because we are entirely interdependent, we cannot realistically say that any part of the body is dispensable. We all need each other. Every person has a rightful place in the body. *"If one member suffers, all suffer together; if one member is honoured, all rejoice together"* (1 Corinthians 12:26).

A small tooth might appear unimportant, but one toothache quickly elevates the understanding of the importance of that little body part. The loss of a tooth brings discomfort and puts added stress on the other teeth, as well as on the digestive system, which is then forced to compensate for the job not done by the missing tooth.

If ever there was an unsung hero, it is the appendix. That little internal organ functions totally in the dark, receives no recognition for its contribution to the body and could live a lifetime without notice — unless it starts to hurt. An attack of appendicitis lets the whole body know that, if something isn't done to remedy the situation, the whole body will be filled with poison and die. Not one cell escapes the effects of the pain!

Jesus likened each member of His body, the Church, to a body part with a specific function, or gifting of the Holy Spirit.

Fitness in the Body of Christ

The world is obsessed with physical fitness. Late night TV channel surfers can flip through countless programs extolling the virtues of perfect physiques. All kinds of contraptions are exalted as the final answer to achieving the body beautiful.

How trite it all appears when compared to the importance of fitness in the body of Christ.

Comparisons are, however, sometimes helpful. It is obvious that a physically fit person is fit all over. Muscular torsos are seldom found atop weak legs. In the same way, the Church is truly fit and healthy only when each person operates for the benefit of all in his or her gifts of the Holy Spirit.

No matter how painful it may be, physical health and fitness requires exercise. Unless the members of the body of Christ work together, exercising their various gifts, the church will be spiritually flabby. Each member needs to be born again, baptized in the Holy Spirit, and using the gifts which he or she has received for the building up and good health of the church.

Just as the right arm of a weight lifter cannot do the whole job without the left arm, no church member can say to another church member, *"I don't need you"* (1 Corinthians 12:21) or *"I am not really needed in this body"* (1 Corinthians 12:15).

Just as every muscle and sinew is recognized as vital to the body, there has to be a recognized place in the church for every born again, spirit-filled, gifted person. No person assembles his or her own cells, but is designed by the Creator. In the same way, no church — no pastor, elder nor lay person — can assign gifts to individuals in the body according to any human agenda. Each person is gifted directly by the Holy Spirit and is placed within the church for a specific function.

The Crippled Body of Christ — Missing Pieces

The Church of Jesus Christ has been crippled. How? People who have been equipped with gifts of the Holy Spirit have not been allowed to use their gifts for the benefit of the church. It's as though someone arbitrarily selected pieces of a puzzle for removal from the box and refused to let them be used to complete the picture.

The result is a weak, crippled religion, rather than a powerful partnership with the Holy Spirit. We have become so handicapped in our efforts that, rather than bringing forgiveness, healing and good health to people and the society in which we live, we have perpetuated sin and sickness, both spiritually and physically, into the lives of other people.

A healthy body functions as a unified whole. Every cell fulfills its specific function for the good of the whole body. There is unity among the members. An unhealthy body is a result of weakness in the system. A malfunctioning group of cells causes disunity or *dis*-ease.

Disunity in the church is not necessarily a result of disagreement in doctrine. It is often caused by the lack of recognition of individual Christians and their spiritual gifts. Time and time again, people who may have tried to use their gifts for the good of all have been put down. Others may have witnessed the procedure and have become fearful of stepping out themselves, for fear of correction.

This is why many people don't fit into churches. They find Jesus Christ as their Saviour and Lord, receive a gift or gifts of the Holy Spirit and then proceed to use what they have received in a local church, in obedience to the prompting of the Holy Spirit. Instead of being guided and nurtured, they experience insensitive attacks and put downs. Not surprisingly, they stay home and lick their wounds.

The potential for the body of Christ has too often been stifled by church leadership who, encouraged by the enemy of our souls, warns that allowing people do the ministry that the Holy Spirit has equipped them to do will result in chaos. They say that people will be turned off and will leave the church. They warn that the pastor will be asked to leave — the offerings will decrease — the Devil will get control of the church.

Why don't people read their Bibles instead of listening to faithless naysayers in Sears Roebuck robes?

Crippled people are often reduced to whiling their hours away with dreams of what might have been. The crippled church has been reduced to a shadow of its original self. It has, for the most part, denied the very components that were designed to give it strength and power. The result has been few revivals and the loss of desire to save souls. Evangelism has been turned into a grotesque form of seasonal entertainment for the saints, a salve to relieve their consciences from the knowledge that they, themselves, should be reaching out to the unsaved and bringing them in.

Jesus Christ has called and equipped the church to carry out powerful ministry through the spiritual gifting of its individual members. Tragically, we have responded like the enormously gifted track star who, guaranteed of a gold medal in the Olympics, determined to run the race on one leg, with the other one hobbled by a self-imposed cord.

Discarded Pieces

Because the leaders of most churches have not taken the time to find out how to encourage the proper use of the gifts of the Holy Spirit, they aren't skilled in teaching people to use their gifts in worship, prayer meetings and various gatherings in the church.

There is tremendous insecurity in pulpits with regard to allowing the gifts of the Spirit to flow. Many ministers are deathly afraid of losing "control."

To eliminate the problem, spiritually gifted people are often discarded from the church. They become the missing pieces of the picture.

As an evangelist, I have seen body (of Christ) parts strewn along the highways and byways of every city, town, and village, from one coast of the United States and Canada to the other.

Where Can I Find a Puzzle with all of the Pieces?

Wherever I go, people ask the same question: "Where can I find a "good church" — a "Spirit-filled church" — where I can fit in and use the gifts that the Holy Spirit has given to me?" Unfortunately, there are few.

Because most pastors, ministers or priests are fearful of what would happen if they were to open up their ministries to the Holy Spirit, New Testament Churches as described by the apostle Paul are rare. In such a church, the Holy Spirit would have the freedom to speak through every church member or body part. It would be an exciting, growing place of worship.

The ideal church, according to Scripture, would fulfill every hope, dream and vision that God ever gave to a pastor. The worship and ministry would resemble what the apostle Paul described in 1 Corinthians 14:26–33: "*When you come together, everyone has a hymn, or a word of instruction, a revelation, a tongue or an interpretation. All of these must be done for the strengthening of the church. If anyone speaks in a tongue, two, or at most three, should speak, one at a time, and someone must interpret. If there is no interpreter, the speaker should keep quiet in the church and speak to himself and God. Two or three prophets should speak, and the others should weigh carefully what is said. And if a revelation comes to someone who is sitting down, the first speaker should stop. For you can all prophesy in turn so that everyone may be instructed and encouraged. The spirits of prophets are subject to the control of prophets. For God is not a God of disorder but of peace."* What pastor or leadership would run the risk of allowing that to happen? Despite the fact that Paul tells us how to do *"everything decently and in good order,"* it is not like the order that most churches follow.

Few of us have ever seen or experienced a church that comes anywhere close to that ideal. It would seem that the worship service Paul describes would be out of order. What very few realize is that this is the only order of worship that Scripture validates as being truly guided by the Holy Spirit, in such a way that all of the body parts can function as designed. This is church with all of the pieces available and usable. This is the whole picture.

Spiritual Athletes — Going for the Gold

I keep hearing people in church leadership say, "God has no superstars today." But, indeed, he has — whether elevated to that status by humans or by God.

Just look at an average church service. The same people exhibit their natural gifts and talents almost every week. A few, but still the same few, exercise their few spiritual gifts to the nodding approval of most people who will go home saying, "That was a good worship service." Unfortunately, many will go home experiencing a frustration, the source of which they cannot identify.

The source is the Holy Spirit who has been nudging them to allow His gifts to flow through them. The frustration is the blockage they have erected, whether from pride, self-consciousness, or fear, and the knowledge that their spiritual lives are not what they should be.

The real superstars should be those born-again, Spirit-filled, spiritually-gifted Christians who go to worship, desiring more than anything else, to be able to serve the Lord effectively and to use the gifts with which the Holy Spirit has equipped them for the encouragement of others. They go looking for an opportunity to be equipped for *"the work of ministry for the building up of the body of Christ"* (Ephesians 4:12).

It is the responsibility of the church leadership to provide them with an arena of freedom in which to operate.

Training for Success

As pastor of the Good Samaritan Church in Kitchener, Ontario, I discovered that by using the gifts of the Holy Spirit properly, the Holy Spirit could show the church where He wanted to guide it. He would show us God's plan for the Church and how to accomplish it. When there were impending problems, He would warn us before they befell us and tell us how to solve them. After He had guided us through, according to God's plan, we would give Jesus our praise and thanksgiving. He did it for six and one-half years. He did it by using and speaking through His body parts, His people.

The result was that we did not have one Sunday without at least one salvation, but usually more. Every week we saw people saved, baptized in the Holy Spirit, healed, and delivered safely from evil spirits.

One morning there, Jesus told me to blow a bugle before I started the service. In obedience I said, "Listen folks, this may sound a little strange, but the Lord told me to blow this bugle and so that's what I'm going to do." This went on for about two months. I would blow the bugle and then we would go into praise and worship.

Of course, blowing a trumpet is a warning of danger or impending attack.

A couple of months later, Ruth and I went to Florida on vacation and while we were gone, some people tried to take over the church. Benny Hinn had asked me to preach in his church on the Sunday and I was to do some teaching there, but one day, when Ruth and I were praying together, the Holy Spirit told us to go home quickly. We obeyed and walked into the church right in the middle of everything. The people who were trying to take over had not had time to get the Elders on board because we arrived home before we were expected. As a result, we were able to expose those people for what they were. After a bit of a kafuffle, the troublemakers left and we were able to continue.

Because we taped every prophesy and tongues with interpretation, we were able to check every one out according to Scripture. We published them in the following week's bulletin if they stood up under scrutiny. We had prophesies about all sorts of situations that arose in the church.

Another time, an outside group tried to buy our property out from under us and they ended up going bankrupt over it. Our lawyer became a Christian because of the way the Holy Spirit guided us through that situation. In the beginning, he would give us legal advice to do this or that. We'd pray about it and the Holy Spirit would tell us to either follow or reject his advice. Confounded, he'd say, "What do you mean you have to pray about it? There's no choice here. You have to do this."

We'd go away and pray again. The Holy Spirit would say, "No, don't do that; or yes, do that." It would generally come through tongues and interpretation.

When we'd tell the lawyer, he'd just shake his head.

This went on for three or four years. Finally, he asked to meet with our Board. I asked him if he'd mind telling me what it was about. He said that he'd prefer to talk to all of us together and just said, "Trust me."

I agreed and called a meeting. He stood up and said, "I just want to thank you people for showing me what faith is. In the legal profession, we call it 'risk.' You were legally unprotected for much of the time through the process of the negotiations concerning your building, because of decisions you made after praying over issues. I watched Jesus carefully and safely guide you through legal problems which you should never have been able to get through."

He accepted Jesus.

Invalid Judgments

There have been all kinds of stories about people who have been offended by the use of the gifts of the Holy Spirit. That might well be true, if the gifts of the Holy Spirit were not used according to Scripture and by the guidance of the Holy Spirit. However, I know from my own experience, observations and reports, that most people who have left the church have done so because the Gospel was not being preached.

These people did not experience what they read about in the Bible. They came looking for God and did not find Him. Nor did they see a demonstration of the power of the Holy Spirit. They did not leave because they were offended by the use of the gifts of the Holy Spirit, but because they never heard them or saw them being used in the church. In fact, they couldn't have identified one if their life depended upon it. They usually left out of boredom and disappointment.

The only people who are truly offended by the movement of the Holy Spirit are those who do not want God in their lives and do not want to see evidence of His reality, or sometimes those who have not received the baptism in the Holy Spirit and simply have not been able to discern truth.

Did you know that it takes, on the average, only seven complaints, whether from individuals or from couples, to get a pastor to shut down a successful church program or worship service? On the other hand, an unsuccessful program, or a worship service that is killing a church and driving people away, can drone on for years on end. The justification for the exodus is that the people who have left were not spiritual enough or were not dedicated deeply enough to the mission of the church.

Evaluation of Criticism

The church leadership — whether pastors, elders, deacons, or lay leaders often does not know how to evaluate criticism. They have not learned how to determine whether criticism is constructive or destructive, positive or negative. Most leaders become so fearful of certain powerful individuals in their congregation, they compromise the Gospel. They discard the preparation they received at Bible college, or seminary, and follow advice of people who have never taken a ministry course and who know nothing about worship or the Christian ministry. They follow unspiritual advice because of fear. They ignore both the Bible and the Holy Spirit. Paul reminds us all that, *"God has not given us a spirit of fear; but of power and of love, and of a sound mind"* (2 Timothy 1:7).

Danger! Danger! Danger! — Pieces that Don't Fit

No matter what God does, it seems that Satan is right there with a counterfeit, trying to spoil God's plans and rob people of His blessings.

The great fear of Christians is that Satan will infiltrate worship services and deceive individuals with his counterfeit gifts. We are warned over and over again, not to let just anybody go ahead and use their so-called gifts of the Holy Spirit, because the Devil might be involved. We have become so paranoid — afraid of being fooled or led astray, blaspheming against the Holy Spirit, or perhaps being so deceived that we'll actually fall away from the Lord — that many people have taken the ostrich position and refuse to participate in any way with the operation of the gifts. Many church leaders have forbidden their use in services.

This determination to protect individuals from Satan's wiles would be admirable if it was entirely scriptural. However, the problem is that it was Jesus who gave real gifts to His church for very specific purposes, not the least of which was for use in defeating Satan. When we refuse to use Gods tools, we are left trying to battle the enemy in our own strength - which doesn't work well at all.

We need to understand that the so-called counterfeits of the gifts of the Holy Spirit come from the occult world and practices. They are so different from the real gifts that, unless we were told they are supposed to be counterfeits of the Holy Spirit, we probably wouldn't recognize them as such.They neither look nor sound like the real gifts of the Holy Spirit, nor do they result in the same mighty works and miracles.

Here are a few examples:

Gift of the Holy Spirit	Counterfeit
Prophesy	Fortune telling, palm reading, crystal ball reading, the practice of seeking out a medium where the so-called medium has to go into some kind of trance-like state.
Healing	A temporary healing that quickly disappears. The person's health deteriorates rapidly and the person dies prematurely.
Tongues	Automatic handwriting, or a person going into a trance and speaking with a voice other than his or her own and coming under the dominating control of a spirit of some kind. Often a woman's voice will come out of a man or a man's voice out of a woman. The person may make animal sounds like the roaring of a lion or a wolf, or sounds that have no meaning in any language.

The best way to get rid of the fear of counterfeit gifts of the Holy Spirit is to become familiar with those that are real. We need to learn to use them, test them and encourage their proper Biblical use. That is our best protection.

When we take the time to learn to use the gifts with confidence, the day comes when we can look back and laugh at ourselves for being caught up in any fear of counterfeits. The Devil delights in our ignorance and lack of experience.

Some years ago, I had a friend who was working for a major bank. He was sent away for a one week course called, "How to Identify Counterfeit Money," which was to be held in Toronto, Canada. Before he left, we speculated that the teacher of the course would probably display all kinds of counterfeit money as examples of what to look for.

That, as it turned out, was not how the course was taught.

Instead, the course leader displayed legitimate currency of all denominations for those on the course to examine. For 35 long, boring hours that week, the participants familiarized themselves with great quantities of Canadian paper money: $1, $2, $5, $10, $20, $50, $100, $500, $1,000, and $10,000 bills. (Today, of course, the $1 and $2 bills have been replaced with coins.)

All week, they rubbed the money between their fingers, examined it, held it up to the light, got the feel of the paper and generally became totally familiar with genuine currency. On the last day, counterfeit money was shown to them for four hours. To the amazement of the students, they could easily spot and identify the counterfeit money. They had become so familiar with the real thing, they could tell at a glance whether the money was counterfeit or not.

The same is true with the gifts of the Holy Spirit. We have to become so familiar with the genuine gifts, and their use, that when the enemy does try to throw in a counterfeit, we can spot it and identify it without any problem. We don't have to get in a panic, or worry about what the Devil will do. We can expect that he will try to throw in some confusion, but for those who are familiar with the Holy Spirit and the way He uses His gifts, there is no concern. They have learned how to cooperate with the Holy Spirit. When He uses the Gifts to encourage, warn or correct them; or to direct them in ministry to one another, they experience great blessing.

Because the so-called counterfeits do not look, sound, or do the work of the Holy Spirit in our midst, the word "counterfeit" is somewhat of a misnomer. The real gifts of the Holy Spirit cannot be copied. We need each other for encouragement, teaching, experience and reassurance, and to make the body of Christ the visible witness to the world that Jesus is our Saviour and Lord.

Christian ministry is war. *"For the weapons of our warfare are not carnal, but mighty through God to the pulling down of strongholds"* (2 Corinthians 10:4). Usually the weapons are explained to be: preaching, witnessing, prayer, Bible study, worship and specific things that help Christians deal with the Devil, evil spirits and sin. These certainly are weapons.

However, the mighty weapons that are overlooked and rarely used are the gifts of the Holy Spirit. These gifts, when used properly, drive away the Devil, defeat evil spirits, and open the way for people to accept Jesus Christ as their Saviour, Lord, King and God. When used under the guidance of the Holy Spirit, they cause Christians to mature and become responsible, reliable church members. When allowed to be used in the worship and work of the church, they result in God's people being obedient and knowing,*"the peace of God that passes all understanding"* (Ephesians 4:7). When allowed to be used according to Scripture, the gifts have an evangelistic purpose that will cause revival in our churches.

The Love Piece

Christian love (agape) is the oil that allows the gifts of the Holy Spirit to operate and be used openly, correctly, and with freedom. Paul's "love chapter" (1 Corinthians 13) is strategically placed between his two chapters of instructions about the proper use of the gifts of the Holy Spirit. To many people's disappointment, this chapter is not a warning against using the gifts. Rather, it is a manual on their proper usage.

"If I speak in the tongues of men and of angels, but have not love, I am only a resounding gong or a clanging cymbal. If I have the gift of prophecy and can fathom all mysteries and all knowledge, and if I have a faith that can move mountains, but have not love, I am nothing. If I give all I possess to the poor and surrender my body to the flames, but have not love, I gain nothing. Love is patient, Love is kind. It does not envy. It does not boast. It is not proud. It is not rude. It is not self-seeking. It is not easily angered. It keeps no record of wrongs. Love does not delight in evil, but rejoices with the truth. It always protects, always trusts, always hopes, always perseveres. Love never fails" (1 Corinthians 13:1–8).

At this point, many who reject the use of the gifts for today are saying, "Go on, go on!" because it is the next part of the passage that they claim as justification for their position.

"But where there are prophesies, they will cease; where there are tongues, they will be stilled; where there is knowledge, it will pass away. For we know in part and we prophesy in part, but when perfection comes, the imperfect disappears. When I was a child, I talked like a child, I thought like a child, I reasoned like a child. When I became a man, I put childish ways behind me. Now we see but a poor reflection as in a mirror; then we shall see face to face. Now I know in part; then I shall know fully, even as I am fully known"(1 Corinthians 13:9–12).

Unfortunately, many glance quickly at this passage and say, "See? Tongues and prophesies are not for today. It says right here that they will pass away!"

What about knowledge? Do we not have any knowledge today? The argument doesn't hold water. Close examination will reveal that it is at the end of life, as we know it, that prophesies, tongues and our imperfect knowledge will pass away. Only then shall we see *"face to face"* and *"know fully."*

God wants us to have all of the benefits of the gifts of the Holy Spirit. They are gifts of grace, distributed by the Holy Spirit. They are righteous gifts, given to us by God to use for our personal building up and the edification of our fellow church members. They are to be used in ministry that has been bought and paid for by Jesus on the Cross of Calvary. Their use is never to be discouraged. They are for the benefit of the Church. Through them people can be saved and healed and protected. Through them the fellowship of the church can be developed. Their use develops spiritual maturity.

Paul has called us to be tolerant of each other. *"Having gifts that differ according to the grace given to us, let us use them"* (Romans 12:6). We must have the same patience with fellow believers that Jesus has with us.

Love completes the picture.

6

Unwrapping the Gifts

Presents for Everyone

"All these are inspired by one and the same Spirit who apportions individually as He wills"
(1 Corinthians 12:11).

It is Christmas at the Smith's. Father and Mother have done everything they can to make things perfect for a storybook celebration. For months they have deliberated over what gifts each child would appreciate and use to the best advantage.

With each purchase now boxed and tied to Martha Stewart perfection, the parcels glimmer in soft reflection of the tiny, golden twinkle lights on the tree. It is finally time to savour the delighted expression on each child's face.

The children are so excited that all they can do is bounce. Nevertheless, they settle expectantly around the tree until each name is called. One by one, the gifts are revealed.

The first child eagerly rips the wrapping paper away, throws the bow to the side, pulls the carefully-chosen gift into the light, examines it and then, pouting in disappointment, crosses his arms as he declares his dislike for what he has been given. The second and third children open their boxes together. They take a look at their gifts, and then, oblivious to the care with which each gift was chosen, they compare what each has received with the other. Having determined to switch gifts, each tries to put on the gift meant for the other, to no avail — neither fits. Howling in dismay, the two protest the perceived injustice.

Child number four is reticent to open her box, having witnessed the disturbing display of her brothers and sisters. She cautiously peers inside. Engaging the others in idle chatter to deflect attention from her gift, she slowly slides the box behind her, hoping that no one will notice that she has opened it. When asked about her gift, she shakes her head, pretending not to have even seen it.

The fifth child is practically jumping out of his skin by now. Christmas is the most important time in the whole year to him and he can't get enough of anything. Having exhausted every drop of patience in his little heart, he finally jumps right into the middle of the pile of gifts and greedily grabs at every package in view, crowing jubilantly, "They're all mine. All of the gifts are mine! Father loves me so much that he meant for me to have every one!"

In the wild melée, as the others attempt to retain what they have been given, Father intervenes and chuckles tolerantly at the child's enthusiasm. When order is restored, he hands his small son the parcel marked with his name and, despite the little one's protestations, he firmly declares that no child could be given all of the gifts.

Father then hands a colourful box to child number six. With studied intensity, the little one pulls each strand of the bow apart, carefully extracts the gift and, with effusive thanks, expresses as much gratitude as he can articulate. To everyone's surprise, he excuses himself, carries his gift to the desk, opens the bottom drawer, takes everything out of the drawer, puts the gift in the very bottom, piles everything else back on top and closes the drawer.

Rejoining everyone under the tree, he smiles as though nothing happened.

"Why did you hide your gift in the bottom of the drawer?" they all ask in shock.

"What gift?" he shrugs his shoulders and pretends ignorance. "I didn't receive any gift."

The seventh child has waited patiently. He is sure that the gift in the one remaining box is for him. Sure enough, Father picks it up, hands it to him and smiles with love as he says, "This is just what you need, my son." The boy unwraps the gift and, with pure delight and inexpressible gratitude, he puts on the garment inside. It fits perfectly. Immediately, he notices that his little brother is shivering, draws him close and cuddles him lovingly within the warmth of his gift.

Christmas all Year 'Round!

In the spiritual realm, Christmas never ends. The gifts that stream from that first Christmas, when God sent His Son to redeem the world, just keep on flowing.

Of course no comparison with earthly gift giving can possibly convey the value of the gifts of the Holy Spirit. When we consider the price that was paid at Calvary so that we could experience salvation and the richness of the gifts of the Holy Spirit, we cannot possibly comprehend the magnitude of their value. Jesus' story of the "Ten Talents" (Matthew 25:21,23) is a description of their value in earthly measures. The talents described are symbolic of the gifts of the Holy Spirit. In Jesus day, a "talent" of gold was a unit of measurement. At today's gold prices, each is worth $1,225,813.12.

The parable goes on to parallel the excitement of what can happen through using the gifts, rather than leaving them to lie dormant. At the end of it all, Jesus will say, *"Well done, my good and faithful servant. You have been faithful over a little. I will set you over much. Enter into the joy of your Master."* Through using the gifts, we can experience the joy of our Master!

According to the apostle Paul, it is the Holy Spirit who decides what gift or gifts each of us needs in order to be equipped to share the Gospel with the world.

In my mind it goes something like this: after a person experiences the new birth and then is baptized in the Holy Spirit, the Holy Spirit looks at that specific individual and, according to his or her God-given ability, ponders what gift He can give this person to show him or her how much he or she is loved, appreciated and trusted by Jesus. He looks at each of the gifts of the Holy Spirit in careful consideration and finally chooses the one or ones that He knows this person needs for use in ministry.

The apostle Paul makes it very clear that the gift or gifts that we receive are no mistake. He says, *"But each has his own special gift from God, one of one kind and one of another"* (1 Corinthians 7:7).

Receiving Gifts

Unfortunately, many of God's children are just as self-centered, foolish and lacking in judgment as most of the Smith children. In comparing their gift or gifts with those that other people have received, some decide that they would rather have what the other person has. When the coveted gift seems totally beyond reach, they pout in disappointment. Oblivious to the enormous value of what they have been given, they don't use their gifts. They *"bury* (them) *in the ground"* (Matthew 25:25).

Others deny receiving anything. The gifts do not fit their theology. They claim that because the gifts are "not for today," they did not and could not have received them. Any thoughts to the contrary are assigned the label of imagination and are accorded no more meaning than that of misguided fantasy. They too, "bury their gifts in the ground." If pressed to explain the source of the gifts others claim to have received, most of these people would be quick to point their fingers at Satan.

Then there are those who say they are thrilled to

have received gifts of the Holy Spirit — but never use them. They love to boast to other people that they have received this or that and wear their claims like lapel pins. Very sadly, however, they never minister what they have received to others. Again the gifts are "buried in the ground."

How it must bless the Father when He sees people receive with thanksgiving, delight and understanding. In humility of heart, these people meditate in wonderment on the realization that the Holy Spirit has entrusted them with powerful ministry gifts. They treasure them as pure gold for use in serving the Master. The knowledge that they have received gives them a feeling of great honour and blessing, rather than any occasion to boast. They begin to use them immediately, by investing them in ministry. The result is that these talents of gold increase and double. The gifts of the Holy Spirit are not only for the building up of the church, but are to be part of the witness that draws people to salvation.

To Use or to Bury — our Choice

Ministering the gifts of the Holy Spirit through us is one of the ways that God answers prayer. Those who have them can be a part of the solution to people's problems, if they allow Him to use their lives. However, we have the choice to use them, or not to use them. The saying, "If you don't use them, you lose them," does not apply here. Paul tells us that, *"the gifts and calling of God are without repentance"* (Romans 11:29). Once given, the Holy Spirit will not take them away from us. They are given to be used or not used until Jesus returns. Only then, *"when the perfect comes, the imperfect will pass away"* (1 Corinthians 13:10).

For now, use of the gifts is one of the wonderful ways that God has provided for us to participate in His ministry and work. If we choose to bury what the Holy Spirit has given, we lose immeasurable riches both here and in Eternity.

The Interdependent Body

Some people who discover the joy of using the gifts of the Holy Spirit get greedy and want all of them. Unfortunately, with one exception, no one person can have them all. That exception is Jesus in whom dwelt all of the fullness of the Holy Spirit. If we could all have all of the gifts, we would not need each other.

As it is, we are meant to be an interdependent body, complementing and cooperating one with the other. That is what fellowship is all about. When the church comes together, as each person uses his or her gifts in ministry for the good of others, every person both gives and receives ministry. That is the plan. Unfortunately, the reality is most often quite different.

Filling in the Gaps

Some people have observed my ministry and concluded that I have all of the gifts of the Holy Spirit. They're often surprised when I tell them that I don't. I just act as though I do!

A problem arises when others, who have been gifted in a particular capacity, do not step forward with their gifts.

In such a situation, adjustments have to be made in order to minister effectively to people who often have very critical needs. What I do is this: I use the gifts of the Holy Spirit that I have been given, and, where I do not have a particular gift of the Spirit in order to deal with a particular problem, I pray. I can get the same results, because God still hears and answers our prayers.

The difference is that the person, who God equipped to function in that particular situation, missed the blessing of being used. Part of the body ended up being more exercised that the rest. It was out of balance.

If I had all of the gifts of the Holy Spirit myself, I wouldn't need anyone else. I would be my own little church selfishly trying to minister to myself and by myself. That is not what Jesus ever intended for His church. He wanted us to come together as the family of God to worship

Him, minister to each other, and then go out to minister to the world.

Wanting More

Often, when the Holy Spirit decides it is time to give another gift to a person, He will give that person a growing desire to receive another gift. I believe that is why Paul said: *"Make love your aim, and earnestly desire the spiritual gifts, especially that you may prophesy"* (1 Corinthians 14:1). That desirous person then can ask God, and the Holy Spirit will give him or her another of His gifts (Romans 1:11). While we are invited to seek a particular gift, God gives us gifts according to His wisdom and purpose for our lives.

Beginning to Use the Gifts

There has been a lot of confusion about how to begin using the gifts the Holy Spirit gives us. When people are newly gifted, there's seldom much encouragement for them to begin using them, simply because the majority of pastors don't have experience in teaching people how the Holy Spirit wants to work through them. Some people think they need a bolt of lightening from Heaven, telling them that it's time for them to prophesy. Others are under the impression that unless they are shaking, with their hearts practically pounding out of their chests, it's not really the Holy Spirit and they dare not speak.

People need to know that the Holy Spirit is very gentle.

Using a gift should almost be like a reflex action. A simple whisper from the Holy Spirit that He wants us to speak out in tongues or give an interpretation or whatever, should be enough to elicit a response from us. He should not need to practically shake us out of our chairs in some frustrating attempt to get us to be obedient in the use of a gift.

For example, in a recent house meeting, a woman was quietly speaking in tongues as the others were praying. I asked her to please speak out a little louder.

"Why?" she asked.

"Because," I said, "I believe that the Lord wants to give a message in tongues through you."

"But I ... I," she sputtered.

"No, really," I persisted. "Just do what you are doing but speak up a little louder."

So she did. A moment later, someone else began to give the interpretation, paused for a breath and a second person continued the interpretation. When that person paused, a third person finished it.

The Holy Spirit is just that gentle, that usually the simple idea, the simple desire to pray in the Spirit, is His nudging to minister to a group or an individual through a gift. That should be all it takes for Him to be able to communicate a message.

Therefore, if a person suspects that a prophecy should be coming or whatever, simply opening the mouth in readiness to speak is all that is needed. The Holy Spirit will supply the words.

People aren't accustomed to it being that easy. They think that there has to be some great sign from God, but that's not the way it should be. In actual fact, it's a very simple thing.

Of course Paul puts limits on the use of the gifts — two or three messages is enough. After tongues have been spoken, the group should wait for the interpretation, and if there's none, then the meeting should simply progress with teaching or preaching or whatever has been planned.

Recently, I ran into a fellow from Orangeville, Ontario, who had been at a house meeting and he expressed some concern about tongues.

"I don't know what to think of all of this tongues stuff," he said.

"Why?" I asked.

Shrugging his shoulders, he said, "I don't know what these people are trying to say."

"Well," I responded, "tongues are legitimate languages

and when they're used properly, there will be an interpretation with them."

"What do you mean 'interpretation'?" he asked. "I never heard anybody say what it meant."

"That's exactly the problem. That's why Paul said that if there are tongues, there must be an interpretation or else people will think it's crazy."

"Yeah," he said. "I think the whole bunch of them are crazy!"

Although this man was a Christian, he had never been baptized in the Holy Spirit and because the gifts were used improperly in his presence, he was not convinced.

Most people are sitting around terrified that they might say the wrong thing. They're so afraid that what they say might not really be from the Lord. If a believer does speak out in tongues out of his own enthusiasm, rather than in response to prompting from the Lord, the worst thing that will happen is that he or she will be praising the Lord in a strange language in public. What is so terrible about that? The other possibility is that there will be an interpretation and then there will be great encouragement for all.

It has to be that easy. The gifts of the Spirit need to flow naturally and easily. They need to be used properly, but they can be opened gently without any great fuss.

Checking the Tag to Confirm the Giver

One of the greatest fears people have is that someone is going to reject their message as not coming from God. They think that if they speak at the wrong time, God's going to kill them or worse.

In fact, God has never killed anyone for honestly trying to cooperate with the Holy Spirit. The Holy Spirit will not kill us. Jesus will not condemn us. In fact, God loves us so much *"that He gave His only begotten Son, that whoever believes in Him should not perish but have Eternal life"* (John 3:16). He is pleased when we try to attune our senses acutely to Him in an attempt to grow in maturity.

The greatest mistake that people make in judging the gifts is that they use their *feelings* as a measuring rod. If something doesn't *feel* quite right, they think it's suspect.

It doesn't matter how a message *feels*. The question has to be whether or not it's scripturally accurate. In actual fact, if a prophesy is from God, it's going to make people feel uneasy because it's going to convict them of sin.

People seem to be under the impression that a word from the Lord has to make them feel good. Well, that will happen too, of course, but if there is a call to repentance, people should feel uneasy. They should feel like Isaiah and want to run out of the building.

When someone makes a mistake in using the gifts of the Holy Spirit, he or she needs to be corrected with a kind attitude. The person should not be confronted with a holier-than-thou approach, but in the manner of a real friend who can sympathize from the experience of having to learn to use his or her own gifts through a great deal of loving patience on the part of the Holy Spirit and fellow Christians. Most would say, as I do, that they still require a lot of patience to this very day!

Having Fun

The joy of the Lord should flow full and free as people begin to discover and use their gifts. The idea that holiness means acting as though one has been baptized in prune juice, has nothing to do with the Holy Spirit. It's supposed to be *fun* using these gifts.

Yes, they are serious business. But, they are also the Lord's way of communicating with His Church and doing ministry through His Church. Working with the Lord should be exciting.

As a good friend of mine once cautioned: "Gord, we have to be careful that we don't become so heavenly minded that we are no earthly good." He was right. The gifts of the Holy Spirit are designed for ministry so that we can be of some earthly good, as we apply the saving work of Jesus Christ to the lives of our church family.

The Fifteen Charismatic Gifts of the Holy Spirit

When people speak of the gifts of the Holy Spirit, they normally talk about the nine gifts listed in 1Corinthians 12:4–11. They forget about the seven gifts in Romans12:6–8. (Note that one of these, the gift of Prophecy, is contained in both lists and so is counted only once.)

In the following two chapters, we are going to focus on the individual gifts; first those in 1 Corinthians and then those in Romans. In both lists, the same Greek word, "charisma," is used for "gifts." It is the word from which we derive the phrase "charismatic gifts" or "gifts of grace freely given."

We shall look at each of the fifteen gifts individually and attempt to clarify:

1. proper procedure for private or personal use
2. proper procedure for public use
3. how in certain situations the need can be answered through prayer.

7
The Nine Gifts of Corinthians

"For to one is given the word of wisdom through the Spirit, to another the word of knowledge through the same Spirit, to another faith by the same Spirit, to another gifts of healings by the same Spirit, to another the working of miracles, to another prophecy, to another discerning of spirits, to another different kinds of tongues, to another the interpretation of tongues" (1 Corinthians 12:8–10).

1. The Word of Wisdom

The Word of Wisdom is a problem-solving gift with a very practical purpose. It is a supernatural solution or "know-how" for an earthly problem. Through this gift, God imparts His wisdom to those close to Him, thus communicating how to deal with particular situations and empowering people to make proper judgments. This kind of wisdom is not natural or earthly wisdom but it is entirely practical.

The Word of Wisdom can be given in any worship service, prayer meeting, Bible study, or any group of people who are seeking God's help. The group may be a small group of two or three, a meeting of thousands, or a simple little family praying together.

The important thing is not the size of the group, but the fact that the word or message is given by the Holy Spirit when He wants to give it, rather than when we want to get it. It operates at the discretion of the Holy Spirit, not ours. We can neither demand nor orchestrate a Word of Wisdom. We may ask for one, but it is still the Holy Spirit's prerogative to determine the *when, where* and *how* of its use.

In times of crisis, when it seems that everything is in a muddle, the Holy Spirit may tell a person who has been gifted with the Word of Wisdom how to solve the problem.

Neither the person with the problem nor the person with the gift would normally know what to do. The solution may not make any sense. It may sound totally crazy, but if followed, the problem will be solved. One of the ways that God answers prayer is through the use of this gift.

A person gifted with the Word of Wisdom may receive the word in a variety of ways. He or she may be worshipping God in a group, when, without warning, the Holy Spirit will tell him or her that someone in that meeting has a particular problem. Because The Holy Spirit is intimately tuned in to every individual need and situation, the person will not necessarily be named to save embarrassment and protect confidentiality. In other situations where personal privacy is not an issue and God could be glorified through public knowledge of what is happening, the person might be named.

It is the gifted person's responsibility to stand up, or at least speak up, at the appropriate time and tell the group that there is at least one person or perhaps a number of people with a particular problem (or problems) and this is the solution. The Holy Spirit might give just one, or perhaps a list of problems with their solutions through the person who has the gift of the Word of Wisdom.

It is not the gifted person's responsibility to follow up on people in order to make sure that they have done what the Holy Spirit has directed. The option is always with the people who have the problem to use, or not to use, the solution or solutions which the Holy Spirit has provided. If they do, then they will be blessed, not only in having a problem solved, but also in knowing that Jesus does care for them.

There is no problem with which the Holy Spirit cannot deal. A Word could be given for anything from fixing a car, investing money, buying a piece of real estate, or solving a church problem, to dealing with the most intimate personal problem.

I was in a church service one evening when the Holy Spirit prompted a man there to stand up and say, "This may sound strange and even unspiritual, but there is a person here who is having a problem with his or her car. Now, I don't know anything about cars, but the Holy Spirit just told me to tell you that if you will look under the dashboard of your car, you will find that there are some wires that need to be connected. Somehow, or other, the mechanics missed them."

Now, that probably doesn't sound very spiritual to many people's ears, but anything that affects God's people and hinders or prevents them from getting on with God's everyday plan is a spiritual problem. People need to get that through their heads. Life cannot be compartmentalized. It is all spiritual because the Holy Spirit is present in every aspect of our lives.

In another meeting, a tent meeting on a Reservation in Northern Saskatchewan, a lady stood up to share a Word of Wisdom. She said, "There is a man here tonight who has been struggling. Nothing has been going right with you. You want to serve God, but you can't. You are considered to be the leading man in your church, but you know that you are not. You can't understand what is wrong. The Holy Spirit has told me that the reason you are having such a problem is that you have been resisting being born again. You have believed that because you were raised in the church, you are saved and going to Heaven. Well, you are not and that is your struggle. You need to come to the altar tonight and be born again. You need to come to the altar tonight and find forgiveness for all of your sins. Your struggle will end and you will know God's plan for your life. You will have the peace of God."

Suddenly, a man whom she did not know burst into tears. Everyone in the tent meeting could hear him. He rushed to the front. When we prayed with him, he asked Jesus to forgive him and come into his heart. He found the solution to his problem. Later on, he told us, "I changed from a religious man to a Christian man."

Sometimes, we think that God is not really interested in the small problems that we have to deal with. Through the Word of Wisdom, He is able to show us that He does care about every detail. Our lives are not made up entirely of big problems, but of an accumulation of small ones.

I do not have the gift of the Word of Wisdom. Thus, I have to rely on other people to use their gift. However, when I do need wisdom, I can pray. This is what James was talking about when he wrote, *"If any of you lacks wisdom, let him ask God who gives to all men generously and without reproach and it will be given to him"* (James 1:5). That speaks of an answer to prayer. I do not have to feel left out just because I do not have the gift of the Word of Wisdom. As James told us, *"The effectual fervent prayer of a righteous man availeth much"* (James 5:16).

Those who have never experienced the Holy Spirit quickening them with a Word of Wisdom are naturally curious as to how it is received or manifested in the gifted person. People who have this gift tell me that the Holy Spirit communicates the word, message, or information in several different ways, depending upon the person involved. Some claim to hear an audible voice, while others say that they hear an inaudible voice — a quiet whispering in their minds. Still others say that they get what they call "impressions." I have had people tell me that they close their eyes in prayer and in their imaginations they see what looks like ticker-tape with words written on it. As they read the words, speaking out loud, more and more words appear until the solution is complete.

As with any gift of the Holy Spirit, people can cooperate and share what the Holy Spirit has shown them, or they can keep it to themselves. It is very common for people to be fearful that they are just making things up in their heads or that they might embarrass themselves or just simply be wrong.

If a person doesn't have the gumption to speak out a Word of Wisdom that the Holy Spirit has given, he or she will experience a deeply uncomfortable feeling that something is wrong, or a profound sense of having failed God. Most importantly of all, however, there are those who will go home not having received an answer to their prayers because gifted people have not trusted and cooperated with the Holy Spirit.

Those who do cooperate, however, know the unequalled excitement of working in partnership with the Holy Spirit in ministering to the needs of the people for whom Jesus died on the Cross of Calvary. What a wonderful experience!

2. *The Word of Knowledge*

The Word of Knowledge is a supernatural "know-what" the Holy Spirit wants to do next in a worship service, a prayer meeting, a Bible study, or a meeting of any kind wherever people are gathered together to seek God's will. The gathering could number as few as two or as many as thousands. It can even be given during a radio or television broadcast. This gift is used by the Holy Spirit to tell us what Jesus wants to do in our midst and allows the person with the gift to participate in God's work. It is knowledge about something that God is doing, wants to do or is about to do at that exact time.

This gift explains what God is doing and wants to do at that moment. As with all of the gifts, it cannot be acquired by study or learned by observation. Most often, it has to do with healing or the provision of something such as finances that will occur immediately and not by means of a person's efforts.

This is a gift that I have been given and I must confess that I am still very uneasy whenever the Holy Spirit shows me what He wants to do. This is because I want to be able to cooperate with the Holy Spirit and be accurate, but I want to be sure that I do not just communicate things that I would like to see God do for people. That is why I do not like people to give me prayer requests before meetings. I fear that my compassion might turn into what I could interpret as Words of Knowledge, but are really just wishful thinking, rather than God's desire for His people. I literally tremble and sweat when the Holy Spirit gives me Words of Knowledge.

Words of Knowledge are important for people to receive because they are given so that people can receive healing for their diseases and infirmities. People's health, yes, and even their lives, can depend upon our sharing of the gift of the Word of Knowledge.

This gift operates in much the same way as the gift of the Word of Wisdom. The Holy Spirit will communicate the message in various ways, according to however He can catch our attention, whether it is in an audible voice, a quiet inner voice, impressions, the spiritual ticker-tape, or in any way He wants. Those with this gift should not be concerned if He speaks the Word of Knowledge to someone else differently than He does to them. The important thing is simply that they get the message and pass it on to the appropriate people at the right time.

For me, the gift operates just a little differently than

for most. When I am praying, I get a picture in my mind's eye, or imagination, of a human body on which various organs light up, or are highlighted to show me what Jesus wants to do. At the same time that I am seeing this, He quietly tells me of specific problems. If I were to take a course in anatomy, I could perhaps give more accurate descriptions of what the Holy Spirit is showing me. On the other hand, most people are like me and don't know what the proper medical terms are for their body parts — they only know where it hurts. Thus, my description usually relays the message adequately to convince them to come forward for prayer.

The responsibility of the person who has the gift of the Word of Knowledge goes only as far as simple sharing with his or her listeners. We are neither required to make people respond, nor to spend an inordinate amount of time encouraging them to step forward for prayer in order to receive the fruit of the Word of Knowledge. Beyond giving people a reasonable time to cooperate, we have no responsibility. Whether they accept the Word of Knowledge or not is up to them, not us.

Recently, I was speaking at a Full Gospel Business Men's Breakfast. The Holy Spirit gave me a Word of Knowledge for several people there. One in particular stood out. I said, "There is a man here who has been told by his doctors that he has an incurable heart problem. The pain in your chest is very severe. It is so bad that you were not sure that you wanted to come to this meeting. Your wife did not want you to come either, for fear that you might get too excited and have another heart attack. Well, the Holy Spirit is telling me that if you will come for prayer this morning, you will be healed."

Sure enough, a man came for prayer accompanied by his wife, who told me that he was the one, and I had described the situation perfectly. Later on, after checking back with his doctor, he told me that his heart was completely healed.

I am constantly amazed that Jesus allows us to participate in His ministry in such an unusual and exciting manner.

3. *The Gift of Faith*

The gift of Faith is a sudden and complete trust and total confidence in Jesus Christ and in the Bible, with all of its promises, as the absolutely inerrant Word of God. The person with the gift of Faith does not waver with the ups and downs that characterize an ordinary Christian walk. Such "faith people" know that there is nothing that God cannot do and will not do, if the conditions of the Scripture are met.

They are what I call "the spiritual cheerleaders" in the church. When everyone else is low on faith and not sure that Jesus will do what He has said, or even if He can, those with the gift of Faith cannot see any reason why He can't. They are so completely positive that they can almost drive you crazy.

These people are heard saying, "Jesus can do it! Jesus will do it! Jesus is doing it! Praise God, Jesus did it! Praise the Lord, it's done!" They generate enthusiasm for the things of God, for the church, for His people, for the Bible, for tithing, for healing, for deliverance, for Jesus' return, for praise and worship, for miracles, for looking after the needs of the poor, for supporting other ministries, for using the gifts of the Holy Spirit, for prayer; in fact, for everything that is a part of the normal Christian life. Their faith is contagious.

The gift of Faith gives a person full access to all the promises of the Bible. This means that such a gifted person has no problems praying within the Biblically stated will of God, for anything or anyone. Although they would not pray for things which are sinful or which encourage people to live ungodly and destructive lifestyles, they do pray constantly for people who are in such states, that they might be saved and find God's plan for their lives.

People who have the gift of Faith are great "prayer warriors" because they pray with great expectations and usually don't take "no" for an answer, knowing that they are praying within the will of God.

No one needs to feel left out if they do not have the gift of Faith. We are told that each person receives a *"measure of faith"* (Romans 12:3). It is important to realize that the word which is translated from the Greek as "to have faith, or believe, or to have confidence in, or to trust," describes a personal relationship with Jesus Christ in which we can talk and communicate with Him. Such communication is called prayer.

Faith is not measured by quantity or weight. It is an intangible. People who claim that with enough faith, any need, including healing, money or whatever, will automatically be filled, lack understanding.

Jesus explained how to get more faith, but His explanation was upside down to what we would have expected. When asked by His disciples to, *"Increase our faith!"* He replied, *"If you had faith as a grain of mustard seed, you could say to this mulberry tree, 'be rooted up, and be planted in the sea,' and it would obey you"* (Luke 17:5,6).

"Mustard seed faith" is not the *gift* of Faith. "Mustard seed faith" grows depending upon the spiritual climate or environment. Some days it grows a lot. Other days, it doesn't grow at all. One day, such a Christian knows that Jesus can do everything that the Bible says. Other days, he or she isn't sure that He can do anything.

A "faith relationship" with Jesus Christ is developed over time through experiencing His faithfulness. Like any relationship, it can have its ups and downs, not from Jesus' side, but from ours. Learning to trust Him and to be obedient is a process.

Although it is not the *gift* of Faith, "mustard seed faith" is completely reliable. Jesus remarked one day: *"It is like a grain of mustard seed, which, when sown on the ground, is the smallest of all the seeds on earth; yet when it is sown it grows up and becomes the greatest of all shrubs, and puts forth large branches, so that the birds of the air can make nests in its shade"* (Mark 4:31–32). Mustard seed trees in Israel can grow to a height of 40 feet. No wonder Jesus picked mustard seed as an example of faith!

When I was pastoring, in order to encourage children and adults to understand the concept of "mustard seed faith," I used to give the children some mustard seed during a Sunday service and ask them to take the seed home, plant it, grow it for three months and then bring the plants to church on a designated "Mustard Seed Sunday." The results were always interesting. The plants ranged in size from about one foot to over six feet. Just like the plants, we grow in faith depending upon individual spiritual nurturing and the spiritual climate.

What do we really mean by 'mustard seed faith'? It is having just enough faith to reach out and cry, "Jesus! I need your help. Here is my problem." It is having just enough faith to *do* what Jesus tells us to do. He said, *"So you also, when you have done all that is commanded you, say, 'We are unworthy servants; we have only done what was our duty'"* (Luke 17:10). In other words, we are to just *do* what Jesus tells us to do without questioning. We're expected to respond just as the servants at the wedding in Cana of Galilee did, when His mother told them to *'Do whatever He tells you'"*(John. 2:5). It's that simple.

Thus, without the *gift* of Faith, prayer can bring the needed result. Gifted in this area or not, each of us can have a vibrant, confident faith that enables us to accomplish everything that Jesus has planned for us. As the faith-tree grows, we can know, without doubting, that all of the promises of God are for each of us, personally. With either mustard seed faith or the gift of Faith, we can become encouragers, God's spiritual cheer leaders, knowing that God's team wins in the end.

Those with the gift of Faith need to have patience with those who don't. They need to encourage their brothers and sisters. *"Love one another with brotherly affection; outdo one another in showing honour"* (Romans 12:10).

4. Gifts of Healing

Gifts of Healing are perhaps the most desired of the gifts. The proper translation of the Greek text is *"charismatic gifts freely and graciously given or bestowed, of healing or remedy."* This is a very important gifting, because other people's lives and ability to serve Jesus Christ in good health can depend upon the faithfulness of those who have the gifts of Healing.

It is interesting to note that this gift is a plural gift. This might mean that a person could be used to heal one particular disease or category of diseases, making him or her a "specialist" in terms of applying God's healing power - or, it could mean that a person has the gifting to heal any number of diseases, making him or her a "general practitioner" in terms of applying God's healing power.

I met a pastor in the Southern States who has the gift of Healing for eyes. No one in his church wears glasses. God uses him in a specialized area. On the other hand, Oral Roberts is a man who, over the years, has prayed for people who have received healing from various kinds of diseases or illnesses. He could be called a "general practitioner."

Whether specialist or GP, however, the Holy Spirit equips people with this gift to be a part of the ministry of the Church — not to go out into the world to open up so-called "healing clinics."

People with gifts of Healing have a responsibility to make themselves available to pray for the healing of sick people, whether through asking a sick person for permission to pray for them, or through responding to direct requests for prayer. Sometimes sick people will feel free to ask, while at other times they may be reluctant to ask, but are in definite need of prayer. Regardless, people with gifts of Healing have to be willing, when they see sick people, to offer to pray for them.

The key is to follow Jesus' example. Although Jesus did have many people go to Him for healing, either for themselves, for a member of their family or for a friend, He did not always wait for a person to ask.

For example, Jesus offered to heal the man with the withered arm in the synagogue in Capernaum (Mark 3:1–5). Then, there was the crippled man who had been sick for 38 years who lay near the pool called Bethesda (John 5:1–17). That man had no idea that Jesus could heal him. He simply complained to Him that he had no one to help him to get to the pool, when the angel stirred the waters. At that point, Jesus spoke healing to him, saying, *"Get up! Pick up your mat and walk."*

A few of those who did ask included: the paralytic who was lowered down to Jesus for healing by four friends who cut a hole in the roof where Jesus was speaking (Mark 2:1–12), 10 lepers (Luke 17:11–19) two blind men at one time in Matthew 9:27–31, and a blind beggar, Bartimaeus, who called to Him through the crowd for help (Mark 10:46–53).

An interesting story of a blind man, who asked Jesus to heal him, is found in Mark 8:22–25. It is unique in that it involved Jesus laying hands on the man twice before he was completely healed. The first time resulted in only a partial healing. Full restoration was received only when the man resubmitted himself to Jesus' hands. Of course Jesus healed many others, too numerous to count.

In our ministry, I have observed that God heals in two different ways: either instantaneously, the first time that we pray for a person's sickness or problem; or a little bit each time that a person has prayer. Francis McNutt calls this "soaking prayer." I simply call it "continuous prayer."

I have discovered that if a person is not healed completely the first time that we pray for them, it is probably necessary for them to continue to come for prayer. The result is, that after having been prayed for repeatedly, they will eventually be completely healed.

When I was pastoring in Englishtown, New Jersey, I visited a man who was dying. McKinley Bryant had a cancerous tumour in his stomach that made him look like he was nine months pregnant. He was in terrible pain and had been sent home to die. After simply praying and asking Jesus to heal him, my friend was totally healed.

As often as we have seen people healed instantly, however, we have seen Jesus heal others over a period of time, as they repeatedly asked for prayer. These people learned from the parable about the widow, who went to the judge day and night, in order to influence him to act in her behalf (Luke 18:1–8). The whole point was, *"He told them* (and us) *a parable to show them that they ought always to pray and not to give up"* (Luke 18:1). The word "always" in this context means "continuously until something is done."

The first time I attended a Kathryn Kuhlman "Miracle Service," it was held in Peterborough, Ontario. I sat beside a woman who had a serious and apparently very painful bone condition. She explained to me that she had been following Kathryn Kuhlman all over North America going from one city after another, because there was no church in her city where she could receive prayer for healing. That night, she was healed.

In 1973, when I was the Senior Minister of St. Paul's United Church in Brampton, Ontario, I suffered a severe heart attack. Upon my release from the hospital, my doctor advised me of the seriousness of his diagnosis. There was nothing more that could be done for me, medically. He warned me about continuing in my ministry as the pastor of a large church. He said, "Gordon, if you continue doing the kind of ministry you are doing, you will be dead within two years. If you want to stay in the ministry and live even for two years, then you will have to find a small church that has no problems."

What a laugh that was! He apparently thought that churches are hotels for saints when, in fact, they are hospitals for sinners. A small church with no problems is pure fantasy. I figured that if I was going to die, I might as well do it serving Jesus Christ right where I was. I didn't even bother looking for that little "church with no problems."

Every three months, I had to have my heart tested. Whenever the technician would see the results coming out of the testing machine, she would almost have a heart attack herself. The only thing that was regular about my heart beat was that it was irregular. I asked for prayer for healing numerous times. I had many pastors and Christians pray for me. During the process, I discovered a very strange thing: if you aren't healed quickly, Christians don't want to continue to pray for your healing. They'll start to pray that God will take you home. Nevertheless, I was persistent.

In 1976, while driving home from a funeral in the neighbouring town of Georgetown, I suddenly experienced pain in my chest and in my left arm. I drove furiously to Peel Memorial Hospital, where I was quickly taken into an emergency room and met by my doctor. He and the technician immediately hooked me up to the heart testing machine. He said, "There's something wrong with that machine." They tried a second one. He stood there shaking his head. "It appears that your heart is perfectly normal now."

Jesus healed my heart completely that day. Recently, I had it tested for my insurance company. The nurse was told by the doctor that I had the heart of a 25 year-old. Persistence in following Jesus' instruction pays off.

"Why does God not heal completely every time?" I am frequently asked. Quite frankly, I don't know, but I suspect that it may be because He wants to develop a relationship with us (or with our care givers) which He knows will deepen over the period of time that a person continues to request prayer. For whatever the reason, it is important to continue to ask for prayer until either healing or Heaven comes.

One night, I was ministering in Swift Current, Saskatchewan. Following the message, I prayed for healing for a man by the name of Bob Davisson. Jesus healed him completely of the malignant tumours in his lung and of several other ailments. Some time later, he had a recurrence of his symptoms. Having heard that I was speaking at a Full Gospel meeting in Edmonton, Alberta, he drove eight hours to Edmonton and, following prayer, the symptoms disappeared and total healing was confirmed by his doctors.

I shall never forget the night in Lakehurst, New Jersey, when I prayed with Helen Harlan and her six-year-old daughter, Jackie. Helen, a widowed mother of three little girls, had been diagnosed with terminal cancer in the abdomen. She had been told that she would be fortunate to live more than three months. The cancer would break out in boils all over her stomach area and the smell was awful. She was in terrible pain.

Jackie, the daughter, had cancer in her eyes. One eye had been removed and the cancer was eating away at the other eye. She, too, often suffered excruciating pain. When we prayed for the two, Jackie was completely healed, but her mother wasn't.

However, Helen knew that if she was going to see her girls grow up even for a few more months, she had to go for prayer. Every time the altar was open, despite her agony, she kept going for prayer. She discovered that God could sustain her and give her strength to live week by week. I don't know how many times we took her to the hospital at Fort Dix. Because her husband had been in the Air Force, she was receiving treatment at the military hospital there. The doctor told me he didn't know why she was still alive, because she was so full of cancer. She became the persistent widow who Jesus described in the parable in Luke 18:1–8, who went before the judge day and night until he acted on her behalf.

Finally, some of the people began to pray that Helen would die — that the Lord would take her out of her pain. In the New Testament, we do not have permission to pray for anyone's death. We have permission only to pray for their healing.

Well, the weeks stretched into months, and the months into years. Finally, after 16 years, Helen was completely healed. She is still living a healthy life in New Jersey today.

Helen learned, as we all must learn, that if we want to be healed badly enough, we will keep on going to Jesus, no matter how many times it takes. We must want to be healed so badly that we'll go to the front of the church, or to the altar, every time the invitation for prayer is given. Most people won't do that. Besides that, most churches don't offer a prayer time around the alter at every meeting. Too often, they have to have a committee meeting to decide whether or not to pray for people. It's frightening. It is imperative that churches give people an opportunity to receive healing at every worship service. People who have gifts of Healing must be given the opportunity to use them so that God's people can be healed and serve Him in good health.

About three summers ago, we went back to New Jersey for a visit and discovered that both Jackie (now all grown up) and her mother were still enjoying excellent health. The only setback Jackie has had since her healing was that when she went to get her driver's license, they put her on a three-week-trial period to see whether the eye, which she had lost prior to her healing, would hinder her driving ability. It didn't and she got her license! She is now married with a family of her own.

Those who have not been given gifts of Healing don't have to feel left out, or that they are second class Christians. They can still pray for others to be healed. That is what Jesus was talking about in the Gospel of Mark when He said: *"And these signs will follow those who believe ... they will lay their hands on the sick and they will recover"* (Mark 16:17,18). He was talking about praying while placing hands on somebody who is sick. This is not necessarily a reference exclusive to the gifts of Healing. It is a sign that will follow all true believers who lay their hands on the sick. It is interesting to take note that the way that this instruction is given in Greek, Jesus is really saying, *"Keep on laying hands on the sick continuously until they are healed."* Isn't it wonderful that Jesus wants us to participate in His healing ministry by being the instruments by which others can be healed?

Besides gifts of Healing and the laying on of hands by believers, another method of prayer that can result in healing is the calling of the elders of the church to anoint the sick person with oil. Unfortunately, not many people are willing to ask their elders to anoint them with oil. Those who do, experience a special kind of ministry.

A few years ago, a doctor's wife in my church became very ill. Her doctor tried everything that he knew of to bring about her healing. After reading in the book of James about the elders' ministry of anointing with oil, she called her husband, who was also a Christian, and asked him if it would be agreeable to him for her to call the elders of their church. He agreed that it certainly couldn't do any harm, and in fact, could do a lot of good. When the elders came and anointed her with oil and prayed for her, she was healed.

There is no special oil that has healing power in it. The key is the act of faithful obedience upon which God acts to heal a person.

A friend of mine, Ed Howard, was an elder in his church. He was a motor mechanic who didn't know very much about church procedure. A friend of his, who was sick in bed, called him to come and anoint him with oil and pray for his healing. Now, the only kind of oil that Ed knew much about was motor oil. So, he purchased a quart of 10-W-30 and went to his friend's bedside. As he poured about one-half of the quart over his friend's head and prayed for his healing, Jesus healed the man, just as the Book of James promises.

Many ask, "Is everyone healed who asks for prayer?"

The answer is very clearly, "No." Not everyone is healed, and the Bible tells us that there are a lot of reasons why. I do not have the space to list them all, but I'll mention a few:

- sin in a person's life (Psalm 66:18)
- wrong motives (James 4:3)
- doubt (James 1:5-7)
- disobedience (John 15:10)
- staying away from worship (Hebrews 10:25)
- refusal to help poor people (Proverbs 21:13)
- pride (Proverbs 16:18)
- unforgiveness (Matthew 18:24)
- treating the spouse improperly (1 Peter 3:7)
- refusing the laying on of hands (Mark 16:18)
- eating the Lord's Supper in an unworthy manner (1 Corinthians 11:27–32)
- occult involvement (Deuteronomy 18:9)
- refusing to tithe ten percent of the income to God (Malachi 3:8–10)
- not calling the elders to anoint the person with oil (James 5:14)
- sexual immorality (Revelation 21:8) Galatians 5:19–20, 1 Corinthians 12:21).

There are many other reasons mentioned in the Bible, too numerous to list. Joni Erickson believes that she has not been healed because God told her that, with her permission, He was not going to heal her because He wanted to use her wheelchair as a platform from which to preach the Gospel to millions of people. That is exactly what she has been doing.

Many ask, "Do people have to be Christians before Jesus will heal them?" I have prayed for people who did not believe in Jesus Christ, but who were healed anyway. The result was simply a healthy unbeliever who then proceeded to rationalize that his healing would have occurred anyway, that it was spontaneous remission that simply coincided with the prayer, or that it was just all a coincidence.

Jesus' grace extends even to the unbeliever who will ask. What a tragedy that they do not value the price that was paid for that grace.

We must never forget that Jesus is still the Healer. There is not a disease on the face of the earth that He cannot heal. Any problem blocking healing usually lies with human issues. For instance, when confronted with highly contagious diseases, we have to set aside our fears and go ahead and pray for those people, so that they can be restored to health through the healing power of Jesus Christ.

I remember the first time that I encountered the AIDS virus. The young man before me was full of fear. He had no hope for his future. I reminded him that Jesus still heals today. I reached out to lay my hands on his head in order to pray for him. The thought crossed my mind, "If you touch him, you'll get it." I instantly replaced that thought with the knowledge that Jesus promises us protection when we serve Him. I went ahead and prayed. Three days later, his doctor told him that the tests showed that there was no more sign of the AIDS virus. Jesus had healed him. We have to be willing to boldly go where others fear to tread and offer the ministry of healing.

We have to expect criticism when we pray for people for healing. I am frequently asked, "Are you not practicing medicine without a license and are you not placing people's lives in danger?" No, we are not practicing medicine without a license. We simply pray for people's healing. We do not tell them to go off medicine that has been prescribed by their doctors. The doctor who diagnosed their problems will tell them when they are healed. His declaration of their healing becomes a very important part of their testimony in terms of establishing credibility.

5. The Gift of Miracles

The gift of Miracles (1 Corinthians 12:10) is probably

the most spectacular of the gifts of the Holy Spirit. This gift is variously translated "works of power," "activities that produce power or call forth miracles," "effects of power," or "working with miracles." However, the word 'miracles' does not appear in the Greek text.

Properly translated, it is "the gift of energizing power." Through this gift, the supernatural power of the Holy Spirit is applied to natural situations. The result is that miracles happen. It is the extraordinary use of God's power.

Many people call the healing of sick people who are suffering from various diseases, "miracles," which of course, in the broadest sense, is appropriate. However, in the strictest sense of the word, a miracle of healing is a different phenomenon.

Miracles of Healing

When healing occurs through the operation of the gift of Miracles, it is a recreative work that is done by the power of the Holy Spirit to parts of the physical body. A healing miracle involves the straightening of bones that have been badly deformed, the correcting of congenital deformities, or the replacing of organs or body parts that have been removed, or are so badly deteriorated through disease that for all intents and purposes are destroyed, or are not functioning.

I once prayed for a police officer, Corporal Neals of the Ontario Provincial Police who had suffered a serious heart attack. He had been told that his heart was too badly damaged for surgery. There was no blood pumping through the bottom one-third of his heart. Right there in the hospital, we asked Jesus for a miracle. The doctors were going to send him home to simply put in time until he died.

After prayer, the man insisted upon another set of X-rays. Much to the doctors' surprise, a new vein had suddenly appeared where there was not supposed to be one!

Nevertheless, there it was, pumping blood through his heart. Despite his protestations that Jesus was his Healer, the doctors insisted on rushing him into surgery to do some corrective work on two valves. Within two weeks, he was home driving his car, while another man, who had had similar surgery the same day, remained in the intensive care unit, still recovering. The Corporal telephoned me after he got home to ask, "When Jesus heals, does He usually complete the job?"

"Why, yes, of course," I replied.

"I knew it," he said. "I tried to tell the doctors that but they wouldn't listen to me. So, they went ahead and operated on the valves without giving Jesus a chance to finish what He started." That Corporal knew first hand the true meaning of a "healing miracle." He went back to work and was soon promoted to Sargeant. He is now retired in Guelph, Ontario.

An elderly lady from my congregation, with whom I had prayed, turned up in her doctor's office healed of her terminal cancer. Shortly thereafter, I was stopped in the hallway of Peel Memorial Hospital in Brampton, Ontario, by one of her doctors. "Gordon, may I ask you a question about faith healing?"

"Of course, shoot away," I answered, wondering at his purpose.

"Well, how does it work? Is it your faith, or the patient's faith — or is it the faith of both of you?"

"Well, this is going to sound strange, but it can be either, neither, or both," I said. I continued to tell him about another woman from our church, Betty, whose doctor had discovered that she had two lumps in one of her kidneys. She had required a biopsy. It had meant inserting a probe that would be very painful. The problem was that, because of an allergy, she had been unable to be anaesthetized. I had prayed with her, just before she was taken into surgery, for the biopsy. I had asked Jesus to take away her fear, remove any pain, and had then said, "Well, let's go all the way, Jesus, and remove the lumps."

During the procedure, she had had no fear, no pain, and, despite the fact that the lumps had been clearly visible on the X-ray, much to her doctor's surprise, she had had no lumps. Jesus had given her the miracle healing that we had requested.

The doctor stared at me with a shocked expression. Unknown to me, this was Betty's doctor.

21st Century Miracles

Jesus continues to perform the same kind of miracles that are recorded in the Bible through believers whom He empowers with the gift of Miracles.

There are reports from various places in the world of people turning water into wine. In his book, *The New Wine of God*, Kurt Koch details eye-witness reports of such occurrences.

Just as Jesus walked on water, there are reports of Indonesian Christians who, in order to reach various towns and villages to preach the Gospel and introduce people to Jesus Christ as their Saviour and Lord, walked on water. Mel Tari shares this in his book, *Like a Mighty Wind*.

We have many reports of Jesus continuing to multiply food even today — not just for a show, but to feed hungry people. In one instance, a pastor, who operates in the gift of Miracles in his ministry to the poor in New Mexico, had to feed 200 men who were unemployed and poor. He had two lasagna casseroles. That was all. He prayed over them asking Jesus to multiply the food. All 200 ate as much as they needed. There were two half-finished casseroles left afterwards. That is the gift of Miracles being used in ministry.

When He is given the opportunity, Jesus even raises the dead today. Most pastors are not called to the bedside of people who are dying or have just died. We are called to the funeral home after the body has been embalmed, a point from which life cannot return, because life is in the blood (Leviticus 17:11) not in embalming fluid. However, at the risk of sounding as though I've lost my marbles, I know from experience that raising the dead is still a valid ministry today.

Some time ago, I arrived at the hospital to see a man from my church who was in crisis. His brain tumour was having its final effect. The doctor came out of his room to explain to his wife, who was also a nurse, that his vital signs had disappeared. "Call whomever you have to call and make the final arrangements," he counselled. She cried. We prayed. She then went to call her family and a funeral home.

I went into my friend's room. I did something that I had never done before. I went over to him, opened his eyes with my fingers, and said to him, "I don't want you to die. I'm going to ask Jesus to raise you up." That is what I prayed. Then, I left.

The following day, I returned to the hospital. I met a friend in the hallway who told me that life had returned to my friend, although he was still in a coma. He went on to say, however, that despite the miracle, another minister had just been up to see my friend and had prayed that God would take him. I was so angry that I ran up the stairs and into the room. Only my friend's wife and one of her friends was there. "The vital signs have returned but they are very, very weak," she explained. We joined hands and I again asked Jesus for a miracle that would bring my friend back. The next day, I called my friend's home. One of his daughters answered the telephone. "I just called to see how your Dad is getting along," I explained.

"Oh! Do you want to talk to Dad? He's home, you know." I was surprised when I shouldn't have been, but pleased. God had truly brought him back from the dead.

Falling Under the Power of God

Those who are new to manifestations of the power of the Holy Spirit are sometimes shocked when they see people falling down during times of prayer around an altar.

They don't understand that when the Holy Spirit comes upon people who are being prayed for by a person who has the gift of Miracles, they often fall to the floor, temporarily unable to stand up. This is what I call "an involuntary physical reaction to the Holy Spirit."

Whether termed, "being slain in the Spirit," "falling down under the power," or "resting in the Lord," it is an excellent demonstration of the gift of energizing power — the gift of Miracles. In the past, this manifestation of the Holy Spirit was called "swooning." Today's trendy phrase is "doing carpet time."

When people are slain in the Spirit, they do not get hurt. The power of the Holy Spirit simply causes them to fall to the floor. This phenomenon has occurred throughout the history of the church. John Wesley describes it in one of his letters to George Whitfield, who had written to inquire about reports that he had heard.[2] Later on, it became a part of Whitfield's ministry as well. Recently, a *Time-Life* book about the civil war showed a picture of an outdoor revival meeting, with many people who had been slain in the Spirit, laying on the ground.[3] The experience of being slain in the Spirit is one of the ways that the Holy Spirit can apply the work of the Cross of Jesus Christ to our lives.

Some years ago, I prayed with a pastor-friend who had often wondered why the Lord caused people to fall down under the power of the Holy Spirit. She told me that He told her why, during that experience. She claimed that He said, "People have a hard time to humble themselves before Me. Anyone can get up and walk away, but not just anyone can humble themselves before Me."

While we are humble before our God, He quietly works miracles in our lives. The greatest miracle of all is the gift of salvation. Many people are born again while they are under the power of the Holy Spirit. Others are baptized with the Holy Spirit. Others receive gifts of the Holy Spirit. Others are healed as they lay before Jesus. God speaks to some about their lives and His plans for them. By this means, the Holy Spirit is able to deal with us in many ways, in order to equip us to be more faithful to Jesus Christ.

My first experience with being "slain in the Spirit" occurred at a meeting which was being held in Toronto, where Charles and Frances Hunter were ministering. At the conclusion of the service, Charles gave an invitation for prayer. I went to the front and stood in the prayer line. He came along and asked me what I would like to have prayer for. I told him and closed my eyes while he prayed. I was suddenly pushed to the floor. Furious that he would dare to do such a thing to me, I got up off the floor and returned to my seat.

"He pushed me down," I complained to my wife, Ruth.

"No, he didn't," she defended him. "I was watching. He didn't push you down. You fell down."

I did not accept that. I know when I've been pushed. She couldn't convince me otherwise.

During the next year, whenever anyone mentioned Charles Hunter, I would get angry and complain that there was something questionable about his ministry because he had pushed me down to the floor. Ruth continued to disagree.

In an attempt to prove my point, we attended the Hunters' meeting the following year. When Charles issued the invitation for prayer, I went forward again. This time, I kept my eyes wide open. He was not going to push me again. He came along to me and asked for my prayer request. I said, "I just want a blessing."

"Okay," he smilingly agreed, as he reached out his hand to lay it on my head. His fingers hardly touched my head and I was thrust, pushed, thrown down to the floor with my eyes wide open.

I couldn't believe what had happened! I knew what it took to knock me over. I had boxed for many years. No one had ever succeeded in putting me down. I couldn't even move. I was wide awake. I began to understand the power of the Holy Spirit in a way that I had never understood before.

The next year, when the Hunters were in Toronto, I was in charge of "the catchers" (see p.103).

That night, I was assisting Charles Hunter. At one point, I asked Charles how this kind of ministry started for him. He told me that a friend, who had a miracle ministry, had prayed with him to receive it. He then asked me, "Would you like to have a miracle ministry?" I wondered if it was possible to pray for such a ministry. Charles said, "Let me pray with you so that the Holy Spirit can equip you with it." He prayed with me, but this time I did not fall down. He then asked me to pray with the next young man who came forward. I did, and he fell to the floor. Charles and I prayed for five people at one time and they all fell to the floor, slain in the Spirit. This continues in my ministry to this day.

My one concern was that I didn't really remember reading about this phenomenon in the Bible. I began a search and found that there were at least 44 verses that describe people who could not stand in the presence of God. To list a few:

- Matthew 28:4 *"The guards were so afraid of Him that they shook and became like dead men."*
- John 18:6 *"When Jesus said, 'I am He,' they drew back and fell to the ground."*
- Acts 9:4 *"He fell to the ground and heard a voice say to him ..."*
- Acts 22:7 *"I fell to the ground and heard a voice say to me ..."*
- Revelation 1:17 *"When I saw Him I fell at his feet as though dead."*

Someone once described this experience as "liquid love" being poured into our bodies. Regardless, when people have this experience, although they temporarily may not be able to move, they are aware of what is going on around them. They can hear what is going on and they can open their eyes. It is important not to attempt to get them up off the floor until they can get up on their own, as it will interfere with what the Holy Spirit is trying to accomplish. Interference may prevent healing from being completed or may prevent a person from hearing what the Holy Spirit is trying to tell them.

In Thunder Bay, Ontario, at the conclusion of a Full Gospel Business Men's Banquet, I prayed with a woman for the healing of her heart and she was slain in the Spirit. She lay on the floor under the power of the Holy Spirit for more than two hours before I left. Before leaving, I instructed the men to let her stay there until the Holy Spirit was finished with her.

After another two hours, the men became concerned about her heart condition. They could not get her to stand up. They called an ambulance and she was rushed to the hospital. The men explained that she had a history of a bad heart. The emergency doctor examined her and said, "There is nothing wrong with her heart. It's perfectly normal." She had been completely healed!

One time I ministered at a camp meeting sponsored by a united Church group near Red Deer, Alberta. The following day, I was approached by a young woman in a lovely white suit, who had not responded to the altar call the night before but who had decided, after some consideration, that she would like to receive the baptism in the Holy Spirit. She had been on her way to work at the cosmetic counter at Sears, when she had spotted me and requested prayer.

We stood talking outside the meeting area, and as it had rained the previous night, the grounds were very muddy. Nevertheless, at her request, I prayed for her right there and she fell backwards where she lay peacefully speaking in tongues right there in the mud. By the time she got up, she was clean inside, but her exterior needed a bit of help.

The Blessed Blight of Criticism

"Blessed are you when people insult you, persecute you

and falsely say all kinds of evil against you because of Me" (Matthew 5:11).

The gift of Miracles is a very powerful gift of the Holy Spirit. That is why those who have received it come under a lot of criticism, attacks, ridicule, and verbal abuse. As Jesus Himself experienced attacks by other people, so also, those of us who exercise this gift can expect attacks.

You will recall that it was after Jesus raised Lazarus from the dead that it was said of His opponents, *"So from that day on they took counsel how to put him to death"* (John 11:53).

Jesus said, *"If I had not done among them the works which no one else did, they would not be guilty of sin; but now they have seen these miracles and hated both Me and My Father"* (John 15:24).

For a number of years, I kept count of the number of people that I prayed with to receive the gift of Miracles. Exactly 50 percent of them came back and asked me to pray and ask Jesus to take the gift back because they felt that they could no longer handle the criticism that they received from church members, clergy, members of their own family, and friends.

I remember a lady who has been a friend for many years who I thought understood the working of the Holy Spirit. She approached me after a meeting in which many people had been ministered to by the Holy Spirit. Many of them had been slain in the Spirit, as I prayed with them. She was particularly irate about it. She wanted to argue about the validity of what was happening, but because of her attitude, I wouldn't even discuss it with her. I told her so, and suggested that she go home and pray about it.

She wrote me a letter in which she apologized. She had prayed, and much to her surprise, the Holy Spirit spoke clearly to her. He told her that she was wrong and told her to read Matthew 22:29 which says, *"But Jesus answered them, 'You are wrong, because you know neither the Scripture nor the power of God.'"* Unfortunately, there are many people in our churches who are in this position. Just like the Sadducees and the Pharisees, they can quote the Bible, but they really don't understand the Scripture or the power of God.

When people have never seen nor experienced miracles in their daily living nor in their churches, it is difficult for them to accept them — especially when Jesus is willing to give what appears to be very ordinary people such a powerful gift. Just as John 3:16 reminds us that *whosoever* believes in Him will not perish but have everlasting life, Jesus uses the *whosoever* to carry out His ministry today. What a wonderful privilege to receive such gifts!

But, again, people who do not have the gift of Miracles do not have to feel left out. They can still pray to the God of miracles who answers prayer and accomplishes miracles in the lives of His people.

6. The Gift of Prophecy

Prophecy is an exciting gift given so that God can prepare us for the future. He always plans ahead. Even His spontaneity is planned. He never does anything without telling His prophets what He is going to do before He does it (Amos 3:7). Today, those who have the gift of prophecy are the prophets.

Prophecy is given for our protection and direction. It is to be used in the fellowship of the church, without fear. The word "prophecy" refers to an uncovering of something that is veiled, a revelation of what is hidden, a foretelling of the future with regard to what is going to happen. The dictionary defines prophecy as *"a prediction of the future under the influence of divine guidance."*

A person with the gift of Prophecy will receive messages from Jesus Christ through the inspiration of the Holy Spirit. He or she then has the responsibility to deliver it to the appropriate church, group of people, or individuals.

Like a telegram messenger who is supposed to simply deliver the telegram and not interpret it, the person with a Prophecy is simply a messenger — not an interpreter of the Prophecy. If he or she falls into the temptation to explain the message, many people could be led off track.

The people who are supposed to receive the Prophecy will be shown or told what it means, if they don't know already. It is the Holy Spirit's responsibility to interpret the Prophecies to them.

A perfect example of misinterpretation is what happened when the prophet Agabus was given a prophecy for Paul. He took Paul's belt and tied up his own hands and feet and said, *"Thus says the Holy Spirit, 'So shall the Jews at Jerusalem bind the man who owns this girdle and deliver him into the hands of the Gentiles'"* (Acts 21:11). He, and the other people at that meeting, thought that it was a warning for Paul not to go into Jerusalem or he would be arrested. In fact, it was a confirmation for Paul that he was supposed to go into Jerusalem and be arrested. Because the Holy Spirit had spoken to his heart, he couldn't be persuaded not to go.

Peter tries to explain this important rule of Prophecy: *"First of all you must understand this, that no prophecy of Scripture is a matter of one's own interpretation because no prophecy ever came by the impulse of man, but men moved by the Holy Spirit spoke from God"* (2 Peter 1:20-21). In other words, anyone with the gift of Prophecy should not try to explain what it means. They will probably be wrong. The Holy Spirit must be allowed to do His own explaining to the person or people for whom it is given.

The gift of Prophecy is given to the church for several reasons. It is for the *"upbuilding (edification) encouragement (exhortation) and consolation (comfort)"*(1 Corinthians 14:3) of the people and the church. It is given so that the church can receive instruction or guidance, as in Acts 13:2, where, during a time of worship, *"the Holy Spirit said, 'Set apart for me Barnabas and Saul for the work to which I have called them.'"*

In my experience as a pastor, we (the church and I) discovered that by using the gift of Prophecy, the Lord could show us where He wanted to lead the church, the kind of problems that we would run into, and how to deal with those problems. The result was that the church grew and our members matured.

Recording Prophecies for Testing and Implementation

All these must be done for the strengthening of the church" (1 Corinthians 14:26).

God told us that, *"Where there is no prophecy the people cast off restraint, but blessed is he who keeps the law"* (Proverbs 29:18).

The gift of Prophecy has been given to us so that we shall always know that God's eyes are on us and that we have His attention because He loves us and *"He gave His only begotten Son so that whosoever believes in Him should not perish but have everlasting life"* (John 3:16).

Just as God instructed His prophets in the Old Testament to write down what He told them, He told Isaiah (Isaiah 8:1) Jeremiah (Jeremiah 30:2) Ezekiel (Ezekiel 24:2) and John (Revelation 1:11) to write down what He told or showed them.

If there was purpose in recording prophesy then, there must be wisdom in recording it now.

When I was pastoring a congregation, we had microphones available at the front of the church. If someone had a prophecy or an interpretation of tongues, that person had the freedom to go to a microphone and, at the appropriate time, was allowed to speak out what the Lord had given.

In some services we had one, and in others we had many messages from God. Regardless, they were all taped, written out, checked out scripturally, and if judged accurate, were printed in the next Sunday's bulletin.

True or False?

If, on the other hand, a prophecy was considered to be unscriptural, the person was told why and corrected. The person was not prohibited or stopped from giving prophecies. We attempted to encourage those who had the gift of Prophecy. We did not "stone them outside the city gates" nor did we tell them to stay away. We corrected them so that they could learn to listen to the Lord accurately.

Besides preventing prophecies from being lost and forgotten, recording them as they are given permits people to check them out to see if they are really from God.

John warns us, *"Beloved, do not believe every spirit, but test the spirits to see whether they are of God; for many false prophets have gone out into the world"* (1 John 4:1).

Before accepting any prophecy, it is important to know the messenger and to be able to ascertain that he or she lives a sincere Christian life. Just because a stranger, who claims to have the gift of Prophecy, visits a church or appears on radio or television, that does not mean that their prophecies are either from God or for any individual.

When I was an evangelist with 100 Huntley Street, I was responsible for the on-air "Scriptural Overview," a scriptural check-up of the guests on our television ministry. I found it rather interesting to see how our guests accepted correction. The few who accepted well, were people whose desire was to serve the Lord faithfully and accurately. The many who rejected correction were more concerned about popularity and their public image.

Even today, because there is no real monitoring of what Christians are saying and doing, no real testing, all kinds of unscriptural things are being said and done. Worse than that, because of the impact of the media, they are being accepted and believed without question.

Every prophecy must be checked out to see if it is scripturally correct. Today, whether we like it or not, there are a lot of false prophets who are tickling people's ears by telling them things they want to hear. I have watched a few of them operate. Their followers will not accept any criticism or correction of their so-called "prophecies" which simply make people feel good instead of calling them to repentance through conviction of their sin and unfaithfulness. True prophecy does not always make us feel good, but it is instrumental in equipping us to serve the Lord.

The proof or test of a prophet, or a person who has the gift of Prophecy is whether or not what they have prophesied happens. It is that simple. I know that no one can set a time limit on the fulfillment of prophecy, because

Jesus' own birth was prophesied several thousand years before the actual event. However, most of the wrong ones usually indicate almost immediate fulfillment. Any true prophecy can stand to be tested. *"When a prophet speaks in the name of the Lord, if the word does not come to pass or come true, that is a word which the Lord has not spoken; the prophet has spoken it presumptuously, you need not be afraid of him"* (Deuteronomy 18:22).

Another sign of a false prophet, or of a person who is trying to exercise the gift of Prophecy out of their own flesh rather than from God, is that they will say, "The Lord has given me a burden" of some kind or another. God gives a severe warning *"But 'the burden of the Lord' you shall mention no more, for the burden is every man's own word, and you pervert the words of the living God, the Lord of hosts, our God...But if you say, 'The burden of the Lord,' thus says the Lord, 'Because you have said these words, 'The burden of the Lord,' therefore, behold, I will surely lift you up from my presence, you and the city which I gave to you and your fathers. And I will bring upon you everlasting reproach and perpetual shame, which shall not be forgotten"* (Jeremiah 23:36, 38–40). In other words, watch out for people who tell you that the Lord has given them a burden. He does not give them: He takes them away (Matthew 11: 28–30).

When a person uses the gift of Prophecy, he or she does not go into some kind of an ecstatic state. The Holy Spirit speaks to prophets in a state of normal reality. Their minds are clear and they hear the voice of the Holy Spirit without going into some trance-like state. In fact, a person with a real prophecy can easily be interrupted and then continue with the message from the place that he or she left off. *"The spirits of prophets are subject to the control of prophets"* (1 Corinthians 14:32).

A prophet (a person with the gift of Prophecy) gains his or her credibility by exercising the gift in his or her local church and should be able to get a positive reference from the pastor there.

Sources of Prophecy

There are at least three sources of prophecy:

1. God
2. Self
3. the Devil or Satan.

That is why we must check prophecies out scripturally. Just because something sounds good or feels good, doesn't mean that it is from God.

A warning is clearly given, but not always taken seriously, in a story about a little known prophet named Micaiah.

Long before the time of Jesus, 400 legitimate prophets were asked to prophesy about whether the king of Israel should go to war or not. They all agreed that it was God's will and that the king would win. God showed Micaiah, however, that because these other prophets would not listen to God, God sent a lying spirit to deceive them (1 Kings 1–37).

I believe that the same thing happens today. If a person with the gift of Prophecy will not listen to the Holy Spirit, then he or she will be deceived and will lead many people in a wrong direction and into trouble. Any prophet, or person with the gift of Prophecy, has the potential of losing the ability to tell whether they are hearing from God, the Devil, or an evil or lying spirit through being influenced by important people or selfish desires.

Today there are still people who want to prophesy concerning the time and date of the return of Jesus - a sure sign of a false prophet. They continue to ignore the fact that Jesus said, *"But of that day and hour no one knows, not even the angels in heaven, nor the Son, but the Father only."* And further, *"Therefore you must also be ready; for the Son of man is coming at an hour you do not expect"* (Matthew 24:36,44).

Christians falling into this very trap have written many different books with differing interpretations of end-time prophecy. Despite the fact that these books change their interpretations from generation to generation, no one seems to want to confront these so-called prophets. When they are questioned, they become defensive and attack those who seek an explanation. Nevertheless, people continue to chase after these people, buy their books and support them financially.

Paul recognized this when he warned us that *"even Satan disguises himself as an angel of light"* (2 Corinthians 11:14). When he speaks, that angel of light sounds so nice. He tells us things that tickle our lives and get us out of God's will for our churches and ourselves.

The Danger of Personal Prophecies

There can be great danger in so-called personal prophecies. There seems to be a growing trend for people to give and receive supposed messages of a personal nature. There are times when Jesus truly does give such messages. However, we have to be careful not to go running after them or we risk seeking prophecies in the same way that fortune tellers are used.

When personal prophecies are valid, they are most often given as confirmation of something that the Holy Spirit has already told a person. When this is not the case, the person has to be very careful not to manipulate circumstances in such a way as to bring the message to pass.

God fulfills His prophecies in His own time. We must learn to recognize the voice of the Holy Spirit so that when he does give personal guidance and direction for our lives, we can receive it and then wait patiently for Him to fulfill it.

The Operation of the Gift of Prophecy

I have talked to many people who have this gift. Some tell me that they hear the voice of Jesus, or the Holy Spirit, speaking to them clearly and audibly. Others say that they hear the quiet inner voice of the Holy Spirit speaking to them.

Still others claim that when they close their eyes in

prayer, they see a message written in their imaginations and they read what they see out loud. Some see a message written on a thin ticker tape. As these people read what they see, more words are added to the message until it is complete. Others say that they get impressions and express them. By whatever method the gift of Prophecy operates in the life of an individual, it is vital for that person to learn to use it carefully and reliably by delivering the prophecy to whomever God had intended it.

The best place to learn to use the gift skillfully and accurately, is in the fellowship of fellow Christians who know us, who worship with us and who we can trust to correct or confirm what we say with Godly love and intent. As Paul instructs, *"Let two or three prophets speak, and let the others weigh what is said...For you can all prophesy one by one, so that all may learn and all be encouraged; and the spirits of the prophets are subject to prophets. For God is not a God of confusion but of peace"* (1 Corinthians 14:29, 31–33).

Those who use their gift faithfully, will experience a satisfaction and the peace of God which passes all understanding. They will grow in faith and will find fulfillment in their Christian life in the church. They will hear the words, *"Well done, good and faithful servant; you have been faithful over a little, I will set you over much"* (Matthew 25:21).

Those with the gift of Prophecy must learn to use it and enjoy it. It's so important to spend time with Jesus, with the Holy Spirit, and with with the Heavenly Father. It's vital to learn to hear His voice in order to be able to share what the Lord gives for fellow Christians. It's critical to write it down with the date on which it was received; then check it out with the Bible, deliver it and share it, resisting the temptation to explain it. The Holy Spirit will do that in the heart of the one for whom it is intended. When the prophecy is fulfilled, it is a time for great thanksgiving that the Lord has entrusted the messenger with such a wonderful gift.

It's wonderful to think that Jesus has given us the gift of Prophecy through which He can express His love, by showing us ahead of time what His plans are, to give us hope and direction for the days ahead.

7. The Gift of Discerning of Spirits

The gift of Discerning of spirits or Discernment (sometimes called distinguishing or differentiating between spirits) is both an offensive and a defensive gift.

With special insight from the Holy Spirit (spiritual x-ray vision) a person with this gift is enabled to tell the difference between things and people who are from God, and things and people who are from the Devil, thus giving him or her a starting point from which to either rout the enemy, or seek God for protection.

As part of the kingdom of darkness, evil spirits live in darkness. People with the gift of Discernment are like army scouts who go out in the darkness with night observation glasses. They are the spiritual policemen who God has appointed for our protection. They have "spiritual night vision" with which they can see into the kingdom of darkness, spot the enemy (the Devil, evil spirits, or people who are either possessed by or under the influence of the enemy), and identify them so that the rest of the army (the Church) can go and cast the evil spirits out and set the captives free.

This gift provides protection against false prophets, false teachers, false doctrine, the works of sin, the works of Satan and the work of evil spirits (demons).

The Kingdom of Darkness

The one thing that we need to keep in mind at all times is that the kingdom of darkness is not well organized like the kingdom of God. Assuming it to be highly structured is the one major blunder that most believers make, when they try to understand the works of the enemy. The lack of organization is evidenced in the story of Jesus dealing with the man possessed by demons whose name was "Legion" (Mark 5:1–19). There were more than 6000 demons in that one man. What a waste of resources. When one believer can cast out 6000 demons and set the captive free, it is obvious where the real strength lies.

The kingdom of darkness is self-destructive. Evil spirits lack persistence and faithfulness. That is the reason why there is only *"pleasure in sin for a season"* (Hebrews 11:25).

What are Evil Spirits Anyway?

There are a lot of mistaken ideas about evil spirits or demons (both names mean the same thing).

First of all, they are not fallen angels. Jude 1:6 declares that *"... these He has kept in darkness bound with everlasting chains for judgment on the great day."* In confirmation of this, 2 Peter 2:4 claims, *"... God did not spare angels when they sinned, but sent them to Hell, putting them into gloomy dungeons to be held for judgment."* Thus, all fallen angels, with the exception of the Devil who was cast out of Heaven and thrown down to earth (Luke 10:18) where he continues to tempt people, are chained up until Jesus returns.

The Bible does not tell us where demons or evil spirits come from. It only tells us that they exist and that they attempt to possess people and to attack and torment believers. However, any born again, Spirit-filled believer has authority over them and can cast them out of buildings or people where they reside, harassing the occupants.

The Reaction of Demons to the Gift of Discernment

Anyone who has actually been possessed by an evil spirit cannot stand to hear the name of Jesus used repeatedly. The demon will cause the person to run away.

One such example was a young woman who came to see me in my office. The depth of her spiritual problem became quickly apparent. When I began to talk about Jesus, she began to scream. The demon drove her, reeling and screaming, from my office. She bounced off the walls, pitching from wall to wall down the long hallway, until she crashed against the entrance doors and broke her arm. I followed her all the way and commanded the evil spirit to leave her. She was set free. Right there, I prayed with her to receive Jesus as her Saviour and Lord and be baptized in the Holy Spirit. She did and she was!

Normally, demon-possessed people cannot sit through a meeting where Jesus Christ is being praised and the Gospel is being preached. If a demon-possessed person cannot escape, the demon will cause the person to fall asleep or appear to faint.

The exception to the rule occurs when a demon-possessed person is sent into a worship service or a meeting to disrupt it.

My wife and I saw this happen on a trip to the Bahamas. There we found a well-attended church and sat down towards the back of it. Before long, we noticed a man who seemed to be suffering from palsy, sitting about three pews from the front. He was making strange sounds which got louder as the service progressed. People around us appeared to alternately ignore or sympathize with him. When the pastor started to preach his message, the man created such a distraction that most people couldn't concentrate on the message. I turned to Ruth and told her that the man had a demon. Quietly, in a voice that couldn't be heard by the people sitting in front of us, I commanded the evil spirit to leave the church immediately, in the name of Jesus Christ.

The people around could not hear me, but the demon could. The man stood up, became silent, turned and looked at me and, keeping his eyes firmly fixed on me, he walked up the aisle of the church and left. The pastor completed his message without further interruption.

Satan's Disguises

One of the problems we have discovered in dealing with Satan is that evil spirits will often disguise themselves by giving the possessed person symptoms of a legitimate physical, psychological or emotional disorder such as schizophrenia, depression, palsy or paralysis. It may be crucial to a person's recovery for there to be Discernment as to when medical attention and prayer for healing are to be applied, or when the situation calls for deliverance.

The problem is that it can be devastating to someone with legitimate psychological and emotional sicknesses to be prayed for for deliverance. The suggestion that they may be filled with something evil could dramatically compound the problem. Unfortunately, there are people who are truly possessed by demons who will not recover without exorcism. Nevertheless, taking the blanket approach of treating each instance of disturbance as a case for deliverance may leave people, who actually need medical attention and counselling, without hope. Trying to cast out demons that are not there leads only to discouragement and intensified problems.

On the other hand, if the possibility of demonic activity is dismissed as superstition, people who are possessed will never be set free.

Thus, without Discernment, we are limited to wishful, misguided, and probably wrongful judgment. Still worse, we risk harming the very people for whom Jesus died and rose again.

Looking for Lodging

Besides living in humans or animals, evil spirits can live in buildings where they will attempt to harass, possess, hurt, and even kill the occupants. However, they can be cast out in the name of Jesus Christ so that those who live or work there, can do so in peace.

There are two reasons why an evil spirit will not leave a person or a building. First, if it discovers that the person attempting the deliverance does not believe in the whole teaching of the Bible, it will recognize that the person has no authority over it and it will refuse to leave.

Secondly, if someone makes the mistake of talking to an evil spirit and asking it to name itself, it will lie. If commanded to leave by the wrong name, it does not have to leave. At this point, it may become silent, pretending that it has gone.

Evil spirits love to give undiscerning people a whole string of names and then laugh at their foolishness, or worse, attack them physically.

Operation of the Gift of Discernment

Some people have "visual Discernment" which means that they can actually see demons or evil spirits, whether disembodied or living in humans or animals. (I know that this is true because I, myself, have been confronted by evil spirits and have seen some of them). Other people are simply told by the Holy Spirit that particular individuals have evil spirits which are harassing or possessing them. Still others simply sense their presence.

When people suddenly realize that they are able to see into the spirit world, they may initially think that they are imagining things. Some get so preoccupied with what they see that they lose perspective and cannot, for a period of time, tell the difference between the works of the flesh (Galatians 5:19–21), meaning sin, and the work of evil spirits (demons).

This has become a major problem today. Many people see demons behind every sin. They identify the works of the flesh as the work of demons. For instance, they will tell a person who has the problem of lust that they have "the demon of lust" and try to cast it out. Lust is a sin of the flesh which must be dealt with through confession and repentance. It can be eliminated only when a person submits him or herself to the power of the Holy Spirit.

The same is true about any sin. Sin is not an evil spirit, it is a work of the flesh. Of course an evil spirit can and will cause a person to do sinful things, but repentance will most often preclude the need for deliverance.

Despite these problems, balance generally comes as people mature in the gift and are taught by the Holy Spirit. It is of the utmost importance that those who are given the gift of Discernment learn how to exercise the gift to avoid leaving people feeling hopeless or fearful.

They have a job similar to that of the prophet Ezekiel, of whom God said, *"Son of man, I have made you a watchman for the house of Israel"* (Ezekiel 3:17). They are watchmen or guards for the body of Christ, His Church. Whenever they see the enemy, it is their responsibility to point him out so that believers can defeat him and cast him out.

Effective Warfare

This does not mean that they have to run around accusing people of having evil spirits wherever they sense spiritual problems. If a person discerns that someone is possessed or is being harassed, he or she can simply exercise the authority given by Jesus and command it to go.

This can be accomplished very quietly and unobtrusively. The voice does not have to be raised. Shouting and screaming has no effect on evil spirits. They are not deaf. Volume does not cause them to leave. In fact they have excellent hearing. Authority exercised in the name of Jesus Christ quietly and firmly used will drive them out and set the person free.

On the other hand, evil spirits love to perform for people. When given an opportunity, they will scream, yell, threaten, hit people and even attempt to kill them. The best way to deal with demons is to treat them the same way that a wise mother treats a child who throws a tantrum, because when demons know that they are going to be cast out, that is precisely what they do — they throw tantrums. They will curse and swear and do all kinds of weird things to throw fear into the person who is casting them out. The best thing to do is to ignore them and command them to leave. They will.

In their frantic effort to stay in a person, demons will often speak in a voice quite different from that of the person they are possessing. It is not unusual to hear a man's voice come out of a woman or a woman's voice come out of a man.

One time at "100 Huntley Street," I was asked to assist Father Bob MacDougall in the chapel. When I arrived on the scene, a woman was lying on her back on the floor. Bob was commanding the demon in her to leave. It was arguing with him in a man's voice. I joined Bob in agreement. As soon as I spoke up and commanded it to leave, the woman looked at me and, in the demonic man's voice, said, "And you, you're stupid."

I laughed and said, "You don't have to be very smart to know that. But you have to leave *now* in the name of Jesus Christ." It left, leaving the woman free to receive Jesus as her Saviour and Lord.

When demons are being cast out, they will sometimes cause a person to cough, choke, bring up, burp or do any number of weird things. However, these physical reactions or manifestations are not necessary to gain a person's freedom. If evil spirits cause a person to scream or to roll on the floor making a great display, one can simply command them to be quiet and to leave. Although it may be necessary to take a person who requires deliverance into another room to reduce disturbing others through a noisy display, most demons leave so quietly that those observing may actually wonder if they have left.

When dealing with either the Devil or demons, we must not be vulgar or rude, nor should we curse and swear back at them. Jude warns us about how to treat the Devil. We have to deal with him, and the demons, in the same way the archangel Michael did: *"He did not presume to announce a reviling judgment upon him, but said, 'The Lord rebuke you'"* (Jude 9).

James says, *"Resist the Devil and he will flee"* (James 4:7). That includes demons or evil spirits.

The casting out of evil spirits is called "deliverance ministry" or "exorcism," which simply means to cast out, drive out, or drive away an evil spirit by adjuration (by command).

Unless a person is a seasoned operator in the gift of Discernment, if they believe that they have found someone who needs freedom from a demon, they should report it to their pastor, minister, or a responsible leader in their church and let the pastor and elders deal with the situation. Many people have charged ahead like bulls in china shops, accusing people of having demons; without the maturity, wisdom or authority to bring resolution to the problem — then they wonder why they find themselves in all kinds of problems.

Why the Church Needs the Gift of Discernment

The Holy Spirit never gives a gift without a purpose. Through the Discernment of spirits, the church is alerted to attack the enemy, by setting people free who are harassed or possessed. Once set free, they are able to transfer out of the kingdom of darkness and into the kingdom of light by becoming Christian believers; or, if they are already Christians, to escape from bondage into freedom.

Besides the offensive aspects of the gift, it empowers the church defensively through enabling it to stop any attacks on it by the enemy.

At the conclusion of a meeting near Sudbury, Ontario, a huge man about seven feet tall came striding through two doors from an outside hallway into the auditorium in which I was ministering. Angrily waving his fist at me, he approached me in the prayer line, hissing, "I'm going to kill you," as he swung his fist at my head.

I sidestepped it, touched him on the end of his nose, and calmly said, "Come out in the Name of Jesus." The man went flying backwards, through the doors which he had just entered, and landed on the floor. I went over to him, knelt down beside him and prayed with him to be baptized in the Holy Spirit and he began to speak in tongues. He was set free. He told me that something had been inside him ever since he was a little boy, telling him to do bad things. He had tried to get help, but nobody could do anything to change him. However, that night Jesus set him free.

Free Indeed

People who have been legitimately possessed with or by a demon usually cannot remember the experience after they have been set free.

A number of years ago, a movie about deliverance was very popular. It was called "The Exorcist" and it was about a young girl who was possessed by a demon while playing with an Ouija board. The movie showed all the progressive steps of demon possession. Unfortunately, it ended with the lie that a Christian cannot get rid of a demon.

I was asked to preview the movie by CTV's "Canada AM," which is the Canadian Television Network's morning news program. My review appeared in several newspapers.

Having seen it, a young mother who was at her wits end contacted me. She had gone to see the movie and had left in terror because what she saw on the screen was exactly what was happening to her three-year-old daughter in her home. She was frantic because, like the mother in the movie, she had taken her daughter to see doctors, counselors, and psychiatrists.

When she brought the little girl to my office, the child was so vulgar and rude that I could see why no one had been able to help her. Her behaviour was virtually uncontrollable.

I agreed to pray for the girl, but said that I would deal with her in her own home. When I arrived, she was in her bedroom, sitting in her crib, bouncing like a basketball. Although it was a very hot day and there was no air conditioning, her room was so cold that I could see my breath. She began hissing at me. I took authority over the evil spirit and commanded it to leave in the Name of Jesus Christ. She immediately reverted back to being a normal three-year-old girl. I then prayed with both mother and daughter to receive Jesus Christ as their Saviour and Lord and to be baptized in the Holy Spirit.

Today, the little girl is a married woman with two children of her own and she and her family are serving Jesus. She has no memory or recollection of being possessed by an evil spirit.

License for a Deliverance Ministry?

One word of caution. Beware of people who boast that they have a "deliverance ministry." It usually means that they are preoccupied with demons and the Devil. In fact, they worship demons without realizing it, because all they seem to think about are evil spirits.

When we look at other Christians, unless we have been given the gift of discernment of spirits, our focus should be on what we see of God in them. Matthew 5:8 says, *"Blessed are the pure in heart, for they will see God."* When we look at people who are not Christians, our focus should be on what God wants them to be when Jesus becomes their Saviour.

Our ministry is salvation. As such, it includes deliverance as should every Christian ministry. According to Mark 16:17, all believers have a "deliverance ministry." *"These signs shall follow those who believe; in My Name they will cast out demons ..."* but not all have the gift of Discernment. It is important to repeat this Scripture over and over, because sweeping it under the carpets of time has resulted only in surface cleansing, rather than the deep washing that Scripture prescribes.

Nowhere in the Bible does it say that only those with the gift of Discernment can identify the enemy and cast him out. The promise is for *"those who believe."* Thus, those who have not been given the gift of Discernment, need not feel left out. If they study the Scripture, they will be able to accurately identify the presence of the evil in any form, whether the enemy appears as the Devil himself, as demons, or as false prophets, teachers or religious people. Those who learn to pray and listen to the Holy Spirit will be warned and shown the presence of the enemy.

We need only to use the authority we have been

given as Christian believers, without apologizing to anybody — just giving the glory to Jesus Christ.

8. The Gift of Speaking in Tongues

While many attempt to dismiss tongues as the least of the gifts, there is no place in Scripture where that assumption is validated. As a matter of fact, Paul clearly states in 1 Corinthians 14:39, that we ought not to forbid speaking in tongues.

The gift of speaking in tongues (1 Corinthians 12:10) is probably the most controversial of the gifts of the Holy Spirit, possibly because it is the least understood, but more probably because this gift, more than the others, represents the Lordship of Jesus over our lives. This gift poses the greatest threat to self-control because it exercises God-control over the greatest outward demonstration of self — our tongues.

It enables people to speak in a legitimate language or language that they have never learned. The amazing thing is that they do not know what they are saying. Their words have to be translated or interpreted by someone else in order to be understood even by themselves.

Some people think that Satan can't understand tongues, but he can. No matter what language people speak, it's his job to test everybody to see whether they are going to be faithful to God. Some people think that because they may be speaking an angelic tongue, Satan can't understand — but he was an angel. Angels must speak the same languages as we do, because they talk to us. The thought that we bypass Satan's understanding with tongues is simply another lie from Satan, because he wants us to think that he doesn't know what we're doing and will let our guards down. The reason we speak in tongues is to give God control of our tongues.

In an attempt to explain this gift, translators have misinterpreted it. It should be simply translated as "speaking in other national languages," but it is variously translated or interpreted as:

- tongues (KJV, RSV),
- different kinds of tongues (NIV),
- strange tongues or ecstatic tongues (GNFMM),
- different kinds of tongues (NKJV),
- ecstatic speech (Barclay),
- to speak in languages never learned (Living Bible),
- various kinds of tongues (NKJV), and
- various tongues (Phillips).

Recently, Jack Hayford has called this gift a "spiritual language." In the original Greek, the word, "ecstatic," is never used and the word, "tongues," is simply an old English word for "languages."

Tongues: Initial Evidence or a Gift of the Holy Spirit?

Because the Book of Acts mentions tongues directly, or indirectly, in connection with four of the six experiences of people receiving the Holy Spirit, the doctrine of "initial evidence" has developed.

Most people who are baptized in the Holy Spirit experience speaking in tongues. Out of this experience has developed the differentiation between "initial evidence" and "the gift of tongues." The understanding here is that all people will demonstrate tongues, at least temporarily, when they are first baptized in the Holy Spirit. What determines whether they have received the gift of tongues, or have simply manifested the initial evidence that they have received the Holy Spirit, is whether they can continue to exercise the language continually at their own will (under the guidance or with the cooperation of the Holy Spirit), or whether they have had simply a one time experience which they are powerless to repeat.

In spite of the fact that it is implied that when a person is baptized in the Holy Spirit, he or she will speak in tongues, there is no place in the New Testament where such a distinction is explicitly made.

To the question, " is tongues the initial evidence or is

it a gift of the Holy Spirit?", I would therefore respond that it is both. It is the only gift that everyone, who is baptized with the Holy Spirit, receives the ability to manifest. The Holy Spirit will distribute all the other gifts at His discretion.

Above all else, tongues is a sign (Mark 16:17) for believers that the people who have this gift are born again, Spirit-filled Christians.

What About Spirit-Filled Christians who Don't Speak in Tongues?

Having said that I believe that people have the *ability* to speak in tongues when they receive the baptism, the fact remains that, like me, not all do speak.

Why?

There are various reasons for this:

- some do not know how to release this new language that they did not learn and need instruction and encouragement;
- some people are told not to expect to speak in tongues and so do not try;
- some are told that tongues is not for everyone and, therefore conclude it is not for them;
- many have been taught that Jesus stopped giving tongues, as well as the other gifts of the Holy Spirit;
- some are told that they do not need to speak in tongues;
- others have been told that tongues are from the Devil;
- some believe that people just make up a so-called language and that tongues aren't real;
- others simply do not want to neither speak in tongues nor turn their "rudders" over to Jesus as Lord.

With these mind sets, most people don't take the step of trying to speak in tongues.

Which raises the question, "Should everyone speak in tongues?"

At one time I did not think so, since I felt that the gifts were probably distributed equally throughout the church. But, the Scripture and experience have taught me to look at this gift somewhat differently.

I have come to believe that we do all need to speak in tongues.

Why do we Need to Speak in Tongues?

According to James, the tongue is the most uncontrollable organ or body part in the whole body. *"The tongue is a fire. The tongue is an unrighteous world among our members, staining the whole body, setting on fire the cycle of nature, and set on fire by hell...but no human being can tame the tongue — it is a restless evil, full of deadly poison"* (James 3:6–8).

If any man were perfect, he would be able to *"bridle the whole body"* (James 3:2) especially the tongue. It is the "rudder" of the ship and requires a pilot who can direct it. It is the steering wheel in a car which requires the driving skill of the Holy Spirit.

No man is perfect except Jesus Christ.

Thus, through the supernatural power of the Holy Spirit, He is the only one who can control the tongue. He wants control of our mouths so that He can really be Lord.

The personal use of speaking in tongues gives us a constant assurance that the Holy Spirit is always with us. Too often, when Christians have bad experiences, when they are overwhelmed with difficulties, or when they succumb to fear and anxiety, they begin to feel defeated, depressed and without hope for the future. At such times, praying in the Spirit or in tongues will give them the assurance that the Holy Spirit is still with them, because it would be impossible to speak an unknown language without His indwelling power. Thus, praying in tongues is a constant reminder of Jesus faithfulness to His promise that, *"I will never leave you nor forsake you"* (Hebrews 13:5).

When we do use tongues daily, as Paul tells us, it

"edifies" (1 Corinthians 14:4) or builds up the believer. It causes our faith to grow and opens us up to the guidance of the Holy Spirit.

That's why He wants everyone to receive and use the gift.

Is it a Common Occurrence to Have People Speak in Tongues Today?

I have been in many, many meetings where I have seen every person who came forward to receive prayer for the baptism of the Holy Spirit, receive the gift of speaking in tongues.

One evening in Fredericton, New Brunswick, Canada, I prayed with more than 200 people individually to be baptized with the Holy Spirit. Everyone spoke in tongues.

Recently, in an Anglican Church in Sussex, New Brunswick, everyone who had prayer to receive the baptism of the Holy Spirit received the gift.

In a Pentecostal Church in the Ternopil, Ukraine, several hundred people responded to our altar call and received tongues. Since those people did not speak English and I did not speak Ukrainian, I had to keep checking with my interpreter to see whether the people were speaking in Ukrainian. She kept saying, "She (or He as the case may have been) is speaking in a language that I do not know. I only know that it is not Ukrainian!"

I can tell you of meeting after meeting, from one coast of Canada and the United States to the other, in small churches and large ones, in Christian meetings and banquets, where all those who requested the baptism of the Holy Spirit received the gift of speaking in tongues. Any who had previously received the baptism, but had not yet spoken in tongues, spoke following prayer.

When Jesus said, *"But you shall receive power when the Holy Spirit has come upon you; and you shall be my witnesses in Jerusalem and in all Judea and Samaria and to the end of the world"* (Acts 1:8). He indicated that without the power of the Holy Spirit, we lack the control and power that we need to speak under the guidance of the Holy Spirit, whether in witnessing to others or in using the gifts of the Holy Spirit.

Operation of the Gift of Tongues

Personally, I initially had a difficult time understanding how the gift of speaking in tongues works. I thought that perhaps God was a ventriloquist and, when a person opened his mouth, the Holy Spirit would appear to be speaking. But of course, He is not.

Speaking in tongues can be compared to witnessing, in that Jesus speaks through our mouths — not by overpowering us or putting us into some kind of an ecstatic state or trance — but with our permission and cooperation. Via this unique communications system, He is able to speak to and through His church.

People speaking languages they have not learned do not know what they are saying. In the beginning, it sounds strange to them, perhaps even weird. Most often, the speaker will imagine him or herself to be"'just making it up." Of course that is not the case.

We can choose either to cooperate with the Holy Spirit, or to not cooperate. We can choose either to use this gift, or not to use it. We can use it as frequently or as infrequently as we wish. A major reason why the gift is not understood is simply that we control its use by our willingness or unwillingness to cooperate.

The reality is that most people who have this gift neither cooperate, nor know how to use it to their greatest advantage.

For some people, speaking in tongues can be a very emotional experience. For others, it is not. Because the Holy Spirit deals with us as individuals, every experience is unique and as such, is valid for the person involved. As a result, when we try to share our experiences with others, we usually do it in emotional terms rather than in spiritual terms. The important thing is that, regardless of the degree of emotion, each person receives all that God has for him or her.

When the gift of speaking in tongues is used publicly, the individual or people whom the Holy Spirit wants to use to deliver a message to the Church will be prompted in some manner to speak in tongues. The way that the Holy Spirit moves a person to speak out a message in tongues may differ from person to person. The important thing is faithfulness and willingness to speak it out so that the people in the Church can hear it.

Some people experience a sense of breathlessness. The heart starts to pound and they can hardly sit still. They may wonder whether they are having an anxiety attack or a heart attack. However, as soon as they speak out in tongues and give the message that the Holy Spirit wants them to deliver, they immediately experience peace.

Others tell me that when the Holy Spirit wants them to give a message in tongues, they start to cry, usually starting off gently, but increasing more and more until they speak out the message in tongues. Then they experience peace.

Still others tell me that they get a feeling or an impression that the Holy Spirit wants them to give a message in tongues. They give it and feel peaceful.

Others tell me that they hear a voice, whether quiet or forceful, telling them to speak publicly in tongues so that the Lord can give a message to His Church.

But, regardless of how the Holy Spirit prompts a person, the important thing is to deliver the message. Someone in the Church needs to receive it. *"So, my brethren, earnestly desire to prophesy, and do not forbid speaking in tongues; but all things should be done decently and in order"* (1 Corinthians 14:39,40).

Having this gift gives us all the potential to develop a relationship with Jesus Christ in a new and different way, thereby achieving a personal maturity which will become obvious to others. It allows us to develop an intimacy with the Holy Spirit that can only be developed through praying in the Holy Spirit (in tongues).

Why is There so Much Division in the Church Over Tongues?

Paul said, *"The unspiritual man does not receive the gifts of the Spirit of God, for they are folly to him and he is not able to understand them because they are spiritually discerned"* (1 Corinthians 2:14).

The word *"spiritual"* refers to a person who has received the Holy Spirit. It is the Holy Spirit who enables a person to understand and receive His gifts. The *"unspiritual"* person is one who has not received His baptism. A person can be a saved, born again, Christian believer, and be unspiritual because he or she has not been baptized in the Holy Spirit. That was the case with the disciples before the Day of Pentecost (Acts 2:4). It is usually the unspiritual believers who have the greatest problem accepting and understanding the gifts of the Holy Spirit and their place in the work, worship and witness of the Church.

The Gift of Languages

There are 5,301 languages currently spoken in the world today. This means that when a person receives the gift of tongues, he or she has the potential to speak in any one or more of those languages or in any language that was spoken in the past as the Holy Spirit gives the language that He chooses.

While conducting the first FGBMFI Airlift to the Ukraine, I prayed with a language professor from the University of Kiev who spoke and taught 14 languages fluently. After I prayed with her to receive the baptism in the Holy Spirit, she carefully and deliberately opened her mouth, spoke a few syllables in tongues, stopped, nodded her head affirmatively, spoke more syllables in tongues, stopped, nodded her head affirmatively again and proceeded to repeat the procedure several times. Finally, she looked at me, grinned and said, "I do not know what I am saying, but I do know a language structure when I hear one!"

I studied Greek for seven years and Hebrew for six years. With all of those years of study, I initially couldn't understand how, when the Holy Spirit comes inside a person, he or she could immediately begin to speak in a language without being taught or having studied it. But, that is exactly what happens.

I can identify only the several languages that I have studied. Once I prayed with a French Canadian woman who was from a small town in Northern Ontario, Canada. This lady did not speak English. Through a friend who acted as our interpreter (since I do not speak French) she asked me to pray with her. She said that she "had to get the Holy Ghost." I asked her to pray along with me, through the interpreter, as we asked Jesus to baptize her in the Holy Spirit. She fell down under the power of the Holy Spirit and, as she lay on the floor, she began to speak in tongues. Her tongues language was English! She praised God and thanked Him for sending Jesus. She thanked Jesus for coming and ministering on earth and dying on the Cross and being raised from the dead and ascending into Heaven. Then she thanked Him for baptizing her with the Holy Spirit.

Just then, her husband came into the chapel and saw his wife on the floor speaking in fluent English. He exclaimed, "That's my wife! She does not speak English!" I explained what had happened.

He said "I need what she's got!" I prayed with him and he got what she got — just with a different tongues language.

Then the woman began to speak in a second language. This time she spoke in Ukrainian and said the same thing that she had been saying in English. That happened about eight years ago. To this very day, she cannot speak English except when she is praying in tongues or in the Spirit.

Many times, I have seen people speak in various languages that either I, or someone else, could identify. In

Kingston, Ontario, I prayed for an English-speaking woman who had no love for French-speaking people. She wanted to be baptized in the Holy Spirit. She began to speak in tongues and her tongues language was French. She now loves the French.

Recently, I returned from a trip to Saint John, New Brunswick. There I prayed again with a woman who had received the baptism of the Holy Spirit several years ago while I was doing some ministry in that city. At that time she received the gift of tongues in Biblical Greek.

We cannot determine what language the Holy Spirit will give us. He gives us what He determines is necessary. It can be in any language, known or unknown to us. The Holy Spirit often gives a person more than one spiritual language when he or she receives the gift of speaking in tongues (other national languages). David Duplesis, who was called "Mr. Pentecost," said that he spoke in nine different languages.

Releasing the Gift

When I received the baptism in the Holy Spirit, I was too stubborn to allow Jesus to release the gift of tongues in me. Eventually, however, He was able to penetrate my lack of understanding.

When I had been in the ministry for some time, Ruth and I and two couples from our church attended a service at Evangel Temple in Toronto. At the end of the service, the evangelist, Charles Hunter, gave an invitation for anyone who wanted to be baptized in the Holy Spirit or to receive a gift of the Holy Spirit to go upstairs into a room where his son-in-law would give instruction on how to receive and pray for people.

I didn't want to go, but Ruth reminded me that I was the Pastor and should look after the two couples with us who wanted to go upstairs. "You wouldn't want them to get involved in anything that wasn't right, would you?" she nudged.

I reluctantly agreed and so the six of us went up into the other room. I made sure that all five of my "flock" were in front of me facing the speaker so that I could be sure that everything was in order. In a weak moment, I, too, prayed along and asked for the gift of speaking in tongues.

I tried three times to make sounds and gave up. I whispered to Ruth, "Let's go to a Chinese restaurant. Maybe we'll hear another language there."

"Don't make jokes about the Holy Spirit," she admonished sharply.

I conceded that she was right and apologized. We did, however, go to a restaurant following the service. Afterwards, we went home and went to sleep. Nothing happened until 3 a.m. when I awoke with a start and realized that something strange was happening inside of me. Since I had already observed that when a person is about to speak in tongues there could be any one of four physical symptoms present (full chest, heart thumping, funny tickle in throat and crying for no reason) I recognized what was happening. I wasn't crying, but three out of four gave me a pretty good clue. I knew that the Holy Spirit was trying to give me the gift of speaking in tongues.

I got out of bed, went down into the family room, got down on my knees and asked Jesus to help me release tongues. I started putting some sounds together and something shifted in my throat. A new language began to flow and I stayed on my knees praying in tongues for an hour.

After awhile, the Lord told me to get up off my knees and phone my friend from seminary and tell him what had happened that night. Denis Baker lived in Plainfield, New Jersey. He was the book editor for Logos at the time. In spite of the fact that it was 4 a.m., I dialed his number. The phone rang a full seven rings before a groggy voice said, "Hello?"

I said, "Denis — you will not believe what happened to me tonight!" and I proceeded to tell him the whole story in detail.

After I had finished telling him everything that had happened, a not-so-groggy-by-now voice said, "Sir, I think you have the wrong number."

I stammered a thank you to him for listening, redialed the number and connected with Denis. Again I shared every detail as my friend listened patiently on the other end. When I had finished, he said, "Can I go back to bed now?"

I don't know who the stranger in New Jersey was, but I guess that he needed to hear my story. If he happens to read this book, I'd welcome a return call from him. (4 a.m. would be fine.)

Ruth had prayed for tongues in the same meeting the night before and later on that morning, she, too, received.

Most people, as I did, have a problem knowing how to release the gift. Some strain their voices and make weird groaning sounds. Others attempt to start speaking in tongues by repeating various words over and over again rapidly, such as "Hallelujah, Hallelujah, Hallelujah!" or "Praise the Lord! Praise the Lord! Praise the Lord!" or "The Blood, the Blood, the Blood," hoping that the fast repetition will somehow or other trigger tongues into action. However, no one can speak two languages at the same time.

Perhaps the simplest and easiest way to release the gift of speaking in tongues (after a person has been baptized in the Holy Spirit) is to simply focus one's attention on Jesus Christ. Then, without straining the voice, simply start to utter sounds the way one would normally speak, without using any known language. Through cooperating with the Holy Spirit by giving Him control, He will take the "made up" sounds and shape them into a new language that the speaker has never spoken before. He or she will not understand the words. In fact, it will sound strange to them. It took me about six months of concentrated effort to get accustomed to hearing myself speak in tongues.

As I mentioned in recounting my own experience in releasing tongues, I have observed that when people have been baptized in the Holy Spirit and are about to speak in tongues, any one, or all, of the following symptoms will be internally present:

- the chest will feel full,
- the heart will thump or beat rapidly with a sense of anticipation,
- the throat will get a funny tickle,
- the person will begin to cry for no apparent reason.

On the other hand, one might not experience any of the above, but will begin to speak in tongues almost effortlessly. Whatever the situation, the person must consciously use his or her own vocal cords, just as he or she does when talking normally. When approached with the right attitude of expectation, the tongues language will begin to flow very easily.

Prerequisites

There is no age limit or requirement as far as receiving the gift of speaking in tongues.

I have prayed with many elderly people to receive. I remember an 84 year-old lady who came forward for prayer in a church in Flesherton, Ontario. She told me that she had been seeking the baptism of the Holy Spirit for 42 years. What she really meant was that she wanted to speak in tongues, as evidence that she had been baptized in the Holy Spirit. I gave her some instruction, but she would not do as I suggested. She had become an expert in not receiving. She kept telling me how it was supposed to happen. I finally spoke strongly to her because she would not listen to what I was saying. I said, "Ma'am, please be quiet and listen to me. You have become an expert in not receiving. If you want to speak in tongues, then follow my instructions, no matter how foolish or strange they might sound."

"Well, all right," she reluctantly agreed. She began to mutter something and then began to speak louder as she fell to the floor under the power of the Holy Spirit — speaking in tongues.

Members of her family gathered around her in prayer. One of her grandchildren came to me with tears in her eyes saying, "Grandma, finally got her tongues after 42 years." Well, praise the Lord that we don't have to wait for 42 years in order to receive the wonderful gifts of the Holy Spirit.

I have also prayed with little children to be baptized in the Holy Spirit and they have spoken in tongues. As I was praying with people at the conclusion of a meeting in Wawa, Ontario, I noticed a little 3 year-old girl wandering among those who had come for prayer. She was looking curiously at those who had been "slain in the Spirit." I asked her, "Honey, did you come here for prayer, or did you just come to look?" She gazed at me with her wide brown eyes and hesitantly asked, "Can I get the Holy Spirit too?"

"Well, yes," I answered. The little sweetheart prayed with me to be baptized in the Holy Spirit. She gently slipped to the floor speaking in tongues as the Spirit filled her. The next night, her mother and eight-year-old sister came forward when I issued the invitation for prayer. Both of them came to receive what the little girl had been given.

I have seen people of all ages and church backgrounds receive the baptism of the Holy Spirit with the evidence of speaking in tongues.

Tongues Used in Private Prayer

There are several specific, practical uses for tongues used in private prayer:

- to build up the believer through a personal prayer language
- to receive direction in prayer
- to receive assurance that God has heard and will answer our prayers

- to enter into agreement with the Holy Spirit
- to break bondages.

Paul says that tongues are given in order to build up the individual believer. Here he is speaking of a private prayer language. *"He who speaks in a tongue edifies himself, but he who prophesies edifies the church"* (1 Corinthians 14:4). When a person learns to pray in the Spirit, that is, in tongues, he or she will grow in faith and relationship with Jesus Christ. Tongues offers a new dimension in prayer and a new intimacy with Jesus Christ through the Holy Spirit. I don't know about others, but whenever I pray in English I soon run out of words. In spite of the fact that I know that I am not finished praying, I don't know what to say. Tongues provides the solution for satisfactorily completing our prayer life.

Jesus told us that the Holy Spirit is supposed to be our Comforter and Counsellor (John 14:25, 16:17). By praying in the Spirit with tongues, the Holy Spirit has the freedom to begin to speak to us and communicate with us. We begin to feel what the Holy Spirit feels. We begin to think as the Holy Spirit thinks. Our personality begins to be shaped by the power of the Holy Spirit within and He develops the fruit of the Spirit in us. We discover that as we learn to use this marvellous prayer language, we are strengthened and grow in faith. We learn to trust the Holy Spirit.

Praying in tongues allows us a new method to use in our prayer relationship with Jesus Christ. After I have prayed in English for whatever I feel necessary, I then think about the people or the things that I have been praying about. I then pray in tongues for each person or need until I experience a peace that comes over me. That is God's way of letting me know that He is going to act upon my requests. Sometimes, it takes a few seconds, sometimes a few minutes, and sometimes an hour or more before I experience His peace.

The amazing thing about this "praying in the Spirit," that is, praying in tongues, is that I experience all sorts of dynamic answers to prayer as well as an intimacy with the Holy Spirit. I believe what happens is that we receive the agreement of the Holy Spirit. According to what Jesus said, *"Again I say to you, if two of you agree on earth about anything they ask, it will be done for them by my Father in Heaven"* (Matthew 18:19).

This is not a way to try to force the Holy Spirit to agree to what we want, but just the opposite. It is a way to discover how to cooperate with Him and find out who needs prayer and for what, and then to pray unselfishly. Through this gift, He can call us to pray for certain people we may know without detailing their specific problem or need; thereby not compromising confidentiality. God is not a gossip who goes around telling other people all of the details of our lives, some of which might be embarrassing. The Holy Spirit has often awakened me in the middle of the night in order to pray for other people. He rarely tells me what the problem is — just for whom to pray. Later on, upon inquiring of the person for whom I have prayed, I usually discover that he or she had a crisis or a problem which was solved through prayer.

A few years ago, the Holy Spirit woke me up at 3 a.m., Christmas morning, to pray for the wife of a friend who lives in Thunder Bay, Ontario. I prayed for her for about an hour until I experienced the peace of the Holy Spirit which indicated to me that I had prayed enough. This happened every morning between Christmas and New Year's Day. On New Year's Day, I called my friend out of curiosity in order to see what was happening with his wife. He told me that she had been in the hospital since Christmas Day and had almost died twice in the middle of the night. I told him that the Holy Spirit had awakened me every night to pray for her and that I was very pleased to hear that she was home and well.

Praying in tongues allows us a powerful method for praying for people who need healing from various physical, psychological and emotional problems, or God's intervention in the circumstances of their lives. Whenever I pray for people, I ask them what they would like me to pray for. First, I pray for them in English, then, thinking of their needs or problems, I pray in tongues until I experience the peace of God come upon me. At that point, I know that the Holy Spirit has gone out to meet the need.

Through praying in tongues, we can break habits that may have been plaguing us and inhibiting our Christian growth. For instance, smoking is one of the most difficult habits to break and from which to be set free. I have discovered that if a person who has been baptized in the Holy Spirit will pray in tongues for the same length of time it takes to smoke a cigarette (between three to five minutes) they can be set free by substituting praying in tongues for smoking. It usually takes the equivalent time in prayer that it takes to smoke two to three packages of cigarettes. Twenty cigarettes per package adds up to about one hour and 40 minutes of prayer. Two things result: first, the habit is broken and the person is set free; and secondly, the Holy Spirit will begin to speak to and through him or her *"mysteries in the Spirit"* (1 Corinthians 14:2).

This method of praying in the Spirit can be used to break almost any unhealthy habit. I have recommended it for breaking drug habits where the person, after having been saved and baptized in the Holy Spirit, has prayed in tongues until the desire for drugs passed away. This often requires exercising the gift for several hours.

Praying in the Spirit is a wonderful way for people to be set free from alcoholism. The real need in such a person's life is to replace the old wine with the "new wine" of the Holy Spirit which, of course, is received through receiving the baptism in the Holy Spirit. When a person with a drinking problem prays in tongues, they can not only be set free from alcohol, but they can receive direction from the Holy Spirit with regard to Jesus' plans for their lives.

Praying in the Spirit can also be used to set people free from overeating. Instead of reaching for food, the person can pray in tongues for whatever length of time it takes for the desire to pass. The result is that the person will gain control of his or her appetite and be able to live a peaceful life. Even more than the loss of weight, the person will treasure a more personal relationship with Jesus Christ and with our Heavenly Father.

Tongues — A Key to Personal Growth in Faith

The apostle Paul saw tongues as a key to personal growth in faith. *"I thank God that I speak in tongues more than you all; nevertheless, in church I would rather speak five words with my mind, in order to instruct others than ten thousand words in a tongue"* (1 Corinthians 14:18–19). In other words, there is a time and a place for both. When properly used, both individuals and the Church will grow and faith will increase. That is why Paul instructed us in the proper use of all of the gifts of the Holy Spirit, but with special concentration on the use of tongues.

In my experience as a pastor, allowing the use of the gift of speaking in tongues (as directed by the apostle Paul) truly does result in the edification or building up of the church. Our people became extraordinarily tuned in to what Jesus Christ wanted us to do within the context of an exciting and unique relationship with Jesus Christ.

Singing in the Spirit (in Tongues)

Paul tells us that we can sing in tongues as well as speak. He refers to this as the ability to *"sing with the Spirit"* (1 Corinthians 14:15). Often during a worship service, people will join together singing in tongues. Each person will sing in their own tongues language and switch back and forth to English or whatever language in which they normally pray. The result is a resounding chorus that sounds like a symphony orchestra. It is quite an amazing experience of praise.

Paul says, *"What am I to do? I will pray with the spirit and I will pray with the mind also; I will sing with the spirit and I will sing with the mind also"* (1 Corinthians 14:15). Like any new expression of praise and worship, people need to have instruction and be taught how to sing with (or in) the Spirit. It is not something that we are naturally comfortable with, but we can grow to express our love through tongues, both spoken and sung in *"spiritual songs"* (Ephesians 5:19).

There are those who misunderstand what happens when people sing in the Spirit because they are concerned about Paul's instructions with regard to making sure that tongues used in public must be followed by an interpretation. What these people have failed to understand is that when a church or group of Christians sing in the Spirit, there will be singing both in the native language of the group and in tongues. The native language is usually the interpretation of the tongues that are being sung. As a congregation sings in tongues, most of the interpretation will be praise, but it often includes a message of direction or encouragement for the church or for individual Christians.

Tongues Used in Public

The public use of speaking in tongues is designed for the encouragement and growth of the Church. It is a vehicle that Jesus Christ uses to communicate with His Church. When used in public, it must be combined with the gift of interpretation of tongues. *"If anyone speaks in a tongue ... let one interpret. But if there is no interpreter, let him keep silent in church, and let him speak to himself and to God"* (1 Corinthians 14:27,28).

The speaking of tongues in public is not to be feared or prohibited. Many people become extremely agitated if they suspect that tongues might be spoken in their church service, when in fact, that is exactly where they were designed to be used. *"If any speak in a tongue, let there be only two or three at most three, and each in turn; and let one interpret"* (1 Corinthians 14:27). In actual fact, it is no more frightening to hear somebody speak in tongues than to hear somebody speaking in a foreign language from any other country in the world.

Through the public use of tongues, God (the Father, the Son, and the Holy Spirit) delivers messages to His people, either corporately or individually. These messages can include prophecy, encouragement, direction for the church, a call to repentance, or whatever God wants to communicate.

When people speak in tongues publicly, the legitimacy of the languages spoken is often confirmed by someone present who hears his or her own native language being spoken by a person who does not know that particular language, whether French, Italian, Spanish, Greek, Ukrainian, Finnish, German, or whatever. Invariably, the hearer is surprised to hear a message directed specifically to his or her circumstances — about which the speaker has no knowledge.

Most often, however, the person speaking will speak in a language which is unfamiliar to the listeners and which requires interpretation through a person with the gift of interpretation of tongues.

Tongues, when combined with the gift of interpretation of tongues is *"a sign for unbelievers"* (1 Corinthians 14:22). There is a spiritual dimension within unbelievers that can be accessed through hearing tongues, which confirm deep within their hearts that what they are hearing is from God. It arouses a hunger in them to know Jesus as their Saviour and Lord and receive the baptism in the Holy Spirit.

9. The Gift of Interpretation of Tongues

The gift of interpretation of tongues (1 Corinthians 12:10) should be more properly translated as the gift of interpretation or translation of languages. The Greek word for this gift means to interpret, explain, or translate.

This is a supernatural gift that is given by the Holy Spirit to certain individuals who have been baptized in the Holy Spirit and who, by means of this gift, will provide the interpretation, translation, or explanation for any messages given by God through the use of the gift of speaking in tongues.

Like prophecy, through the gift of interpretation of tongues, we can receive edification, exhortation, and comfort. We can also receive instruction and prophecy.

Interpretation of tongues is the ability to give the sense of what has been said in a message given in tongues. Just as the Holy Spirit leads a person to speak in a language that he or she does not understand, so He also leads someone present to interpret what has been said.

A person who has the gift of interpretation of tongues or languages will not necessarily be able to interpret every tongues language that is used by the Holy Spirit. Usually there are a number of people who have this gift in an assembly, but for different languages. As people learn to cooperate with the Holy Spirit and the people in their fellowship, they will soon discover who the people are who have the tongues language that they can interpret.

Some people will have both the gift of speaking in tongues and the gift of interpretation for their own tongues language. However, it is usually recommended that if a person delivers the message in tongues, he or she should let somebody else give the interpretation. This eliminates any appearance of someone attempting to manipulate a church or fellowship of believers. It also allows more people to gain experience in using their gift of interpretation of tongues.

Usually, there will be more than one person in a church who has the gift of interpretation of tongues. When this is the case, two or three people can confirm the interpretation that is given. What will often happen is that one person will begin to give the message in tongues and will pause; then, a second person will pick up the interpretation. When the second person pauses, a third person might pick up the interpretation, even a fourth. They will all be in agreement about the message that the Lord has sent.

When I first invited Jesus Christ to be my Saviour and Lord and was baptized in the Holy Spirit, I told Him that I did not want to receive the gift of speaking in tongues. I knew that all of the gifts of the Holy Spirit were legitimate and for today. However, because I did not understand the gift of tongues, I did not want to receive it. Sometimes, Jesus will answer foolish prayer requests in order to teach us a lesson. And so, He did not give me the gift of speaking in tongues; instead, He gave me the gift of interpretation of tongues. Thus, when people would speak in tongues, I would usually know what they were saying. It was the strangest experience.

When I finally did ask Jesus to give me the gift of speaking in tongues, He did. Now, of course, like others who have been set free from similar misgivings, I look back and shake my head at my lack of willingness to receive and use such a wonderful gift. It has opened my life up to the Holy Spirit in an exciting and beautiful way.

Orderly Worship According to Scripture

The opportunity should be given in all worship services for messages or words to be received through the gifts of speaking in tongues and the interpretation of tongues. There is only one place where instruction is given about what constitutes how *"all things should be done decently and in order"* (1 Corinthians 14:40) and that is given by Paul (1 Corinthians 14:26–33). From what he describes, there are very few, if any, churches that do things decently and in order.

According to Paul, *"decently and in good order"* involves the following: *"What then, brethren? When you come together, each one has a hymn, a lesson, a revelation, a tongue, or an interpretation. Let all things be done for edification. If any speak in a tongue, let there be only two or at most three, and each in turn; and let one interpret. But if there is no one to interpret, let each of them keep silence in church and speak to himself and to God. Let two or three prophets speak, and let the others weigh what is said. If a revelation is made to another sitting by, let the first be silent. For you can all prophesy one by one, so that all may learn and all be encouraged; and the spirits of the prophets are subject to prophets. For God is not a God of confusion but of peace"* (1 Corinthians 14:26–33).

Thus, truly orderly worship allows a time not only for prophecy but also for tongues and interpretation.

Personal Messages from God via the Interpretation of Tongues

Occasionally, there is a private interpretation given for a specific individual in a church. Most frequently, it is for the person who originally gave the message in tongues. Like prophecy, any personal messages or words from the Lord must be examined very carefully. Like private prophecy, private interpretation of tongues is usually a confirmation of something that Jesus Christ has already told the person. Regardless, the Scripture tells us not to act upon anything unless there are two or three witnesses who can confirm the advice or instructions that the Holy Spirit has given. Anyone who simply chases off after personal guidance without two or three witnesses to confirm it and without the Holy Spirit telling them beforehand, is open to getting themselves into trouble.

Several years ago, I was one of the speakers at a Church Renewal Conference held in Haliburton, Ontario. We had a tremendous move of the Holy Spirit during the conference, throughout which there were many salvations, baptisms of the Holy Spirit, giftings by the Holy Spirit and many healings and miracles.

Following the conference, when I arrived for work at "100 Huntley Street," I received a telephone call from a man who had been part of the leadership of the conference. He told me that he had a dream while he was asleep the night before. In the dream, Jesus had come to him and said, "Maurice, I have something that I want to say to you."

He said, "Yes, Lord. What is it?" He told me that Jesus opened His mouth and began to speak in a language that he did not understand. He asked, "Lord, what does that mean?"

Jesus said, "Call Gordon Williams and he will tell you."

I was shocked, to say the least. I asked him, "Do you remember what the language sounded like?"

"Yes," he quickly responded, "the words are burned in my memory."

Since I had to be in the studio for the start of our television program, I told him that I would write down the words phonetically and pray over the message when I had a few quiet moments. Later on that day, I called him back with the interpretation.

The message which I interpreted for him did not make sense to me. This is what I interpreted: "My son, Maurice, when I call a man to come and follow Me, I do not always require everyone to go and sell all that he has to come and follow Me. I want you to come and follow Me just the way you are. I love you."

Maurice, however, knew exactly what it meant. He had been called by Jesus into full-time ministry and had been trying for a couple of years to sell his farm and business so that he could go and study on a full-time basis. Other people were selling their farms and businesses on both sides of him, but his wasn't selling. He had become very frustrated because he had assumed that God's calling was for immediate full-time study and service. As a result of the message, however, he relaxed and met the responsibilities that were at hand. Eventually, in God's time, he became an ordained minister and is serving Jesus Christ on a full-time basis today.

Operation of the Gift of Interpretation of Tongues

So how does the gift of interpretation of tongues operate in a person's life? Well, many people tell me that when they hear somebody speaking in tongues, they hear the quiet voice of the Holy Spirit giving them the interpretation. Others tell me that when they hear a message in tongues, they ask the Holy Spirit to show them and He does by means of impressions. Others tell me that when they hear a message in tongues, they close their eyes and can see words in their imaginations which they read out loud so that other people can hear the interpretation.

Yet others, like me, hear tongues spoken the first time, but when the person speaking repeats the message, we hear it in English and then speak it out so that others can hear the message and receive it.

Normally, the gift of interpretation of tongues is a permanent and ongoing gift. Those who have this gift will discover that when they are in worship, if the gift of tongues is allowed to operate, they will often be able to give the interpretation.

If, however, there is a message in tongues but there is no one present who has this gift, the Holy Spirit may give the interpretation of a particular message on a one-time basis to someone who prays for the interpretation. That is an answer to prayer. The person will discover that it was not a permanent gifting because he or she will not be able to interpret tongues regularly.

The gift of interpretation of tongues is an interesting, exciting, and unusual means for God to communicate with His Church. He first gave it on the Day of Pentecost and will continue to use it until Jesus returns.

8

The Seven Gifts of Romans

"We have different gifts according to the grace given us.If a man's gift is prophesying, let him use it in proportion to his faith. If it is serving, let him serve; if it is teaching, let him teach; if it is encouraging, let him encourage; if it is contributing to the needs of others, let him give generously; if it is leadership, let him govern diligently; if it is showing mercy, let him do it cheerfully"

(Romans 12:6-8).

Everyone talks about the nine gifts of the Holy Spirit as outlined in 1 Corinthians. However, many people overlook the fact that Paul listed seven charismatic gifts in Romans 12:6-8, only one of which is a repetition of a gift listed in 1 Corinthians, that being the gift of Prophecy.

These, too, are distributed by the Holy Spirit individually as He wishes. They are not given by mistake, *"But each has his own special gift from God, one of one kind and one of another"* (1 Corinthians 7:7). They are to be earnestly desired and used *"for the profit of all"* (1 Corinthians 12:7).

They are not to be neglected, according to the exhortation in 1 Timothy 4:14, but are to be stirred up and carefully used.

1. The Gift of Prophecy

The gift of Prophecy is the only charismatic gift that appears in both the Romans and the 1 Corinthians lists. (For a full treatment of this gift, please refer to Chapter Seven.)

Jesus Christ will give those with this gift a message about future happenings in the fellowship of the church, whether for particular individuals or for the entire body.

Paul tells us that the gift of Prophecy is for our *"edification, exhortation, and comfort"* (1 Corinthians 14:3, KJV) or *"upbuilding, encouragement, and consolation"* (RSV). He said, *"Now I want you all to speak in tongues, but even more to prophesy"*(1 Corinthians 14:5).

The purpose of prophecy is guidance and protection, a vehicle through which Jesus Christ can prepare His Church for the future. This must be distinguished from enlightenment, which is the purpose of the occult counterfeits.

The Faith Factor in Prophecy

Prophecy operates through faith. Only from within a personal relationship with Jesus Christ can a person recognize the voice of the Holy Spirit who relates the prophecies, and deliver the words with confidence that the message is from God. It takes faith to be obedient and speak out a prophecy because anyone with experience knows that people often react negatively to prophecy. *"A prophet is not without honour, except in his own country, among his own kin, and in his own house"* (Mark 6:4).

A Gift — or an Answer to Prayer?

Occasionally, during a time of prayer, the Holy Spirit may give someone without the gift of Prophecy a prophetic word or message for a body of believers or for an individual within the assembly. This kind of prophecy is not to be confused with the *gift* of Prophecy. It may happen when there is no one present who has the gift. In such a situation, the Holy Spirit may use someone who is simply available, though not gifted with the particular spiritual equipment needed at that time.

Obedience to instructions given in prayer is an important aspect of our prayer relationship with Jesus Christ. Anyone receiving a prophecy in this way should write it down, date it, check it out scripturally and share it with the person to whom it was directed. When God does what He said He would do, the date should be recorded and thanks should be given to God for using the vessel.

While a person receiving prophecy through prayer may never be used in this manner again, the gift of Prophecy operates continuously through the gifted person.

2. The Gift of Service

The gift of Service is a gift of practical help. Those who have this gift have the ability to see those things which need to be done in everyday life. These are the "charismatic Marthas and Martins." They see the necessity of getting the housework done when other people don't see it. However, unlike Martha, they are balanced in knowing when to spend time with Jesus in worship and prayer and when to get the practical things done.

These people are supernaturally gifted by the Holy Spirit to help others with everyday needs like business problems, repair work, household chores or preparing meals for those who are sick, shut-in, or too busy serving the Lord in other areas of ministry to look after their own practical needs.

People with the gift of Service are worth their weight in gold in freeing up people who have other gifts of the Holy Spirit, to carry out their ministries.

Deacons as Servants

Church deacons should be people who are equipped with the gift of Service. The original deacons were people chosen for the practical work of waiting on tables to serve food to people who were being fed by the church. *"It is not right that we should give up preaching the word of God to serve tables. Therefore, brethren pick out from among you seven men of good repute, full of the Spirit and of wisdom, whom we may appoint to this duty"* (Acts 6:2,3). The office of deacon was initiated to free up the apostles so that they could devote themselves *"to prayer and the ministry of the word"* (Acts 6:4).

The Attitude of Service

Those who have the gift of Service never grumble or complain when they see work that needs to be done. They just dive in, singing and praising God for giving them such a wonderful ministry.

It is of the utmost importance to the life of any church that anyone given such work as that of caretaker or janitor, be gifted with the gift of Service. If "ungifted" people take on such chores, they will invariably complain about the work and the "inconsideration" of the church people for "leaving such a mess behind them." Then they'll complain because "not enough people came out to help" and "the tools are inadequate for the job." Of course those who do show up to help them will be criticized for their imperfect workmanship.

In contrast, those with the gift of Service delight in serving. They have the eyes of God with which to see what needs to be done. When they see the aftermath of a church meeting, a church supper, or a youth meeting, they rejoice in seeing the hand of God at work, touching the lives of those who were there. They can see by the amount of garbage and debris left behind, that, in the fellowship of the Holy Spirit, people's lives have been touched, saved, healed, and transformed. These people make it a delight to use the house of God.

I shall never forget such a man. Arthur Squires was our church caretaker in St. Paul's Church in Brampton, Ontario, and he had the gift of Service. Arthur saw his work as ministry. Nothing was too great or too small for him to do.

One winter morning when I arrived at our church, the place was a disaster. The hallways and floors of a number of rooms, including our gymnasium, had mud tracked everywhere through them. There was leftover food and debris all over the building — a grim reminder of the previous night's Sunday School meeting.

When Arthur arrived, I watched with curiosity to see how he would react. Sure enough, it was predictable. He rolled up his sleeves, picked up his broom and, with a broad smile on his face and a special twinkle in his eyes, he glanced at me and said, "Praise God! Praise the Lord! Isn't Jesus wonderful, Pastor? Look at all the little footprints and the big ones too! The Holy Spirit touched all of these people in our church last night. Isn't it wonderful!" Off he went, singing hymns and choruses and praying until he was finished. I never heard Arthur complain, because he had a gift of the Holy Spirit. He had discovered that when he used his gift, God blessed him. The beautiful part about it was that God blessed everyone whose life touched Arthur's life. He was a blessing in the true sense of the word.

Arthur never saw himself as a second-class Christian. He was first-class all the way. He had a ministry second to none. Arthur told me one day, "Pastor, I never look sideways. I just look straight ahead to what my Lord Jesus wants me to do." He never compared himself to others. He exercised the charismatic gift of the Holy Spirit with which he had been entrusted and was, therefore, a most valued minister on my staff. His joy of the Lord was felt by everyone.

If all of the gifts of the Holy Spirit were exercised with such enjoyment and diligence, there would be no limit to what God could do through us.

The Gift of Service — or an Answer to Prayer?

While they are praying, the Holy Spirit will occasionally show people some practical things that need to be done for an individual or for the church. Jesus may want these people to help to clean someone's home or the church building. Perhaps He wants them to drive a person to a Bible study or prayer meeting. If we ask Him to show us how we might help someone and meet a need, He will. However, simple obedience to the Lord when He speaks to us in prayer and asks us to do some practical work for Him to benefit someone is not the *gift* of Service. That is an outworking of prayer.

The gift of Service, becomes like an integral trait of one's character. The person is recognized as a consistently helpful soul.

3. The Gift of Teaching

The gift of Teaching is the supernatural ability to explain the Gospel of Jesus Christ. Those exploring Christianity, as well as Christians in every stage of growth, need people who are equipped with a special gift to explain both the simplicity and the depth of the Gospel message.

Preaching and exhortation of the Gospel, followed by an invitation for acceptance of a personal relationship with Jesus Christ and the baptism in the Holy Spirit, are essential in leading people to faith. However, we need people who can, line upon line, explain Biblical doctrines to new believers. Those people can explain such truths as the normal Christian life, our hope of salvation and the promise of Heaven, as well as give insight into the prophesies of the Bible in a way that truly reaches the heart.

Temporal Educator or Holy-Spirit-Gifted Teacher?

There are teachers and there are *teachers*. Not everyone who may want to be a teacher can be a teacher. One of the biggest mistakes that has been made in the church of Jesus Christ is to think that because someone is a professional teacher or educator, he or she would make a good teacher in the Church.

The apostle Paul tries to warn us about the problem that has developed in many churches where people who were not gifted by the Holy Spirit have been allowed to explain the Gospel and the things that God does. He says, *"Now we have not received the spirit of the world, but the Spirit is from God, that we might understand the gifts bestowed on us by God. And we impart this in words not taught by human wisdom but taught by the Spirit, interpreting spiritual truths to those who possess the Spirit. The unspiritual man does not receive the gifts of the Spirit of God, for they are folly to him, and he is not able to understand them because they are spiritually discerned"* (1 Corinthians 2:12–14).

The key here is that the things of God *"are spiritually discerned."* Thus, in order to be able to teach spiritual things, one must be spiritually gifted.

The gift of Teaching is not a natural gift or ability. The *"unspiritual"* person is a person who may, or may not be a Christian but who has not been baptized with the Holy Spirit. We know this because it is the Holy Spirit who explains the Gospel of Jesus Christ and the doctrines of the Bible to the person who has the gift of Teaching.

I have known many people with the gift of Teaching. It is awesome to watch these supernaturally gifted teachers. They attract people like flies.

I remember a young man who had been removed from the membership of his church because of what he was teaching. He simply took passages of Scripture and explained clearly what they meant, without realizing that what he was teaching was contrary to what his pastor was preaching and believed. He was teaching simple Bible truths under the guidance of the Holy Spirit. He was deeply hurt and his parents were very embarrassed by the whole situation.

The young man asked a fellow school teacher to ask me for permission to sit in on one of my Bible Study meetings. He was looking for correction. Following our Bible Study, he was puzzled. "You believe and teach what I believe and was teaching in my church. Do you mean that what I was teaching is right according to your understanding of the Bible?" he asked.

"Your explanation of the Bible was correct," I replied. "Your pastor does not want to believe what the Bible teaches is for us today. Unfortunately, he is the one who is off track."

"Then, what shall I do now?" he asked.

"Welcome home," I said. "You are welcome in this church."

We recognized Bruce's gift of Teaching. He was a delight to watch and hear. His enthusiasm was contagious when he began to talk about the Bible and how exciting it was. His class grew. He asked for, and received, permission to have a Bible study class in his public school classroom, after school was over, for any of the students who might be interested. He made Bible Study so exciting that the class soon filled up with students and teachers. There was no question but that he had the gift of Teaching.

Practical Application

Because the gift of Teaching is a supernatural gift, those who have it will attract people to Jesus Christ as they explain the hope that is within them. They make the Gospel understandable for people of all ages. They encourage people to get excited about reading or studying the Bible. They are able to explain or interpret it in such a way that people can understand its message *"precept upon precept, precept upon precept, line upon line, line upon line, here a little, there a little, that they may go, and fall backward, and be broken, and snared, and taken"* (Isaiah 28:13).

There is no question that people will be taken into the Kingdom of God because a spiritually gifted teacher has explained the truths of the Gospel and the promises of God to them under the guidance of the great Teacher, the Holy Spirit. Jesus said, *"But the Helper, the Holy Spirit, whom the Father will send in my Name, He will teach you all things, and bring to your remembrance all things that I said to you"* (John 14:26).

The gift of Teaching allows believers to get solid answers to their questions about God — who He is, what He does and how He does His work.

Besides teaching, people with the gift of Teaching study to present themselves to God as workmen who have nothing to be ashamed of, *"rightly dividing the word of truth"* (2 Timothy 2:15).

Gift of Teaching or an Answer to Prayer?

Occasionally, during a time of prayer, Jesus will give an individual a particular teaching or revelation on a certain subject which they are supposed to share with someone in the church. The person to whom the teaching is given will be able to explain some particular spiritual truth which needs to be explained, or help a fellow Christian understand something about our faith. This may be either an occasional, or a one time experience in the person's life. However, this is not the gift of Teaching. It is obedience through prayer and Bible study and is helpful to those who make up the body of Christ.

When believers understand God's Word, they are more able to grab hold of God's great plan with confidence and then share the same hope with others who will need to be saved.

What a wonderful gift!

4. The Gift of Exhortation

Miss Hazel Grimmon, who helped to finance my university education, had the gift of Exhortation. She was my encourager, but not mine alone. I later discovered there were many others to whom she devoted her attention and care. Whatever was needed, she gave.

Miss Grimmon was an artist as well as a teacher. She had a dream that someday, when she retired from teaching, she would build herself a lovely little house with a large art studio where she could enjoy her sunset years through expressing her inner creativity.

For some reason, she never seemed to get around to fulfilling her dream. I asked her one day about the house with the art studio. She blushed with embarrassment as she explained that she had invested her retirement dream in the lives of many, many, young people who God had shown her needed her encouragement and help. She had a greater vision. She lived a fulfilled life. Like the apostle Paul, she can now say, *"I have fought the good fight, I have finished the race, I have kept the faith"* (2 Timothy 4:7). The crown of righteousness is hers.

People who have the gift of Exhortation do not usually stand out from the crowd. They see with the eyes of Jesus. Often, they appear to be shy, quiet people with a knowing-what-you-are-supposed-to-do look. They smile with a gentle certainty. They will take people who are struggling with God's call aside and encourage them to go ahead. They will invite those who need confirmation of their call to join them for tea, a meal, or a talk and pray for those who are fighting or running away from their call.

When it is necessary to encourage a church to get on with God's vision, these people can step forward before an entire congregation in the boldness of the Holy Spirit, declaring whatever He gives them to say. When leadership is discouraged, those who have the gift of Exhortation are there to give encouragement. These are positive Christians who confirm God's calling on Christians of all ages. They are a tremendous encouragement to anyone attempting to understand why Jesus would call them into a particular ministry.

These people are not just talk. Their encouragement often comes in the way of financial or other practical assistance. They will do whatever they can to help those who are called by God to get the required training, preparation, or education. If they can't provide for the full need themselves, they will help to find the resources to enable the person or people to accomplish what God is calling them to do. They'll do whatever it takes to get on with what Jesus wants, whether it means baby-sitting, house cleaning, doing office work or whatever will release people to go on and get prepared for their calling.

If God is calling someone to be an elder, a deacon, a Sunday School teacher, an executive in a church group, or to give leadership in a particular area, these people are there to say, "Yes, Yes, Yes, God is calling you to do it and yes, yes, yes, you have the talent, ability, and gifts of the Holy Spirit that equip you to do what He wants you to do."

The gift of Exhortation is a supernatural gifting of the Holy Spirit. Because it gives the ability to recognize the calling of Jesus upon a person's life, people gifted in this way are eager to continuously encourage others to do what God wants them to do by giving sound advice or a warning to do what is proper or required. This validation and encouragement motivates others to start praying for the person whom God is calling and to support him or her in whatever way possible.

People with the gift of Exhortation can see clearly when the Holy Spirit is directing someone to start a ministry, or to do some particular work in the church. This enables them to recognize the source of a person's motivation. They can tell whether the Heavenly Father is telling a person to give leadership in the Church or whether the person is being guided by the Devil, an evil spirit, self, or some other person.

The gift of Exhortation enables people to see the potential in others. Despite the fact that many see themselves as inadequate, ill-educated, unprepared or unattractive with no potential, people who have this gift see those people with the eyes of God and can list all the reasons why He is calling a particular person to engage in a certain kind of ministry. They are described by Jesus in Matthew 5:8: *"Blessed are the pure in heart, for they shall see God."* They not only see God; they see God's people in light of what He has called them to be and to do.

The Gift of Exhortation or an Answer to Prayer?

It is important to understand that when someone is praying, Jesus can ask him or her to give an exhortation, despite the fact that that person does not have the *gift* of Exhortation. The Holy Spirit might impress someone with the need to encourage another in the church to get on with some ministry or position of leadership. Obedience in encouraging him or her could mean the difference between the ministry happening or not happening. This is simply a situation where, through prayer, the Holy Spirit is using someone on a one-time or occasional basis to encourage another to serve the Lord in a special way and is not an example of the gift of Exhortation in action.

The difference between the two types of manifestations of the Holy Spirit is understood essentially in terms of consistency. If someone is given exhortations for others continuously, he or she is recognized as having the gift of Exhortation. If it happens only occasionally, it is seen as an outworking of the Holy Spirit in response to prayer, particularly in a situation where no one is available who has been given this particular gift.

5. The Gift of Giving

Some years ago, I needed a new car. The one that I owned was just about worn out. I was involved in a television ministry which did not pay enough to allow me to purchase even a good used car. But, Jesus had promised to make up any difference in salary and meet our financial needs and so I prayed.

One day, two men came to see me. We talked about cars. In the midst of our conversation, one of them asked, "Gordon, if you could go and buy any car that you wanted with cash in your hand, what kind of car would you buy?" Greedily, I thought and said, "I would buy a Cadillac Seville!" I always liked that car.

"What would you do if you really had one?" he continued.

"Well, the first thing I would do is this: I would go by the dealership and pick it up, go and get my wife and go for a drive. Then," I thought for a moment "then, I would drive by the Honda dealership and trade it in for a small Honda Civic and use the rest of the money for the Lord's work!" We laughed and parted, as I had to go "on air."

When they were leaving the studio after the telecast, one of the men approached me and said, "Well, Gordon, you really blew it today."

"What do you mean?" I asked.

"Well, our friend came in here today to buy you a Cadillac, but your answer persuaded him not to."

"Well, the least he could have done was to buy me a Honda," I laughed.

The other man had told our friend that he believed that the Holy Spirit told him to buy me a Cadillac.

It was not my friend's responsibility to decide whether I was worthy to receive the gift or not. It was not his responsibility to approve, or disapprove, of what I would do with it. It was his responsibility to be obedient to the Holy Spirit. He was the one who was under scrutiny by the Holy Spirit, not me. He lost his opportunity to be entrusted with greater responsibility (Matthew 25:21,33).

The result was that this man fell away from Jesus Christ because He was disobedient. I discovered in my travels that two other men had been instructed to give me cars. They both told me themselves. But, they didn't. Both of them were disobedient to Jesus Christ. Both of them have financial problems and have also fallen away from serving Jesus Christ. Our need was met by another man who was directed by Jesus, while he was praying to help us financially.

A manifestation of the gift of Giving is a situation where no questions are to be asked. The Holy Spirit points out the people who require help, whether that might mean meeting the basic necessities of life, such as food, clothing, housing, transportation and educational costs or whether it might involve helping to support Christians who need financial or other assistance in their ministries. He then tells the person with the gift of Giving what and how much to give. The person who has the gift responds in simple obedience.

The Centurion understood this kind of obedience when he asked Jesus to heal his servant. When Jesus offered to go to his house in order to comply with the request, the man told Jesus that he was a man under authority and he understood how it worked. *"But say the word, and let my servant be healed. For I am a man set under authority, with soldiers under me; and I say to one, 'Go', and he goes; and to another, 'Come,' and he comes; and to my slave, 'Do this,' and he does it"* (Luke 7:7,8).

The apostle Paul tells us that *"God loves a cheerful giver"* (2 Corinthians 9:7) because God Himself is a cheerful giver. He wants His body, His church, to have that same heart attitude. He wants us to enjoy giving not only to Him for His ministry but also to Him for the needs of His people.

People with the gift of Giving give with generosity, not begrudgingly. They do not ask, "How much do I have to give?" Rather, they ask, "Lord, are you sure that this is enough? Should I not give more? After all, we don't want them to run out, do we."

They don't ask, "How little?" They ask, "How much?"

When Jesus says, "Give," the "Giving-gifted" person gives. When He says, "Don't give," he or she doesn't give. This is a spiritually-discerned gift which is activated not through the natural eye, but through hearing what the Holy Spirit is saying.

The Attitude of Giving

Giving must be carried out with simple kindness, liberality, and with single-minded generosity. The original Greek implies giving with both simplicity and generosity (Barclay).

Respect for privacy is another important attitudinal consideration. When the Holy Spirit imparts the gift of Giving, the person to whom it is given is not directed to pry into the needy people's circumstances and attempt to give a moral lecture of criticism along with the gift. Neither is it acceptable to follow up and make sure people use whatever is given to them in such a way that would meet with the giver's approval.

Spiritual Gifts vs. Human Schemes

Because "Giving-gifted" people do not give unless the Holy Spirit instructs them to do so, people who approach these people and make requests regarding their needs don't get very far. People with genuine needs should take them to Jesus in prayer and trust Him to supply the need, either directly or indirectly.

Paul said, *"But my God will supply all of your needs according to his riches in glory by Christ Jesus"* (Philippians 4:19).

It is pivotal to remember that it is God who supplies our needs: it is not those through whom He gives His gifts. Although God uses these people, we are to go to Him and tell Him what we think our needs are. He will then supply our real needs.

Giving: the Responsibility of Every Christian

Helping people who have needs is not the responsibility of just those who have the gift of Giving. It is the responsibility of every Christian believer.

One of the conditions for having our own prayers heard and answered is found in Proverbs 21:13: *"He who closes his ear to the cry of the poor will himself cry out and not be heard."* Thus, we need to have the same compassion for people who have needs that Jesus had. When we pray, the Holy Spirit will tell us to help those people. He will tell us what to do for them, whether we have the *gift* of Giving or not.

The gift of Giving is not to be confused with those random acts of kindness that we perform when the Holy Spirit asks us to respond to special needs from time to time. Those are responses to Jesus' guidance obtained through times of prayer.

It is also not to be confused with tithing. It is not an excuse for a person to withhold their tithes, giving 10 percent of the income to the Lord's work. Nor is it an excuse not to give offerings and alms. The gift of Giving is separate and distinct from those.

We need to see people who are poor and needy as Jesus saw them. They represent Him. He sends them to us, as His body, for help. If we ignore them, He will judge us for how we have treated those in need.

Remember the last judgment which Jesus describes in Matthew 25:31-46. Take a close look at the stinging judgments that He pronounced in that passage: *"Truly, I say to you, as you did it to one of the least of these my brethren, you did it to Me,"* or worse, *"Truly, I say to you, as you did it not to one of the least of these my brethren, you did it not to Me."*

Why Have Some Been Given the Gift of Giving if it is the Responsibility of All?

I believe that the Holy Spirit found it necessary to give the gift of Giving to particular people in order to make up for the rest of us who were unreliable in giving to others in need.

When we see someone who needs help, it is very important to remember that, for all intents and purposes, that person is Jesus Christ for us at the most, and for the least, that person has been sent by Jesus Christ. He sends people to individuals and churches to see if He can entrust us with them. If He can, then we can have a revival. If not, then we cannot have revival.

No matter what, Jesus wants us to be obedient to the promptings of the Holy Spirit. Presenting us with opportunities to give is one way that He teaches us obedience. As we respond, we can know the joy that comes through submission to His will and giving to others.

The Operation of the Gift of Giving

The gift of Giving operates under the direction and guidance of the Holy Spirit. People who have this gift tell me that the Holy Spirit will tell them who to help, how to help, what to help with, and when to help.

Some hear the quiet voice of the Holy Spirit speaking to them. Others tell me that they get distinct impressions. Others say that when they are praying with their eyes closed, they see something like a sheet of paper with people's names on it and a list of what they need. They will then take God's shopping list, obtain the necessary items and then deliver them to whomever the Holy Spirit said should receive them. They usually will simply say, "The Holy Spirit told me to give these things to you."

Where does the money come from for all this giving? It comes, first of all, out of the bank account of the person who has the gift of Giving. After the person has obediently fulfilled the need, the Holy Spirit will replace the money from different, unexpected sources. His gift requires faith working through unquestioned obedience.

It is very interesting to watch a couple I know who have the gift of Giving. The Holy Spirit speaks to both of them, independently of each other. He gives them the name of a person or people to whom they are to minister with the gift of Giving. They then confirm with each other that the Holy Spirit has given them both the same instructions. The Holy Spirit tells each of them what is to be given. It might be a gift of a certain amount of money, groceries, clothes, a car, or whatever else they are to give. This couple is not rich but they are faithful. The Holy Spirit gives them specific amounts which they are to supply. They give, even if it means emptying their bank accounts.

After they have gathered together whatever the Holy Spirit has told them to give, they arrive unexpectedly at the door of the people whose needs they are supplying. They give the gift or gifts with sensitivity to the situation and go on their way. Some people have made the mistake of approaching them later, when they had some other problem and asked them to meet the new need. However, they cannot meet that need unless they are directed by the Holy Spirit.

Ruth and I will never forget the time that Audrey and Graham ministered to our own family with their gift of Giving. It was unexpected because they are friends who drop in to visit from time to time. We know about their ministry of giving and we pray for them. One evening, they dropped in for a visit. They were in the area dropping off a gift.

These people did not know that we had a severe financial crisis. We were completely out of money and groceries. We couldn't even offer them a cup of tea or coffee or a glass of milk because we had run out of everything. We didn't even have a slice of bread left. The only person we had told about our need was Jesus, in prayer. When they dropped in for a visit, we didn't think anything about it except that it was good to see them and visit with them.

As they were leaving, they paused at the door and hesitated for a few minutes, as though they did not want to leave. Gently, Audrey asked, "Would you be offended if we gave you some groceries?"

Shocked, we said, "Well, no, of course not!" It still didn't register in my mind what was going on. They went out to their car and began to bring bag after bag of groceries into our kitchen.

They had no idea that we had any kind of a problem, until the Holy Spirit told them through prayer that morning that we had a financial need.

Now, I want you to understand how specific the Holy Spirit is when it comes to meeting our needs. Ruth kept a shopping list on the refrigerator door with all of our food needs. The Holy Spirit had told Audrey and Graham what was on that list right down to the brand names. Audrey laughed as she told me that when she was reaching for the brand of ketchup that they normally buy, the Holy Spirit said to them, "No, they use Heinz ketchup." Our friends use margarine instead of butter. As they reached for margarine, the Holy Spirit said, "No. Gordon likes butter." So they bought butter. The Holy Spirit also told them to give us a specific amount of money.

This is what the gift of Giving is like. The Holy Spirit allows the gifted person to participate in meeting people's practical needs in such a manner that they share the same experience of joy that God receives as He meets our needs. What a wonderful gift of the Holy Spirit!

6. The Gift of Administration

Two years ago, I was invited to participate in the first Canadian Full Gospel Business Men's Fellowship International Airlift to the Ukraine, one of the former Russian Republics.

The whole trip was prayerfully organized by Olaf Peterson from North Battleford, Saskatchewan. Under the guidance of the Holy Spirit through the gift of Administration, he was able to plan the trip for the three of us who were going to do the ministry, along with his own family. He not only filled the 10-day trips full of meetings, but he managed to obtain the cooperation of the Baptist, Pentecostal, Roman Catholic, and Charismatic churches in the Ukraine.

Besides organizing meetings in several different churches from different denominations, meetings in public and high schools, in a trade school, in an orphanage, and in several town and city public squares (formerly called Red Squares) Olaf organized three banquets in different cities and meetings with leading Ukrainian politicians with whom we were able to witness and pray. Besides all of this, he was the one who scheduled all of our accommodations and air and bus travel.

The results were awesome. We lost count after 1,460 people accepted Jesus Christ as their personal Saviour and were saved. We ministered to thousands of people of all ages.

I have seen Olaf do the same thing when he has organized week-long meetings for my own ministry. It is fascinating to watch my friend use this gift of Administration through prayer.

The gift of Administration (Romans 12:8) is referred to as the gift of leadership or aid in various translations. It is one that is tremendously important in the Church. The Greek word from which it is translated literally means "to stand in front," "to lead," or "to rule."

Again, this is a supernatural gifting of the Holy Spirit. People who have this gift have the ability to organize and assist the different ministries that are being developed by their churches.

These people help to assist those who are called to develop the ministries, both within the church as well as those that are directed outside to reach the unsaved. These people help the Church get organized, equipped, mobilized, and achieve the vision that God has given them. *"Where there is no vision, the people cast off restraint, but blessed is he who keeps the law"* (Proverbs 29:18).

People with the gift of Administration have the responsibility to keep the congregation focused on the vision for ministry which Jesus Christ has given them. These people can organize ministries in minute detail for other people. They can organize local ministry programs which are complete with dates, times, resources, people, meeting places, budgets, and whatever else is required.

When they organize evangelistic ministries, it is awesome to see the contacts that the Holy Spirit leads them to make, the number of meetings they are able to organize and the precision of the necessary travelling schedules and documentation they schedule.

Order and Direction in the Church

Like the other gifts of the Holy Spirit, the gift of Administration brings order and direction to the Church's ministry. The Church needs people who can pull together people with different gifts and abilities and direct them into ministry. These people do not feel that it is necessary for them to do everything, but rather, that it is their responsibility to delegate duties to those in the church who have the gifts required to do what God has shown the eldership. They help those who are called and gifted to achieve their goals. They are wonderful at developing "mission statements" along with the necessary people and resources that are required. The results can be remarkable. In this way, the ministry of the Church can be successfully accomplished as directed by the Holy Spirit.

We need these people in our Christian education programs to organize Sunday Schools, youth programs, men's and women's ministries, outreach programs, evangelistic programs and mission programs. Although people who have the gift of Administration can be used in the ministry of the church, they do not necessarily carry it out themselves.

Those who have been given this gift must learn to use it with a contagious zeal and enthusiasm which will instill confidence in those who have to work and do ministry with them.

Operation of the Gift of Administration

This gift is available to use at all times for the gifted person. When faced with an administrative or leadership problem, the Holy Spirit directs them to organize and provide solutions which will result in God getting the increase. Those who have the gift of Administration tell me that it operates in a manner very similar to the other revelation gifts. The Holy Spirit speaks to them in His quiet voice telling them when, where, and how to organize or give leadership.

Some hear an audible voice. Others get impressions or ideas that they know are not their own. Others instinctively (spiritually speaking), know what has to be done and who is to be involved in various ministries. Some see written instructions in their mind's eyes and follow them. No matter how it is activated in individuals, it really doesn't matter how the gift operates, as long as we cooperate.

The Gift of Administration — or an Answer to Prayer?

A person who does not have the gift of Administration, when confronted with the problem of giving leadership or organizing a program, can pray and ask Jesus, the Holy Spirit, or the Heavenly Father, to show them what to do and how to do it. He will show them and direct him or her. That is an answer to prayer. As with the other gifts, gifted or not, we can pray when necessary and Jesus will show us how to administrate or give leadership in particular situations. This occasional ability differs from the gift of Administration in that it comes as an answer to prayer and is not continuously available to the person.

The body of Christ, the Church, needs people who have the gift of Administration to provide an ordered environment within which Christians can worship, receive teaching and fellowship, and then be sent out to share the Gospel of Jesus Christ with other people. These too, can then be saved, baptized with the Holy Spirit, healed, and set free to know God's plan for their lives. What an awesome gift of the Holy Spirit!

Christians with the gift of Administration have to be the most like the Holy Spirit in exercising their gift. The Holy Spirit is invisible and it is His responsibility to do all of His administrative work without being seen. The only person who should be seen when the Holy Spirit does His work is Jesus.

People with the gift of Administration will have programs put in place and rooms set up for ministry without even being noticed, much less complaining. They exercise their gift without looking for praise from people and their reward is received in seeing Jesus get the glory for their work.

7. The Gift of Mercy

Jesus tried to teach us about showing mercy to people through the parable of the labourers in the vineyard (Matthew 20:1–16).

This is the story about workmen who were hired at different times of the day by a particular householder to work in his vineyard. Some worked for 12 hours, some for nine hours, some for six hours, and some only worked for one hour. At the end of the day, the householder instructed his foreman to pay them all the same wage.

Some of the workers complained that it wasn't fair. They grumbled at him, saying, *"These last worked only one hour, and you have made them equal to us who have borne the burden of the day and the scorching heat"* (Matthew 20:12). What they had forgotten was that, first of all, the householder did not have to hire any of them and secondly, he paid them what he had promised.

That was an act of mercy. This is what mercy does: it supplies an undeserving person's needs happily and unbegrudgingly. That is the reason why the householder who is Jesus, replied to the grumbling workers (us), *"Friend, I am doing you no wrong; did you not agree with me for a denarius? Take what belongs to you, and go; I choose to give to this last as I give to you. Am I not allowed to do what I choose with what belongs to me? Or, do you begrudge my generosity? So, the last will be first, and the first last"* (Matthew 20:13–16).

This is a picture, clear as glass, of Jesus' mercy. Despite the fact that there are Christians who begrudge His generosity to those who may have worked less than they have, He rewards us all equally, who have been saved at different times, and gives us all eternal life at the same time. Each of us, regardless of our own merit, receives the same reward or payment for the work that we do in His Vineyard (the world) reaping the harvest of souls. He gives us all the same promise, *"And my God will supply every need of yours according to his riches in glory in Christ Jesus"* (Philip. 4:19). That's God's Gold Card guarantee!

Instead of holding our sins against us, He forgives us. That is what the hiring is all about. His mercy gives undeserved payment and work in the Kingdom of Heaven to those who were sinners (unemployed through their sins and destined for hell).

The point of the story is that, in order to be like Jesus, we all need to show mercy and forgiveness to those who have hurt us, who have hurt other people and who have hurt themselves.

Natural judgment says that people deserve what they get. It's called "just desserts."

I am certainly glad that I never got what I deserved. Too many of us forget where we have come from. We have come from sinful lives.

Too often, like the labourers, we complain that it isn't fair for people who have done something unacceptable to be forgiven. But what is fair? God's law says that *"the wages of sin is death"* (Romans 6:23). In other words, what is fair is not God's favour but His judgment and Hell. To break one of God's commandments is to break them all. To make it even worse, when we break God's laws or His commandments, there is nothing that we can do to compensate for our sin. Our only hope is His mercy.

Too often, after we have been forgiven, however, we revert back to living according to the law instead of grace. Grace-living means living a life that is directed and guided by the Holy Spirit. *"If we live by the Spirit, let us also walk by the Spirit. Let us have no self-conceit, no provoking of one another, no envy of one another"* (Galatians 5:25–26).

Paul gives us this caution because we get conceited, provoke others, and envy each other when we start to compare ourselves with the other workers in the vineyard. We become jealous because they may not have worked as long and as hard as we have. Such a state of heart crowds out mercy and forgiveness.

When we see God rewarding other people, it should bless us to see that God is meeting their needs. When God blesses someone else in the church, I get blessed. When God meets other people's needs, I get blessed. Whenever God supplies any of our needs, that is His mercy that we are observing. This should bring a warm smile to our faces and a "Hallelujah!" to our lips. We should be able to point our finger to the Householder and say, "That's my God! That's my Saviour, Jesus! Isn't He wonderful!"

We all deserve judgment. When we forget that we

are still sinners who still sin and act as though we have not sinned or are not sinning any longer, our hearts are hardened from a deep appreciation for the forgiveness that has been extended to us. In such a state, we are hardened to the situations of others and fail to show mercy and forgiveness to them. We fall into such a trap.

For this reason, we must learn to pray so that we can be in constant contact with the Holy Spirit, whose responsibility it is to *"convince the world concerning sin and righteousness and judgment"* (John 16:8). We need to be constantly aware of our own undeserving state and not fall into the trap of begrudging God's generosity when it is directed towards people other than us.

The gift of Mercy (Romans 12:8) is the *super*natural gift of showing or extending forgiveness to other people with gracious kindness — gladly, not begrudgingly.

In the *natural realm,* it is possible to forgive a person and at the same time to give criticism and show contempt. It is possible to tell someone that we forgive them yet not show compassion and understanding. It is possible to talk about forgiveness and yet fail to do it with the love that Paul speaks about — a love which does not keep a record of wrong (1 Corinthians 13:4–8).

To be consistently merciful in heart takes a *supernatural* gift from God.

The Straining of Mercy

Many Christians are repelled by other people's sin, especially when they see them blatantly and arrogantly living destructive lives which hurt so many innocent victims. Today's mass murderers and criminals seem to get away with their crimes. Children are physically and sexually abused. Wives are badly mistreated. Husbands are wounded. Parents are hated and blamed for their children's sins.

When hurting people share their disastrous lives, many Christians discover that their forgiveness and love has limits beyond which they refuse to go, because they see that their own lives might be at risk. Like Peter, they cry out, *"Lord, how often shall my brother sin against me, and I have to forgive him? As many as seven times?"* In other words, how much is enough?

Unlike Peter, they close their ears to Jesus' answer which is still hard to swallow. *"I do not say seven times, but seventy times seven"* (Matthew 18:22) — that is 490 times every day for every person in our lives. Is that not impossible? It is for anyone who has not been saved and empowered by the Holy Spirit.

For most Christians, it is difficult to offer mercy and forgiveness to others who have sinned and whose unrepentant lives reflect it. Sexual sins seem to be a particularly difficult area to forgive.

Today, I believe that the disease of AIDS is a plague upon our society world-wide, regardless of its origin. Our churches have done virtually nothing to minister to and care for its victims. In fact, the opposite has occurred. Adults and children in our churches who have contracted the deadly virus have been ostracized and have had to leave their churches. Others, knowing what would or might happen if it became common knowledge that they had the AIDS virus, have kept the deadly secret to themselves and have told no one, not even their pastors, priests, or ministers, about their suffering and pain. They have suffered unto death. They have watched their loved ones, yes and even themselves, slowly, agonizingly, quietly, and, often alone, pass from life to death.

There has been little mercy, little forgiveness, little help and little love extended to them. Oh, what a shame is upon us! As George Whitfield once said while watching a convicted prisoner being taken to the gallows for his execution, "There, but for the grace of God, go I." I believe that we are being called to minister to AIDS victims with love, cheerfulness, and mercy.

In the past, whenever any kind of plague killed hundreds of thousands of people, the Christian Church set up hospitals in order to care for the sick and dying. Today, even people with physical or mental handicaps find it very difficult to be accepted and welcomed into our churches. The blind, the deaf, people in wheelchairs, do not receive the kind of ministry that they need. We lack mercy in our ministries.

Today, homosexuality has angered many Christians and they have become aggressively hostile towards "gay" people. They forget that their own sin, before they were saved, was equally obnoxious to God. We need to seek the guidance and help of the Holy Spirit in order to love and forgive those who have chosen the gay lifestyle. We are still in the healing business. I have personally seen God heal AIDS through prayer. How can we offer the grace and love of Jesus Christ without the compassion (Matthew 15:32) that demonstrated His love.

"The works of the flesh" that Paul listed are still with us today: *"fornication, impurity, licentiousness, idolatry, sorcery, enmity, strife, jealousy, anger, selfishness, dissension, party spirit, envy, murder, drunkenness, carousing, and the like"* (Galatians 5:19–21). Many Christians say, "Hate the sin, but love the sinner." However, that is not what is usually experienced by the sinner.

What About Mercy for Christians who Fall?

Even Christians who "fall" are not shown forgiveness and mercy in the way that God gives it and meant us to give it. A "different gospel" comes into play. A different standard is applied. These people are heavily penalized. "They should have known better," says the deacon at the door.

Since when were Christians exempted from sinning? Many people tell me that they forgave Jimmy Swaggart or Jimmy Baker once, or twice, or even three times. After that they wouldn't forgive them again. When they meet Peter in Heaven, if they tell him the same story, they may get a little embarrassed by his response to them. After all, when he complained to Jesus about one of his brother-disciples and asked, *"Lord, how often shall my brother sin against me, and I have to forgive him? As many as seven times?"* Jesus response was, *"seventy times seven"* (Matthew 18:21,22). That's a far cry from three. However, even with his offer of seven times, Peter was more forgiving than most Christians I meet.

When we withhold forgiveness, a root of bitterness develops unnoticed and we are defiled, which means that we are no longer fit for holy use (Hebrews 12:15-16). Not only do we defile ourselves, but we contaminate others so that they cannot be used by God either. Our unforgiveness becomes our "bowl of potage." When Jesus said to forgive every person 70x7=490 times every day, He was not kidding, because that's how often He has to forgive you and me. Believe it.

Jesus is our greatest example of mercy. Even on the cross, after the agony He had endured at the hands of mankind, He said, *"Father, forgive them; for they know not what they do"* (Luke 23:34). As His people, who claim His Name, we need to show such mercy, even to Christians who have fallen.

King David, who had a very close relationship with God, sinned doubly. Not only did he commit adultery with his neighbour's wife, but he also had that neighbour killed (2 Samuel 11:12). However, when he repented, God forgave him and immediately restored David to his Kingship. Today, Christians are removed from further opportunity to serve God in their churches because of the absence of mercy. We begrudge God's generosity. We play by our own new laws. This lack of loving, forgiving, caring mercy, turns people away not only from our churches, but also from the very Kingdom of God. Sadly enough, it also causes God to keep people away from some of our churches because they can be very dangerous places for both sinner and saint.

Supernatural Mercy

People who have been given the gift of Mercy never tire of caring for broken people; those who are sick, suffering, and dying. Drunken alcoholics sleeping over warm grates, bag people pushing their shopping carts around the streets, runaways living under bridges in our cities and abandoned seniors in nursing homes are precious souls to these gifted people.

Although a merciful heart should be a characteristic of every Christian, the handicapped, the mentally retarded, the disabled, the blind and the deaf are confined to their homes because *those who were sent out into all the world* are so wrapped up in their own lives that they go only to visit their friends.

It seems that the Holy Spirit has to supernaturally gift certain Christians, in order for those who need mercy to receive it. These people do not judge. They save. They minister. They heal. They look after the broken and the sick. They look after us.

The gift is seen in the life of people like Mark Buntain and Mother Theresa who have spent their lives amid the squalor of Calcutta, India, ministering to the poor, the sick and the dying. Bill Wilson built his church in the Bronx, New York, by ministering to hundreds of children of the poor. William Stringfellow, the Christian lawyer, expended his life working among the poor in East Harlem, New York.

The gift of Mercy was demonstrated when a Christian transport driver came upon an accident that involved another trucker and an automobile. The truck driver was unconscious behind his steering wheel. The vehicles were being enveloped in flames. He stopped his rig and ran to get the injured driver out of his truck cab before the fire killed him. Other truckers and automobile drivers who were standing back, afraid to go near the burning vehicles, attempted to stop him from going to the burning truck. He pushed them aside, saying, "Don't worry! I must do this! God will protect me because He said, *'When you walk through fire you shall not be burned, and the flame shall not consume you'"*(Isaiah 43:2).

And He did! The trucker doggedly pulled the injured driver out of the truck and dragged him to safety. Neither were even singed by the flames that engulfed them! You see, the person who has the gift of Mercy does not measure the cost. Mercy-gifted people know, as do the rest of us (when we stop to remember) that there can be no cost considered because Jesus Christ has paid an unrepayable debt and their lives are not their own.

The Operation of the Gift of Mercy

There are people with the gift of Mercy who are constantly, every day, offering it to people everywhere they go, both inside and outside the church. They are usually warned that they should not be so generous because somebody will take advantage of them. They smile when they agree that somebody will take advantage of them, because they know that that is what we are here for — to be taken advantage of for the Kingdom of God.

They apply 70 x 7 every day to everyone. They are spendthrifts when it comes to mercy. Their mercy and forgiveness and love result in meeting people's needs and finding opportunities to introduce them to Jesus as their Saviour, Lord, Healer, and Deliverer.

Those who have this amazing gift of Mercy or forgiveness tell me that they are shocked when the Holy Spirit gives them such a gift because all of their defenses go down. They forgive almost automatically — but not without counting the cost. They do not give "cheap grace." They are very aware of the depth of its richness because it was purchased by Jesus Christ at the price of Calvary, dispensed in the love of the Heavenly Father and poured into their hearts by the Holy Spirit.

This gift of Mercy or forgiveness allows the body of Christ to wear its heart on its sleeve where all can see it and *"know Him* (Jesus) *and the power of His resurrection and share the fellowship of His sufferings"* (Philippians 3:10).

Those with the gift of Mercy or forgiveness become hypersensitive to the sin, hurt and pain in the world around them. It brings them to tears which remind them of the day when Jesus forgave them or cared for them in their weakness — again, and again, and again.

The Gift of Mercy — or an Answer to Prayer?

For those of us who do not have the gift of Mercy or forgiveness and sometimes find ourselves struggling with judging others, there is an alternative. It is called prayer. We can ask Jesus to help us to forgive the person who has hurt us so badly. We can turn to our Comforter, the Holy Spirit, and ask Him to give us the power that we need to forgive and to minister to the person who has hurt us to the core of our being. We can turn to our Heavenly Father and ask Him to give us the courage to forgive as we have been forgiven. It's not easy, but He will help us do it. That is an answer to prayer. That is an act of faith. That is ministering the Gospel of Jesus Christ.

If we dare, we can pray and ask Jesus to give us the *gift* of Mercy.

What a wonderful gift with which to deal with the pain of the world!

9

Renewal Through Orderly (Powerful) Worship

"When you come together, everyone has a hymn, or a word of instruction, a revelation, a tongue or an interpretation. All of these must be done for the strengthening of the church" (1 Corinthians 14:26).

The Church of Jesus Christ is sitting on a gold mine — and in most cases has absolutely no idea what to do with it. When conducted and expressed as it was meant to be with the gifts flowing freely forth, worship leads to an inexpressible richness of relationship with Jesus and harvest for His Kingdom.

If the gifts of the Holy Spirit were ever grasped and used in the way they were meant to be used, many more people would enjoy the bounty of having Jesus Christ as their Saviour and Lord. Countless numbers would receive ministry that no fortune can buy.

Tragically, the gifts have been at best, tolerated in worship, at worst banned, but most often simply ignored. Certainly, they have been misused and abused.

The fear in many quarters has been that if the gifts are allowed expression, there will be excesses. The fact is that excesses have occurred simply because those in leadership in most churches have never learned how to use them properly. They have mishandled, misunderstood and misdirected their use to the degree that their effectiveness has been tragically short-circuited. On the other hand, when they have been used as Paul directed, lives are truly changed.

Opposition to True Worship

Whenever the Holy Spirit is being poured out, spiritual warfare abounds. The apostle John warned, *"Beloved, do not believe every spirit, but test the spirits to see whether they are of God; for many false prophets have gone out into the world"* (1 John 4:1).

Recently, I was at a worship service where some strange things were happening. The man who was speaking made it clear that we were to accept what was happening without questioning. He implied that we were to set aside our brains, boasting, "At one time I was educated, but now I'm anointed." He didn't seem to know that the two are not mutually exclusive. Many highly educated people have been anointed by God for ministry.

It soon became clear that he had indeed set aside his education, as he proceeded to share a very poor message which he blamed on the anointing of the Holy Spirit. His message was punctuated, from time to time, with jerking head, shoulder, and arm movements, after which he would exclaim, "Oh! The anointing is still on me!"

Weird jerking movements are not necessarily caused by the presence of the Holy Spirit, although such movements have been associated with certain church developments which often went wrong in the past, hence the names "Quakers" and "Shakers." However, when they are encouraged by particular churches that do not like to call themselves churches, people can be misled.

I know that both historically and in my own ministry, there has often been some shaking or trembling when people experience the presence and power of the Holy Spirit. However, these physical movements are neither exclusive to the ministry of the Holy Spirit nor to be encouraged. They could be a physical response to an evil spiritual presence.

In order to determine the source, our discernment has to line up with Scripture, which indicates that when the Holy Spirit is the source of the manifestation, there will be *"peace"* (John 14:27) and *"self-control"* (Galatians 5:23).

During the particular service I was in, several people were called upon to share. In the midst of their so called testimonies, they would almost invariably fall down on the floor shaking and trembling. They never did tell us what Jesus had done for them. When they would fall, the leader would exclaim, "That's the Holy Spirit! Nothing to worry about." The falling down was supposed to be confirmation that what the man or woman was experiencing was from God.

When one man fell to the floor, he started to growl and roar so loudly that he could be heard all over the auditorium. The leader laughed and said, "Isn't the Holy Spirit wonderful! Listen to him roaring like a lion. Oh, yes! It's the Lion of Judah. Yes, he's a Lion of Judah!" People clapped and laughed throughout the congregation. This was followed by others roaring and screeching.

Quite the contrary. These people were not lions of Judah. That title is reserved for only one person: Jesus Christ.

Roaring and growling have been in evidence many times in our ministry. In every instance, the disturbance has been caused either by evil spirits manifesting through people or by people making noises in the flesh. People have forgotten that Peter warned us about one who likes to roar. *"Be sober, be watchful. Your adversary the Devil prowls around like a roaring lion seeking someone to devour"* (1 Peter

5:8). He will roar in anyone's meetings who cannot, or who hesitates to identify him. Besides that, he loves to trick anyone he can into roaring instead of praising and worshipping Jesus Christ.

As the meeting progressed, the leader told the congregation that if anyone were to experience a tingling sensation, a shaking of the limbs or numbness in the lips, fingers, or any part of the body, this would be indicative of the presence of the Holy Spirit. We were instructed to raise our hands for prayer from one of their ministry team should we experience anything like that. These individuals then spread throughout the auditorium, laying hands on people and praying for them.

I wandered freely among those who were doing the praying and observed that there was no invitation to repent and no instruction given about prayer. People were lying all over the floor. Now, I have no problem with that, because the Holy Spirit will cause some to fall down. However, as I watched, I saw that many were trying to cooperate by falling down themselves. Many of the people who were lying on the floor were yelling, roaring and screeching. Others were jumping up and down continuously while still others were attempting to run around despite the lack of space. Some exhibited exaggerated physical jerking movements which several told me were uncontrollable. This was continuously encouraged by the leadership.

One woman, who I did not know, tried to convince me that this was really the result of the Holy Spirit. I had to wonder what she would have told Paul, who, when describing the fruit of the Holy Spirit, included *"self-control"* as one of the fruit (Galatians 5:23).

It was very obvious that this was spiritual warfare taking place right in the church sanctuary and those in leadership were totally oblivious to it. Operating hand in hand with the spiritual warfare, was a lot of human nature looking for a religious experience.

It has been well-documented throughout the years that these kinds of excesses usually accompany any movement of the Holy Spirit. The problem arises when they are left unchecked because they will provide a hindrance to what Jesus Christ is attempting to do.

The leader continued to reassure us with phrases like, "Isn't it wonderful what the Holy Spirit is doing!"

It may have been wonderful what the Holy Spirit was doing, but it was not wonderful what the leadership of the meeting was doing or not doing. They obviously did not recognize that there were some people there with evil spirits who needed to be set free. Satan's work was routinely misidentified as being the work of the Holy Spirit.

The leadership seemed totally unaware of the fact that the chaotic, noisy manifestations were a call to minister to the people. Some required prayer to be saved, others needed the baptism of the Holy Spirit, some needed healing and others needed deliverance. This is the sort of behavior that Paul was trying to warn us about when he specifically mentioned the abuse connected with the gift of speaking in tongues (1 Corinthians 14:18–19). Too often the gifts of the Holy Spirit have been used inconsistently and erratically without proper teaching, direction, and correction.

Without understanding what they are doing, people allow themselves and others to be trapped by their limited understanding of ministry. The lack of discernment is frightening when people mistake a noisy, loud meeting for the work of the Holy Spirit whose powerful ministry is characterized by a calm, peaceful order — not always quiet, but certainly calm and orderly. In my travels I have observed this lack of discernment becoming more and more widespread.

C.S. Lewis, in his preface to his book, *The Screwtape Letters*[5], warned of the very problem that exists today. "There are two equal and opposite errors into which our race can fall about Devils (evil spirits or demons). One is to disbelieve in their existence. The other is to believe, and to have an excessive and unhealthy interest in them. They themselves are equally pleased with both errors and hail a materialist or a magician with the same delight."

The particular ministry which I was visiting, teaches that diseases and sicknesses are caused exclusively by evil spirits or demons. Because those involved are preoccupied with looking for demons, they are vulnerable to them.

Kathryn Kuhlman used to say, "The Holy Spirit is a gentleman. He will never do anything to embarrass or hurt you." Her meetings were always conducted in an atmosphere of peace and power without disruptions. She would not tolerate people doing weird things which they attributed to the Holy Spirit. The fruit of her ministry bore witness to its validity. Countless participants experienced permanent changes in their lives.

Satan's Strategy #1 — Divide and Conquer

The leadership of the ministry I visited, told those who were there, both pastors and laymen, to "take this back to your own churches."

Many have attempted to do just that so that "spiritual experiences" will abound in their churches and hopefully fill them up. They have gone back home with a fresh spiritual manifestation tucked in their belts and have attempted to duplicate it in the lives of their congregations. The result has been that many have lost their ministries and church after church has been divided.

One woman who attended, told me that she found the meeting "too chaotic." Another felt that it was very disruptive with all of the shouting and screeching. Yet another Christian said that the meeting was like going to a party where you were the only person who didn't know what was going on. The underlying message was that the "insiders" really knew and understood what was going on while the "others" needed to learn and get on track. An "us" and "them" atmosphere is so destructive to the body of Christ. The majority of visitors were loving Christians who, while trying not to be critical of the service, simply did not know what to make of the unfamiliar experience. They did not have the confidence to trust the discernment they were given.

Why are Abuses Allowed in Worship?

Too often, those in leadership do not have enough Biblical knowledge and experience to be able to adequately examine what is happening in their worship services and ministries. They misinterpret manifestations and cannot differentiate between what is from God and what is of the Devil or the flesh. Confusion is rampant. *"For God is not a God of confusion but of peace"* (1 Corinthians 14:33).

However, the simple fact that there is some abuse does not mean that we should stop using the gifts. We don't stop using automobiles because they're misused, even though the degree of irresponsibility may lead to some people being killed. The same thing is true with the gifts of the Holy Spirit. Despite what others may do, our responsibility is to use them as God intended so that people can be brought into the Kingdom of God.

In some situations, lack of knowledge, lack of discernment, fear or just plain negligence has resulted in a blind eye being turned to counterfeits and misuses of the gifts of the Spirit. In such groups, the leadership has tolerated blatant misuse and allowed people to do things that have frightened some or absolutely disgusted others. They have been viewed like the "king's new clothing" with no one willing to do or say anything that will shock the king back to reality. Finally, someone will speak out in a loud whisper, "Why is the king not wearing any clothes? He's naked."

Quenching the Holy Spirit vs. Quenching the Unholy Spirit

Although some argue that, "our ways are not His ways," the fact that everything has to line up with Scripture has never changed and is indisputable. One of the primary arguments of those who hesitate to decry unscriptural manifestations is that we must not quench the Spirit because God is doing a "new thing."

I am not suggesting that we should "quench the Holy Spirit" (1 Thessalonians 5:19) but we must quench the spirit of evil and enter into true cooperation with the Holy Spirit in our worship so that the harvest will be plentiful.

When I talked with several people who had experienced some of the strange manifestations I have outlined, they told me that they felt wonderful so it must have been of God. When I questioned them further, however, it became evident that they had not experienced any conviction of sin.

Whoever said that when we experience the presence of the Holy Spirit we are always going to feel good, warm and wonderful? When Isaiah went into the Temple to pray, he was looking for an experience with God and he had one. However, he experienced something that he had never expected.

He had a vision of God: *"I saw the Lord sitting upon a throne, high and lifted up; and his train filled the temple"* (Isaiah 6:1–8). It certainly didn't make him feel good, warm and wonderful. Quite the contrary. He wanted to run out of the temple and escape.*"Woe is me! For I am lost; for I am a man of unclean lips; for my eyes have seen the King, the Lord of hosts."*

Feelings cannot be trusted when assessing a move of God because Satan can give good feelings while true conviction is very uncomfortable. Discernment is more than feelings — it is a rock solid inner "knowing."

We must be willing to speak out when we see abuses of the gifts and ask, "Why is the Church not wearing any clothes? Why is everyone saying this bizarre behaviour is OK when it's not scriptural?"

I believe that the time has come for us to use the powerful gifts of the Holy Spirit, properly, powerfully, and according to Scripture in our worship.

Daring to Challenge the Naked Emperor

Recently, when I questioned what was being allowed to happen in a worship service because I did not believe that it was being done by the Holy Spirit, a friend became upset with me.

"Why can't God do something new that's not in the Bible?" he asked.

"That," I replied, "is just the problem. If it isn't in the Bible, it isn't from God" (1 Corinthians 4:6).

For many people, that seems to be a little narrow-minded. Sure it's narrow, but what's wrong with that? It's for our protection. It's Biblical. *"Enter through the narrow gate. For wide is the gate and broad is the road that leads to destruction, and many enter through it. But small is the gate and narrow the road that leads to life, and only a few find it. Watch out for false prophets. They come to you in sheep's clothing, but inwardly they are ferocious wolves"* (Matthew 7:13–15). The Devil would love to get us involved in so-called worship that misleads people and results in them falling away from God.

The Bible has many warnings. Jesus said, *"For false Christs and false prophets will arise and show great signs and wonders, so as to lead astray, if possible, even the elect. Lo, I have told you beforehand"* (Matthew 24:24,25). The elect can be led astray when they do not examine everything to see whether or not what is happening in their churches is scriptural. When we look to our emotions or feelings as a barometer of God's presence, we become vulnerable to the wrong god — *"the god of this world"* (2 Corinthians 4:4).

The apostle Paul warns that there are *"false apostles, deceitful workmen, disguising themselves as apostles for Christ. And no wonder, for even Satan disguises himself as an angel of light"* (2 Corinthians 11:13–14). The people about whom Paul was talking were probably convinced that they were from God. They no doubt thought that they just believed differently and were more correct — more spiritual — than Paul.

Too many people view worship as some kind of mystical trance that one dare not disturb with reality. There is a great difference between carnal mysticism and true worship in Christian spirituality. Unless the scriptural order for worshipping God is followed, people become vulnerable to the consequences of occult mysticism.

We need to follow the example of the believers in Berea, of whom it was said, *"Now these Jews were more noble than those of Thessalonica, for they received the word with all eagerness, examining the Scripture daily to see if these things were so"* (Acts 17:11). Too often, our experiences interpret the Bible rather than the other way around.

When I had the responsibility on the "100 Huntley Street" Christian Television Ministry to do a "Scriptural Overview," a scriptural check-up about what our guests were saying, I had to give Biblical verses to support or correct (as discreetly and gently as possible) what the guests shared. Some accepted correction gracefully and with appreciation. Others refused to accept that they were "off base" according to Scripture.

In our worship services, if we examine everything according to Scripture and make the necessary changes, we shall be seen, like the Bereans, and like those who accepted scriptural direction at "100 Huntley Street" as *"more noble."* If we retain our own wisdom regardless of Scripture, we shall be seen as being out of God's will.

When we submit ourselves to Scripture rather than seeking after spiritual experiences, abuses of the gifts will not be in evidence.

The gifts of the Holy Spirit are God's unique guidance system. That is why their use must be continually monitored. All messages received through the gifts must be checked out according to the Bible. God is not going to reveal anything to us or tell us to do anything that runs contrary to Scripture.

Paul's College of Applied Gifts

The apostle Paul took the time to write to the

Corinthian Church because he wanted to give them, and us, directions for the proper use of the gifts of the Holy Spirit. He knew that they were powerful when used properly and directed by the Holy Spirit as they were intended. However, he knew that there was a lack of understanding about them: *"Now concerning spiritual gifts, brethren, I do not want you to be ignorant"* (1 Corinthians 12:1). He wanted to educate the Corinthian Christians, and us, so that believers through the ages could take full advantage of the wonderful gifts which allow us to participate in the miracle ministry of Jesus Christ.

Godly Repentance — The Foundation of True Worship

To this day, the conviction of sin is still the first reaction to the presence of the Holy Spirit. I experience it every time the Holy Spirit moves. *"For godly grief (sorrow) produces a repentance that leads to salvation and brings no regret, but worldly grief (sorrow) produces death"* (2 Corinthians 7:10).

The lack of Godly repentance results in the divisive phenomenon of people who, because they may have had a spiritual experience but do not know their Scripture, decide that through their experience, they are somehow superior to those who have not manifested any type of unnatural behaviour. They assume a disturbing "holier-than-thou'"attitude. Rather than being equipped to return home and use their new-found faith to develop their local churches, they do just the opposite. They become "faithful complainers," knowing neither the Scripture nor the power of God. They become critical and unreliable, especially when their pastor does not provide the same type of worship service in which they have had this "spiritual experience." Too often, they leave their church because it's not providing "the real thing."

Unfortunately, because of the lack of sound instruction, the "real thing" has come to mean a so-called ministry where feelings and spiritual experiences are more desired than a consistent relationship with Jesus.

What's Wrong with this Picture?

Unbelievers can see very clearly after a simple reading of the Bible, without any discernment at all, that the worship service of today is a far cry from the New Testament model. True revival is characterized by great numbers of people becoming Christians. The effective result of the correct use of the gifts of the Holy Spirit is salvation: *"But if all prophesy and an unbeliever or an uninformed person comes in, he is convinced by all, he is judged by all. And thus the secrets of his heart are revealed; and so, falling down on his face, he will worship God and report that God is truly among you"*(1 Corinthians 14:24,25).

Nowhere in Scripture is there an example of the outpouring of the Holy Spirit without at least a few, usually many people, even hundreds and thousands, becoming Christians. Without people being saved there is no revival. In many of our churches, seekers are hard-pressed to find people whose lives have been truly transformed by the new birth. Most are struggling to develop a moral life that they have been told they must demonstrate. Our churches are filled with second and third generation members who are best described as "God's grandchildren," which is a contradiction in terminology because, according to the Bible, God has no grandchildren, only first-hand believers.

Honest seekers search out worship services looking for the healing ministry of Jesus Christ that is described in the Bible only to be disappointed, because there is rarely, if ever, an opportunity for people to receive prayer for healing. It is not unusual for people to be told that "God doesn't do that anymore." No more healing of the sick and no more raising of the dead has become the hallmark of our modern churches.

That Which has been Lost Needs to be Found

In a world mesmerized by the hoards of spirits which clamour *"to steal and kill and destroy"* (John 10:10) people chase after the occult in deadly fascination. In the midst of it all, our churches turn unbelieving backs and deafened ears to cries for help. They have rejected or lost understanding of how to use the very tools that God gave to remedy the situation.

So-called "worship services" often consist of a ritualized opening prayer, one hymn, a solo, offering, announcements, a twenty minute sermon, a closing hymn and a benediction which sends people on their way no better than they arrived. The scriptural model of a worship service is totally ignored, replaced by the fruitless plans of man. If anyone were to come forward to contribute in the manner of 1 Corinthians 14:26, where *"everyone has a hymn, or a word of instruction, a revelation, a tongue or an interpretation,"* people would look for his or her spaceship after church.

We must follow the directions that the angel gave to the apostles when he was releasing them from prison: *"Go and stand in the temple and speak to the people all the words of this life"* (Acts 5:20). *"All the words of this life"* mean just that. Not some of the words. Not just the words with which one feels comfortable. Not only do we have to speak *"all the words of this life,"* but we must also demonstrate *"all the words of this life."*

Because Paul knew that words would not always suffice to convince people of the Gospel, he said, *"And I was with you in weakness and in much fear and trembling; and my speech and message were not in plausible words of wisdom, but in demonstration of the Spirit and of power, that your faith might not rest in the wisdom of men but in the power of God"* (1 Corinthians 2:3–5).

Just as few of us would be willing to purchase a car solely on the word of a car salesman, few people are willing to turn their lives over to Jesus without a demonstration of the power and reality of His Holy Spirit. People buying cars want to test-drive the demonstrator in order to gain some certainty that what the salesman says about the car is true. A demonstration of God's power through the operation of the gifts during worship point people to the reality of God and their need for Him. Sadly, they have been the best-kept secrets in the Church.

Use of the Gifts in Every Aspect of Church Life

The gifts of the Holy Spirit can and should be used not only during the Sunday worship services but also in prayer meetings, Bible Studies, meetings of elders, the Church's Christian Education program and all congregational meetings where a Church is seeking God's guidance for its future. Of course the most foundational meeting of the Church — each individual family in its home — will discover that use of the gifts in simple devotional times will ensure the Holy Spirit's guidance for families in day to day life.

Every aspect of our lives should be pleasing to God and in that sense should be worship unto Him. No matter whether we are driving along in the car by ourselves or participating in corporate worship within a congregation or dealing with issues in a church board meeting, we need to be sensitive to what the Holy Spirit wants to do and be ready for instant obedience to His leading.

The Source of Disbelief, Excess and Disorderly Worship

Who would encourage us to believe that the gifts of the Holy Spirit are not for today, or that they are not from God? Who would encourage the unexamined use of the gifts of the Holy Spirit and the use of their counterfeits so that people would end up being embarrassed, or frightened, or confused by their experiences?

The answer is obvious. When a person reads the New Testament, in Greek or in English or in whatever language, it is apparent that there is only one person who would want us to stop using the gifts of the Holy Spirit and so leave us vulnerable and weak in spiritual warfare. There is only one person who would want us to misuse the gifts of the Holy Spirit. Of course it is our enemy — Satan, the Devil.

The Devil uses people in our Churches who *"disguise themselves as servants of righteousness"* (2 Corinthians 11:15).

Using reasonable logic based on experience and mixed with a works-righteousness, they claim that any supernatural manifestations described in the Bible are no longer to be expected, because God stopped using them at some vague period in history. Any present day supernatural manifestations are not from Him.

While many of the people who use this "spiritual reverse psychology" are well-meaning individuals, they need to understand that Satan is using them to block what Jesus wants to do in the lives of His people today. They are pawns in the Devil's crafty game.

What Happens if it's Not from God?

The practice of recording all interpretations of tongues, prophecies, revelations, and any other messages which are received through the gifts of the Holy Spirit so that they can be examined according to Scripture, is a vital key in keeping a congregation on track. When messages are found to be accurate, the Church needs to be informed that they have been found to be so. Keeping a record of the date when a prophecy was received through the Holy Spirit, as well as the date when God fulfills it, enables the Church to give Him the glory and thanks.

If, however, a message is determined not to be scripturally correct, the person who is in charge of the service must say so. The person who gave the message must be told why the message they gave was wrong according to Scripture.

We do not stone errant prophets today, we correct them in love. Anyone who really desires to be used by God through the use of the gifts of the Holy Spirit will accept correction. The experience will help them to become faithful, mature believers. Those who will not receive correction should not be allowed to use their gifts publicly in any meetings. It is vital that everyone in the church has the security of knowing that the leadership will not allow anyone but Jesus Christ to guide them.

Renewal in Worship

Using the gifts of the Holy Spirit — as they were meant to be used — results in not only a renewal of individual Christians' lives but also brings a renewal in our worship. Far from begrudgingly fulfilling their "church duties," Christians look forward with great anticipation to worshipping God when they know that He will truly meet them in that place of praise. They no longer ask, "Do I have to go to church?" but look forward with eager anticipation to going to worship as "the Church, the body of Christ" because they are the church.

When the gifts are allowed to flow in worship, there is a new freedom. Each one has something to contribute. Dynamic worship springs out of worshipping together in *"spirit and in truth"* (John 4:24).

Because ministry to the believers overflows into evangelistic use of the gifts in worship, the result is not only personal growth, but also congregational growth.

Scriptural Order

Without the gifts, the scriptural design for worship is missing. The problem through the ages has been that when the gifts have been allowed to operate, it is often a sloppy thing without regard for scriptural direction. That is why they came into disrepute.

1 Corinthians 14:26–33 says, *"When you come together, everyone has a hymn, or a word of instruction, a revelation, a tongue or an interpretation. All of these must be done for the strengthening of the church. If anyone speaks in a tongue, let there be two or at the most three, each in turn, and let one interpret. But if there is no interpreter, let him keep silent in church, and let him speak to himself and to God. Let two or three prophets speak, and let the others judge. But if anything is revealed to another who sits by, let the first keep silent. For you can all prophesy one by one, that all may learn and all may be encouraged. And the spirits of the prophets are subject to the prophets, for God is not the author of confusion but of peace, as in all churches of the saints."*

Thus, when there are messages in tongues, there should be no more than two or three allowed in each meeting. When a message in tongues is spoken, those who have the gift of interpretation must be allowed to interpret. The same thing is true with regard to the gift of prophecy. Only two or three who have the gift of prophecy should be allowed to speak and let the other people weigh what is said, which means to check out or judge the prophecies to make certain that they accord to Scripture. If someone else has a revelation from God, that person should be allowed to share it, but *"All of these must be done for the strengthening of the church."*

When we dare to risk what Paul encouraged the Corinthian Church to do, a whole new understanding of worshipping in the Spirit will be experienced.

The old and new can blend together in traditional hymns and new choruses *"addressing one another in psalms and hymns and spiritual songs* (singing in the Spirit, ie. in tongues) *singing and making melody to the Lord with all your heart, always and for everything giving thanks in the name of our Lord Jesus Christ to God the Father"* (Ephesians 5:18–20).

What we have come to call "praise and worship" gives us entry through His gates and into His courts. *"Enter into His gates with thanksgiving, and into His courts with praise"*(Psalm 100:4).

The Word in Worship

A worship service must always include preaching of the Word or the Gospel. Today, there is a tendency to down-play the importance of preaching. What many don't understand is that preaching is a supernatural activity. It initiates and activates faith. That is the reason why Paul encourages us with what in the world's eyes is foolish. *"For after that in the wisdom of God the world by wisdom knew not God, it pleased God by the foolishness of preaching to save them that believe"* (1 Corinthians 1:21). *"So then faith cometh by hearing, and hearing by the Word of God"* (Romans 10:17).

Opportunity for Ministry During Worship

During times of praise and worship, sensitivity to God's call to minister to various needs within the meeting is imperative. Getting so immersed in one's own good feelings in the presence of the Lord can short circuit the fullness of His blessings. A time of ministry at every worship service is vital.

There must be a time where seekers are given the opportunity to accept Jesus Christ as their Saviour and Lord, where people can be baptized in the Holy Spirit and receive the gifts of the Holy Spirit and when people can have prayer for healing or other needs.

Very few churches have a time for ministry in every worship service. Can you imagine going to purchase a car and the salesman saying, "I only close the deals a few times a year. Please come back at a later date." That never happens.

When I was in pastoral ministry, we had an invitation for ministry at every worship service, with the result that there was not one Sunday when we did not see at least one person saved. There were people baptized in the Holy Spirit, delivered from evil spirits, healed, and ministered to in whatever areas of their lives needed attention.

Impartation of the Gifts of the Holy Spirit During Worship

Paul had a particular ministry of imparting spiritual gifts. This is a part of my ministry as well. I have discovered that the Holy Spirit will give believers a desire for particular gifts of the Holy Spirit and, if they will come to receive prayer and ask in faith, they will be equipped with the gifts as I pray with them to receive. Paul said, *"For I long to see you, that I might impart to you some spiritual gift to strengthen you, that is, that we may be mutually encouraged by each other's faith, both yours and mine"* (Romans 1:11-12).

People need the opportunity to receive the gifts during worship services because the gifts of the Holy Spirit allow Jesus Christ to exercise His Lordship over us daily and allow us to participate in His ministry.

Fulfilling worship

People can be saved, baptized with the Holy Spirit, gifted with the amazing gifts of the Holy Spirit, and still not be satisfied. Unless their worship is lifted to God out of freedom of expression of the gifts they have been given, they will feel a gnawing dissatisfaction — a void, within. While it is the duty of leadership to make sure that an environment of freedom is available to worshippers within the church, it seldom happens.

Perhaps the most frequent complaint that I hear from Christians as I travel is, "I don't get fed at my church." What they're saying is, "My pastor doesn't feed me." Most of the complaints are from people who go to evangelical, conservative, Bible-believing, Pentecostal, or Charismatic churches, where the Gospel is being preached but no opportunity is given to people to use their faith and gifts. However, as sympathetic as I can be, there would be nothing to be gained by agreeing with the complainers by voicing my frustrations with their leadership.

I have to point out to these people that if they really want to be fed and satisfied, then they will have to get fed at the same place where Jesus ate. He was fed every time He ministered to somebody else. After talking with the woman at the well in Samaria, Jesus' disciples brought him some food to eat. He said, *"My food is to do the will of Him who sent me, and to accomplish His work"* (John 4:34).

I tell people, "If you really want to get fed, then do some ministry. Do something for God. Lead somebody to Jesus."

Christianity is not a "spectator sport." We were saved so that we could help other people know Jesus Christ as their Saviour, Lord, Healer, and Deliverer. Every time we participate, we will be satisfied. *"Blessed are those who hunger and thirst, for they shall be satisfied"* (Matthew 5:6).

God equips people with His gifts for the purpose of getting those around them saved and into the Kingdom of Heaven.

Growing Through Dynamic Worship

Growing in the Spirit is dependent on learning to exercise the gifts of the Holy Spirit and allowing Him to develop the character of Jesus through the development of the fruit of the Holy Spirit in each person. Learning to use the gifts skillfully both in private and in public, finding a Spirit-filled church (one that is open to the Holy Spirit and His gifts) and serving a function in the church is very important to growth.

A truly Spirit-filled church will help not only in the discovery of spiritual gifts, but in the development of their use. It will encourage people to truly look for opportunities to serve Jesus Christ. It will impress upon them the importance of studying the Bible both privately and in a Bible study group so that people will be able to rightly (correctly) divide the word of truth. It will teach them to develop their "listening-to-God skills," called prayer through opportunities to pray with other Christians, both with the mind as well as in the Spirit (tongues). It will model the most effective way for people to cooperate with the Holy Spirit through sensitizing them to look for others who need not only spiritual help but practical help.

Spiritual growth in private life comes most quickly through simply making oneself available for God's use. Availability, grounded on solid scriptural knowledge and obedience, goes hand in hand with the guidance of the Holy Spirit and the blessing of Jesus.

Let's do what Jesus Christ has equipped us to do. He told us to, *"Go therefore, and make disciples of all nations, baptizing them in the name of the Father and of the Son and of the Holy Spirit, teaching them to observe all that I have commanded you; and lo, I am with you to the close of the age"* (Matthew 28:19,20).

Worshipping God through exercising the gifts of the Holy Spirit provides us with one of the means by which we are able to do *"greater works"* (John 14:12) than Jesus did, as He guides us in their use.

God has given us awesome tools to carry out the ministry of His Son. Let's do what He has equipped us to do!

Learning to Enjoy Praise and Worship

Besides allowing the gifts to move freely according to the scriptural order, there's a depth to praise and worship that has not been understood because of shallow teaching. The key comes through understanding the real meaning of praise and worship according to the original Greek and Hebrew in which the Bible was written.

There are five Hebrew words for praise. Each of these are indicative of particular body movements as well as attitudes of the heart. "Normal" praise, according to God, involves practicing these physical-spiritual exercises.

Unfortunately, while we have lost much of the original meaning of how to approach and praise our God, the eastern religions have capitalized on their counterfeit. They know that by doing certain physical things, like yoga, they gain entrance to the spirit world.

In Christianity, God showed us in the Bible, in the original Hebrew and Greek, that certain physical positions and exercises, when carried out in an attitude of praise to Him, would open us up more fully to the Holy Spirit, thus enabling Him to deal with us in beautiful ways. This is a critical aspect of praise and worship that we have, for the most part, forsaken.

It is unfortunate that so much has been lost in our English translations of Scripture. Unless pastors are familiar with the original Hebrew meanings of the words that are translated as "praise" in our Bibles, they will stand up in front of their congregations on a Sunday morning and say "Well, let's all praise the Lord this morning," and then proceed to lead in a song-service which has little to do with truly praising God as God wants us to praise Him.

Whenever I have taught on God's real directives for praise and worship, it has been fascinating to see what has happened. The Holy Spirit moves with awesome power. People are healed and their lives are changed.

One time, I was teaching a group of teenagers at a Youth Rally in Alliston, Ontario. After teaching them some of these principles and giving an altar call, many of them began to rush to the front. In speaking with some of them afterwards, they said that they had been sitting in their chairs thinking, "There's no way I'm going up there," when, all of a sudden, it was as if somebody just picked them up and carried them towards the front. They accepted Jesus as their Saviour and were filled with the Holy Spirit and all kinds of amazing things happened.

Let's take a look at six words: five Hebrew words that have been translated as "praise," and at the original Hebrew word for "worship."

i) "Yadah" Praise

The Hebrew word, "Yadah," has been simply translated as 'praise', although it means to throw your hands wide in victory and carries with it the implication of an attitude of adoration, gratitude and thanksgiving. It is used over fifty times in the Old Testament. Psalm 106, *"Give thanks to the Lord, for He is good,"* is 'Yadah" praise, as is Psalm 18:2,3 which says, *"Come bless the Lord."* Psalm 134:1,2 is another example of 'Yadah': *"Thy loving kindness ... ."* It was "Yadah" praise that led God to bring confusion into the ranks of the enemy and bring victory to His people.

"Yadah" often involves a sacrifice of praise, thanking God with a firm belief in His faithfulness to be true to His promises, not only for things received, but for answers yet unseen.

Whenever we lack faith or have inner rebellion or doubts, we need to break into "Yadah" praise. It dispels unbelief and is described as putting our arms around God's neck and thanking Him. "Yadah" praise is very powerful.

It is important to note that this is the only Hebrew word translated as "praise" that carries with it any connotation of thanksgiving. In general, praise is not thanks. People are thanked for what they have done. They are praised for who they are.

We Christians are, in general, the most unthankful people around. We get so caught up in ourselves that we misunderstand what is going on in us. We stew about getting into God's presence and churn up the sins of the past, all the while cooking up a great pot of guilt.

The ability to remember the sins of the past was never meant to stir up guilt. After we have received forgiveness, the memories are left within us to remind us to thank Jesus for what He has done in our lives. If every time a thought of past sin comes to mind we say, "Thank You, Jesus," we will find ourselves immediately thrust into His presence.

2) "Hallel" Praise

"Hallel" is the Hebrew root of "hallelujah" and means "to praise the Lord raising the arms and moving them around." There is a great deal of misunderstanding about the word "hallelujah." Of course it is one of the most common words we use to praise God. When it begins with an "h", it means "praise the Lord." However, many people drop the "h" and sing "allelujah" or "alleluiah." What they don't realize is that in so doing, they change the meaning of the word to "the Lord is weak, unworthy and unable."

I've had many people ask why, if this is true, anyone ever dropped the "h" in the first place. I believe it may be because some with a very sketchy understanding of the language have said that in Greek there is no "h" sound at the beginning of the word. However, any scholar will tell you that there is. When written, it looks like a reverse apostrophe that goes above the "a." Interestingly enough, Strong's Concordance has dropped the "h" and that's probably where a lot of people get confused. I generally really like Strong's, but that is one mistake I have found.

"Hallel" is used in over 200 Scriptures where it is simply translated as "praise." The implication of the word can be compared to the attitude of a young man who has fallen in love and is totally absorbed in the object of his attentions. When people try to carry on a normal conversation with him, they can't, because he is entirely engrossed in his love. That's the way our praise to God should be. We need to be so wrapped up in our love for Him that nothing can distract us from praising Him for who He is.

1 Chronicles 16:4 tells of David appointing certain Levites to give thanks and praise the Lord. Psalm 135 begins with a command to *"Praise the Lord."* When Christians are filled with the Holy Spirit of God, no one has to tell them to praise Him. They do it because they want to. It is a wonderful release of the fullness of their hearts.

"Hallel" has been called a fanatical type of praise by mockers because when people praise God the "hallel" way, they tend to rave on and boast about how good the Lord is. This is the kind of praise in which the Lord dwells.

Psalm 22:3 says *"the Lord inhabits the praise* (hallel) *of His people."* When we *"enter into His courts with praise"* (Psalm 100:4) Scripture is talking of "hallel" praise. When we *"enter His gates with thanksgiving,"* it means we go in His front door and right into His living room with praise. That's how quickly we can get into His immediate presence with this kind of praise.

As we sing, "hallelujah," both in the spirit and with understanding, we find unity, strength, fellowship, healing, rest and deliverance. With "hallel," God fills His house with His glory.

iii) "Shabach" Praise

"Shabach" is found over 300 times in Scripture. It means *"to shout, to speak in a loud voice, or to command."* "Shabach" praise means to shout the walls down! Psalm 20:5 says *"We will shout for joy ... ." "The oil of joy for mourning"* in Isaiah 61:3 is "shabach" praise, as is the promise of *"garments of praise,"* in the same verse.

How can it be normal to sit quietly for one hour on Sunday morning, rising only to sing three mournful hymns at appointed times in accordance with a carefully scheduled church bulletin, when Scripture is full of jubilant exhortations to shout for joy?

iv) "Zamar" Praise

"Zamar" means to "praise with your whole being" and includes everything from dancing before the Lord, to playing instruments unto Him, chanting, singing, moving the hands and feet and all sorts of wonderful things. In 1Chronicles 15:16, David appointed singers with instruments to sing joyful songs. Psalm 47:1 exults, *"Clap your hands, all you nations; shout to God with cries of joy."*

v) "Barak" Praise

"Barak" means "to bless, to kneel before the Lord, an act of adoration, to bow down in worship expecting a miracle."

In my last church, I had a fellow in my congregation with a bad heart, who would never come to the altar for prayer. One Sunday night, I was teaching about the real meanings of praise. I was aware of Bob sitting in his pew with his arms crossed in front of him. When I got to the word "barak," I explained how, when people bow before the Lord in a worshipful attitude expecting a miracle, praising Him with this word, healing is available from God.

I don't know how he got there without my seeing him walk to the altar, but at one point I caught some movement out of the left corner of my eye, and there was Bob, kneeling at the altar, lifting his hands before the Lord and praising Him, saying, "Barak, barak, barak, barak." He went to see his doctor the next week and discovered that his heart was healed!

God will heal people as they truly praise Him out of hearts of adoration, using this word. Psalm 72:12–15 says, *"For He will deliver the needy who cry out* (barak) *the afflicted who have no one to help. He will take pity on the weak and the needy and save the needy from death. He will rescue them from oppression and violence, for precious is their blood in His sight."*

Praise is an act of the will. When we learn to use this key, we open the door to the power of God in our lives. Lest someone think that this is just another formula for a self-centered approach to God for his or her own purposes, be warned that the attitude of the heart is pivotal. True praise is always God-directed — never simply a tool to get what we want. It simply opens the door to allow God to work more fully in our lives.

Although the New Testament is God's new covenant with us, there are certain things, like tithing and praise and worship, that have been brought through the Cross and still apply. In Matthew 4:10, Jesus says, *"Worship the Lord your God, and serve Him only."* Further along, in John 4:24, He tells the woman at the well that, *"God is Spirit, and His worshippers must worship in spirit and in truth."*

It's tragic that counterfeit, occult religions have maintained their physical-spiritual exercises in communicating with evil spirits, while we Christians have, for the most part, forsaken our physical-spiritual exercises of praise which bring health, healing and a beautiful openness before the Lord.

vi) "Shachah" Worship

The Hebrew word for worship is "shachah" and it means to bow down or prostrate oneself before the Lord. The Greek word for "worship" means to get down on hands and knees like a dog, before God. That is difficult with our style of services today where we alternate sitting and standing and expect comfortable chairs and pews to fill the sanctuary.

One of the main difficulties we encounter when trying to teach according to scriptural directions for "nomal"praise and worship is the fact that we have pews in our churches, while the temple in Jerusalem had no pews or chairs. Thus, we are restricted in our freedom. Besides the space restrictions, few people comply with the way God wants us to worship Him because they have never been taught His directives properly.

For those wishing fuller teaching on this subject, I have prepared a booklet on *Praise and Worship,* which is available from the address at the back of this book.

When we take time to search the Scripture and understand it in light of its original meaning through direction of the Holy Spirit, a richness in relationship with Jesus begins to emerge that is sweeter and fuller than we had ever dreamed possible.

10

From Caterpillars to Butterflies: A Revitalized Holiness

"I appeal to you therefore, brethren, by the mercies of God, to present your bodies as a living sacrifice, holy and acceptable to God, which is your spiritual worship. Do not be conformed to this world but be transformed by the renewal of your mind, that you may prove what is good and acceptable and perfect" (Romans 12:1-2).

A woman out walking on a warm spring day found a branch with a cocoon on it. She carefully extricated the tiny, mummy-like structure and took it home so that she could watch the new life emerge.

It wasn't long before she noticed the butterfly trying to get out. In a valiant struggle to free itself from what appeared to be impossible encumbrances, it pushed and fought with painstakingly slow progress.

Feeling sorry for the poor thing, she decided to help. With the aid of a sharp pair of scissors, she deftly snipped the corners of the imprisoning cocoon. The magnificent creature first slipped out easily; then flipped, flopped, and died.

Too late, the woman realized that her compassion had exceeded her wisdom. Without the struggle of fighting its way out of the cocoon, the butterfly was denied the God ordained process of strengthening its wings so that it could fly free.

Christian Caterpillars

When a person becomes a born again believer, he is like a caterpillar — justified (forgiven) but just in the first stage of the process of sanctification. Although a person is sanctified (set apart for God's purposes) from the moment God calls him or her into service (it happened with Jeremiah while he was still in the womb! *"While you were yet in the womb, I sanctified you."* Jeremiah 1:5) the process of sanctification is an on-going development of the character of Jesus within each willing Christian. It is the process of being prepared for holy use.

Jesus calls each of us to grow from the "justified" caterpillar stage and to emerge from our old lives as new creatures. He calls us to a life of "holiness" or "holy living" as sanctified, holy, beautiful butterflies, flying far above the circumstances of this life. Becoming a Christian is just the first step in what should be a dynamic transformation.

One very important function of the Church is to serve as a cocoon for caterpillar Christians, nurturing and protecting them as they grow through the process of sanctification. Within this (hopefully) supportive environment, they are subjected to the heat and pressure of the Holy Spirit as they are changed from a lower order into a higher order of being: from the natural into the spiritual, from the carnal to the holy.

A New View of Holiness

Some time ago, I came into an understanding of holiness that has, I believe, been overlooked.

It began with fresh insight into Paul's exhortation to Christians in Romans 12:1: *"I appeal to you therefore, brethren, by the mercies of God, to present your bodies as a living sacrifice, holy, and acceptable to God which is your spiritual worship"* and the command which immediately follows it: *"Do not be conformed to this world but be transformed by the renewal of your mind, that you may prove what is good and acceptable and perfect"* (Romans 12: 2).

Most caterpillar Christians try to transform their minds through their own efforts. They know what kind of lives mature Christians lead and so they try to effect that lifestyle in their own lives. They study the Bible, read Christian books and literature, pray and meditate, participate in worship services and perform all manner of activities which they perceive as serving Jesus Christ and "cooperating with God" in their transformation.

However, I believe that Paul is trying to communicate something radically different to our understanding of how the change takes place. In this passage, he is attempting to tell us how to cooperate with the Holy Spirit in a way that transcends our earthly efforts and effectively results in the transformation that God desires to make in each person.

The problem is that most people, including myself until now, have missed what Paul is trying to tell us. He wants us to understand what our *"spiritual worship"* is. The problem is that the translation is not quite accurate. The original Greek word is not "pneumatikos" which would mean "spiritual" rather, the word used is "logiken" which means "logical" or "reasonable." Also, the normal Greek word for "worship," "proskuneo," is not used here. Instead, the Greek word, "latrian," meaning "service," is used. The proper translation for this phrase is *logical or reasonable service* rather than "spiritual worship".

Thus, Romans 12:1 should read *"I appeal to you therefore, brethren, by the mercies of God, to present your bodies as a living sacrifice, holy, and acceptable to God which is your reasonable service."*

Thus, what Paul is saying is that the logical, reasonable way to serve God according to His requirements is to submit our bodies — every appetite we have, whether physical, emotional, intellectual or spiritual, every goal we have, every moment we have, every thought — as a living sacrifice to Him.

Changing our lives from self-directed to God-directed requires a monumental change. It is such a radical change that it is *impossible* to accomplish by our own means.

A Holy Spirit Metamorphosis

The Greek word, "metamorphoomai," which is translated, "transformed," is the word from which we get the word "metamorphosis." Metamorphosis is a process by which an insect, creature, or person is subjected to heat and pressure in order to change its form from a lower level to a higher level of life. It is this process which changes a caterpillar into a butterfly.

The problem with the metamorphosis from a "justified" Christian to one who has truly surrendered the "self" is that "Christian caterpillars" usually, whether intentionally or unintentionally, interfere with the process which God has prescribed. They want to do things their way. However, unless they submit themselves to God's plan, they do not get transformed into "Christian butterflies." They remain caterpillars all their lives.

Christian caterpillars never experience the exciting "normal Christian life" described in the New Testament. They never see miracles, signs, and wonders. Oh, yes, they may tell others about Jesus and the great things that God did in the past and see many people become caterpillars through sharing their great knowledge. They may take their places in the church, carry out their "obligations" to God and know their Bibles better than all other caterpillars put together — but what they read simply becomes part of a clean-living, Godly life. They never turn into butterflies.

When Jesus was approached by a lawyer who asked Him, *"Teacher, what shall I do to inherit eternal life?"* Jesus answered, *"You shall love the Lord your God with all your heart, and with all of your soul, and with all of your strength, and with all of your mind; and your neighbour as yourself"* (Luke 10:25–27). In other words, in order to be able to cooperate with God in everything He wants us to do, and especially with our transformation, we have to be willing, with an act of the will, to submit every aspect of our being — heart, soul, strength and mind — to the Potter's hand.

To Change or Not to Change? — A Matter of the Will

Not every Christian is willing to change. Although all have been willing to take the first step in the process of transformation by becoming*"born again"* believers (John 3:3,5,7) willingness to take the next step by receiving the power of the Holy Spirit is more commitment than many want to make.

However, according to Jesus in Acts 1:8, *"You will receive power when the Holy Ghost comes upon you ... ."* Only after people have received the Holy Spirit or have been baptized or filled with the Holy Spirit, can the change begin.

The apostle Paul tells us, *"The unspiritual man* (the person who does not have the Holy Spirit, the natural or carnal person) *does not receive the gifts of the Spirit of God, for they are folly* (foolishness) *to him, and he is not able to understand them because they are spiritually discerned"* (1 Corinthians 2:14). By *"spiritually discerned"* he means understood through the Holy Spirit.

Many Christians are *"unspiritual people,"* meaning that they have not received the Holy Spirit into their hearts or lives or they have not been baptized with the Holy Spirit. There is no doubt that they are saved. However, they are in the same state that Jesus' own disciples were in before the day of Pentecost (Acts 2:1–4). They are like the Samaritans who believed in Jesus Christ and were baptized with water by Philip but who did not receive the Holy Spirit until Peter and John laid their hands on them (Acts 8:12–17). They are like the disciples of John who met Paul and received the Holy Spirit, spoke in tongues and prophesied when he prayed and laid hands on them (Acts 19:17).

Such Christians are what Paul describes as *"unspiritual," "carnal"* or *"natural"* in the sense that they have not received the Holy Spirit. They usually neither understand nor accept the gifts of the Holy Spirit. They frustrate, beyond understanding, those Christians who have been baptized with the Holy Spirit and have received gifts, because those who have received know how greatly these people would benefit if they would only receive. They know how simple it could be for them and they know from personal experience that the gifts are available to everyone who believes today. They also frustrate the working of the Holy Spirit in the life and fellowship of their churches.

Because *"unspiritual"* Christians do not understand the importance of the gifts of the Holy Spirit in fellowship and evangelizing the world, they quench both the Holy Spirit (1 Thessalonians 5:19) and those Christians who have been baptized with the Holy Spirit.

Spirit-filled Christians (often called charismatics or pentecostals) are often looked upon as being divisive. They often have to leave their churches and try to find other churches where the leadership is open to the work and gifts of the Holy Spirit.

As was mentioned in an earlier chapter, the two experiences, salvation and the baptism of the Holy Spirit, can occur at the same moment as happened with Cornelius and his household (Acts 10:44-46). However, it can not always be assumed that simply because someone has had the salvation experience of becoming 'born again' that he or she has been baptized with the Holy Spirit.

The reaction of traditional Christians to Spirit-filled Christians is similar to that of the Israelites to Moses. The Israelites said to Moses, *"You speak to us, and we will hear; but let not God speak to us lest we die"* (Exodus. 20). They do not want God to get too close to them. They do not want God to speak too directly and too clearly to them.

Spirit-filled Christians are a constant reminder that God does want to speak directly to every Christian. Every time the gifts of the Holy Spirit are used, they bring God's voice and direction into a church. Every time that occurs, traditional Christians will react badly because they want to keep a comfortable space between them and God. The gifts of the Holy Spirit remove that comfortable space.

Spirit-filled Christians are also a constant reminder to traditional Christians that Jesus wants more from them than they are willing to give: all of their hearts, minds, souls, and strength (Luke 10:27).

Many claim that they want nothing more than to change, but that God doesn't seem to do anything in their lives. Without exception, these people would experience total transformation if they were willing to totally surrender their lives. Refusing to sacrifice any part of the self to God blocks Him from the work He wants to do.

The Process of Change

As Christians submit their wills to His, the power of the Holy Spirit begins to work inside of them. He gradually changes their natural characters into the character of Jesus through developing the fruit of the Holy Spirit in them (*"But the fruit of the Spirit is love, joy, peace, patience, kindness, goodness, faithfulness, gentleness, self-control"* Galatians 5:22,23) and giving them special ministry gifts (1 Corinthians 12:11).

A common problem is that people think that they can make a choice between using the fruit of the Spirit and the gifts of the Spirit. They don't understand that it is not an either/or situation, but rather a both/and situation. Both the gifts and the fruit are absolutely essential to a Christian's transformation and ministry. While the fruit of the Holy Spirit make the gifts of the Holy Spirit acceptable and effective in ministering to other people, the gifts prove the authenticity of our faith in Jesus Christ. These two together develop fellowship so that *"these signs shall follow those who believe. In My Name they shall cast out demons; they shall speak with new tongues; they shall take up serpents; and if they drink any deadly thing, it shall not hurt them; they shall lay hands on the sick, and they shall recover"* (Mark 16:17–18).

It takes all of the combined effort of heart, soul, strength, and mind working in cooperation with the Holy Spirit in order to be *"transformed by the renewal of the mind"* and not to be *"conformed to this world."* When people willingly cooperate with the Holy Spirit, they will not be conformed to this world but will be transformed by the renewal of their minds and can then truly offer themselves as living sacrifices.

How can I Cooperate with the Holy Spirit in Such a Way that my Mind will be Renewed and I Will be Truly Transformed?

When asked this often posed question, many well-meaning Christians will counsel in a "New Testament form of legalism." They make all sorts of suggestions: "Do this. Don't do that. Try this. Try that. Keep the Ten Commandments. Keep the church rules. Read and study your Bible more. Pray more. Don't miss worship. Go to Bible study meetings. Go to prayer meetings. Go to men's or women's fellowship meetings. Witness to other people. Give more. Go out on a mission field. Visit the sick, the lonely, the shut-ins. Help those in need. Do. Do. Do. Do more."

The more that people try these things, the more they fail and are conformed to this world. The more they fail, the more they are condemned. The more they feel condemned, the more guilt they feel. The transformation is always just beyond their reach.

The answer can be found in Romans 12:3 where Paul encourages Christians to look at the *"measure of faith"* which has been given to them and then to use the *"measure of faith"* that they have received.

The *"measure of faith"* or *"measures of faith"* that Paul is talking about here are the *"gifts of the Holy Spirit."* Romans 12: 6–8 says, *"We have different gifts according to the grace given us. If a man's gift is prophesying, let him use it in proportion to his faith. If it is serving, let him serve; if it is teaching, let him teach; if it is encouraging, let him encourage; if it is contributing to the needs of others, let him give generously; if it is leadership, let him govern diligently; if it is showing mercy, let him do it cheerfully."*

According to Paul, if we want to prevent ourselves from being conformed to this world and be transformed by the renewal of our minds, we must use the charismatic gifts as we are led by the Holy Spirit. The Greek word for "gifts" (charismata) used in Romans 12 is exactly the same word that Paul uses in 1 Corinthians, Chapter 12, where the most commonly recognized gifts are found.

Thus, Paul's answer to this question is some hard practical advice. Whoever wants to cooperate with the Holy Spirit in the process of transformation or metamorphosis into a "Christian butterfly" must begin to use the gifts of the Holy Spirit in logical or reasonable service.

Pressure to Conform to the World

Using the gifts in logical service is not always an easy thing to do. Even in most churches, Spirit-filled believers are pressured to conform to the world and not to use the supernatural gifts of the Holy Spirit, whether in public worship services or in smaller Christian meetings. This pressure does not come from non-Christians but from "caterpillar" Christians. (The "butterfly" variety encourage them all the way.)

Even the second and third generations of churches that were established to be open to the direction and guidance of the Holy Spirit have begun to conform to the world by either not using or not allowing the use of the gifts of the Holy Spirit. It is easier to control a church full of Christian "caterpillars" than Christian "butterflies" who fly on the wind of the Holy Spirit. Most pastors, ministers, priests or church leaders do not see the need for the gifts of the Holy Spirit in their congregations.

The result is, of course, that there are thousands and thousands of frustrated Christians who are trying to cooperate with the Holy Spirit by using their spiritual gifts, but who are not encouraged or even allowed to do so.

Because of the criticism that charismatic (gifted) Christians fear from "offending" others by using their spiritual gifts, they usually cave in to the pressure, hold back and conform to worldly expectations. The irony is that the supernatural gifts are designed to draw and attract to Jesus Christ the very ones these people are afraid of offending.

The gifts all have an "evangelistic edge" or purpose to them which is meant to establish faith in Jesus Christ in non-believers, when combined with the preaching of the Gospel. The supernatural aspect confirms to people that the Gospel of Jesus Christ is really true.

Despite all of the concerns people have about offending others through using the gifts, I have never seen an unbeliever offended by their use. However, I have seen unbelievers, involved in such practices as witchcraft and satanism, turn away from the occult when they have seen or heard the gifts of the Holy Spirit being used. Over and over again, I have seen them accept Jesus Christ as their Saviour and Lord and be baptized with the Holy Spirit.

The same impressive result was evident with Simon the Sorcerer. He was so impressed when Peter and John prayed with the Samaritan believers to receive the Holy Spirit that he wanted what they had. He offered to pay them money if they would empower him with the same gift to pray with people as they had (Acts 8:2–24). Since the bench mark of authenticity of the baptism of the Holy Spirit was the events of the Day of Pentecost (Acts 15:8–12) it has to be assumed that those believers began to speak in tongues and probably prophesied as well. Without those signs, there would have been nothing visible to impress Simon.

The gifts of the Holy Spirit still have the effect of demonstrating the power of the cross to all unbelievers and drawing them to believe in Jesus Christ as their Saviour and Lord.

Most of the non-Christian world knows that there is a supernatural dimension to life and they are hungry to find it. Because they have never seen or experienced the supernatural in Christian churches, however, they wander off to the occult and false religions that expose them to demonic and satanic supernatural experiences.

Paul never suggested that we should stifle the gifts for fear of offending anyone. He encouraged their use wholeheartedly. He knew that with proper, skillful use, they would break through the walls of cynicism to reach unbelievers with Jesus.

That is why he said both to the Corinthians and to us, *"And my speech and my message were not in plausible words of wisdom, but in demonstration of the Spirit and of power that your faith might not rest in the wisdom of men but in the power of the Holy Spirit"* (1 Corinthians 2:4,5).

Paul was the one who preached the Gospel to the Corinthians and introduced them to Jesus Christ as their Saviour and Lord; but he was also the one who introduced them to the Holy Spirit and taught them how to use the gifts of the Holy Spirit effectively. Conforming to worldly pressures, either inside or outside the church, was never part of his message.

Another Kind of Pressure — Pressure to be Transformed

Most people do not like the experience of being transformed. Although the pressure of the Holy Spirit does not go beyond what we can bear, it is usually very stressful. The process places the believer between God's pressure to be transformed and the world's pressure to conform. Heaven's gates are pounded regularly with the prayers of believers crying, "Oh God, isn't there an easier way for you to change me? Why do I have to go through all of this? Don't you love me, God?"

It often seems that there is no budging those gates. There is no easy way. Transformation means crucifixion —

nailing the "self" to the cross — putting the desires of the flesh to death. Crucifixion means cooperation with the Holy Spirit. It places people at odds with the world.

While the world pressures Christians not to cooperate with the Holy Spirit in this often lonely and painful process, resistance to its pressures to conform to the worldly standards, attitudes, goals and behaviours means transformation and *"the renewal of your mind, that you may prove what is good and acceptable and perfect"* (Romans 12: 2).

The Choice — Cooperation vs. Self-Will

Christians have the choice to either cooperate and be transformed or remain carnal caterpillars. Many refuse to cooperate with Jesus. They think they have been made to crawl for the rest of their lives. They look up at the butterflies and say to themselves, "There is no way that you'll ever catch me flying in one of those things. They're too dangerous. People criticize, attack and kill them. No, they are not for me. No, God wants me to stay just the way that I am: safely saved."

God never meant for butterflies to remain safe little caterpillars, crawling along on their bellies, oblivious to the joys that await them.

Life in the Cocoon

It has been my experience that 'Spirit-filled' Christians need "Spirit-filled" pastoring. They need fellowship, teaching and supervision in using their gifts so that Jesus' plan for them and their churches can be accomplished. Jesus warned us, *"So for the sake of your tradition, you have made void the word of God"* (Matthew 15:6).

Inflexible traditions and doctrines too often prevent God from equipping His people His way — the way that is described in the Bible. We must be willing to accommodate the changes that the Holy Spirit wants to accomplish because He does not always accommodate our Church practices or traditional ways of worship. He has his own "order" of worship (1 Corinthians 14:26–33) which is quite radically different from the orders of worship of almost all churches. Those who have experienced the true "order" of worship can never be totally satisfied with many of the so-called traditional or non-traditional worship services.

Jesus warned, *"And no one puts new wine into old wineskins; if he does, the new wine will burst the skins and it will be spilled and the skins will be destroyed. But new wine must be put into new wineskins. And no one after drinking old wine desires new; for he says, 'The old is better'"* (Luke 5:37–39).

Traditionally and historically, the new wine is the Holy Spirit. The wineskins are people — temples of the Holy Spirit. Just as new wine has to go through the process of fermentation, the Holy Spirit causes people to be stretched and changed by His power. This is the process of "holy fermentation" in people, which transforms and equips them to carry out God's will.

The new wine will not fit into people or wineskins that have lost their flexibility to cooperate with the Holy Spirit. Like wineskins, people who are not open and flexible to the Holy Spirit and the disruptions that He causes in transforming their lives, and carrying out Jesus' plan through His church, will burst open like inflexible wineskins and the wine of the Holy Spirit will be lost.

The Holy Spirit causes a "holy dissatisfaction" with traditions which block the freedom of the Holy Spirit. This "holy dissatisfaction" can be satisfied only when the person who has been baptized in the Holy Spirit is free to live and worship freely using the gifts in ministry.

When people become born again Christians, it means that they have become new wineskins, flexible and ready to be filled with the new wine of the Holy Spirit through the baptism of the Holy Spirit. However, it is surprising how quickly even new wineskins can become old wineskins if they are not quickly filled with the Holy Spirit. For, as Jesus cautioned, such people will remember their old ineffective and unsatisfying ways of serving and worshipping God and will wistfully say, *"The old is better"* (Luke 5:39). They are reluctant to change from their traditional religious habits and try the true Gospel. They will either go back to their old ways or they may try to combine the old and the new in an ineffective and inoffensive way so that they conform to the world.

For those who dare to grow in Jesus, it takes time, practice, and encouragement from pastors and fellow Christians, as well as cooperation with the Holy Spirit in order to learn how to use the gifts of the Holy Spirit skillfully. When Christians first receive any of the gifts, they typically experience much anxiety, apprehension, perspiration and risk-taking as they agonize in their attempts to use the gifts publicly in obedience to the Holy Spirit. No matter whether in worship services, Bible study meetings, prayer meetings, fellowship meetings, house meetings, cell groups or any other kind of meeting, they have an excitement, an expectation, that the Holy Spirit might want to give a demonstration of the presence of God for whatever His purpose.

Using the gifts does not happen automatically or naturally. Most people are uncomfortable with the gifts until they learn how to use them. Even gifts such as tongues attempted all alone in the privacy of one's own home can be an agonizingly new experience in discovering a new and sometimes threatening intimacy with the Holy Spirit.

To learn to use the charismatic gifts publicly in worship, small groups, or ministry requires all of the heart, soul, strength, and mind. That is why Paul appeals to us, *"to present your bodies as a living sacrifice, holy and acceptable, to God"* (Romans 12:1). That is what we do — we present our bodies as living sacrifices — when we use the gifts of the Holy Spirit under His guidance.

Thus, cooperation in the transformation process requires one to be a sacrifice on the public altar of criticism;

vulnerable to rejection from people who do not accept, receive, recognize, or discern that the gifts truly are to be used in worship. Transformation involves willingness to lay down one's pride before those who will deny that the gifts are from the Holy Spirit, but who claim that they come from a person's self, vain imagination, or perhaps even that they are from the Devil or an evil spirit.

Verbal abuse, accusations and rejection from these Christians who are offended by the use of the gifts of the Spirit are routinely heaped upon those who try to be obedient to His leading. Some gifted Christians persist in spite of the criticism. Others conform and stop using their gifts because they can't take the pressure.

Those who persevere and learn to use their gifts skillfully and cooperatively under the guidance of the Holy Spirit experience lives which are never dull or boring but are full and exciting. Their daily living and their Church worship resemble the Book of Acts and Paul's letters. They fly free of the cocoon, soaring as butterflies in the "normal Christian life."

Breaking Free

Paul used the term, *"renewal of your mind,"* because cooperation with the Holy Spirit requires an alert, willing, determined, obedient mind. When the Holy Spirit prompts, tells, guides, or somehow indicates to a Spirit-filled Christian that He wants that person to use one of the gifts, it takes a willing and obedient mind to say, "Yes, Holy Spirit, I'll use my gift as You direct me, regardless of the criticism that I may receive."

There are few churches in Canada and the United States, let alone in other countries, where Spirit-filled Christians are welcome and encouraged to use their gifts as Paul directed. It is a tragic scene. That is why there are so few truly "full-Gospel" or "Spirit-filled" churches.

It is the Holy Spirit's purpose to transform God's people by the renewal of their minds so that they will not be *"conformed to this world"* but will *"prove what is the will of God, what is good and acceptable and perfect."* It was never Jesus' purpose that His church should conform to the world — but that it should *transform* the world in the manner of the first century Christians of whom it was said, *"These men who have turned the world upside down have come here also"* (Acts 17:6).

The Holy Spirit needs our cooperation to effect genuine transformation. Whenever we see an area where one of the works of the flesh is affecting us, we usually try our best to get control of our life in that area. We pray. We read the Bible looking for a way to handle the problem. We try to control ourselves, but the more we try to stop a bad habit or sin, the worse it becomes, until it threatens to drive us to distraction.

There is a natural principle which says that the more time and energy one puts into trying to change a habit or characteristic, the stronger it will become. Most people have experienced Paul's desperation in saying, *"I can will what is right, but I cannot do it. For I do not do the good I want, but the evil I do not want is what I do. Now if I do what I do not want, it is no longer I that do it, but sin which dwells within me"* (Romans 7:18–20). He expresses the frustration of each of us when he cries, *"Wretched man that I am! Who will deliver me from this body of death?"* (Romans 7:24). Under the old traditions of legalistic holiness, there was no hope, only frustration and failure.

But we can break free! *"Thanks be to God through Jesus Christ our Lord"* (Romans 7:25). The answer lies in turning any offensive area over to Jesus Christ and letting the Holy Spirit make the change. When we tell Him what the problem is and give Him permission to make the change, transformation happens.

Cooperation in fellowship with Jesus is the key to holy growth. When we use the gifts of the Holy Spirit, He not only speaks through us in the Word of Knowledge, the Word of Wisdom, Tongues, Interpretation of Tongues, and Prophecy, but He also encourages us through the gifts of

Faith, Teaching, and Exhortation. He protects us with the gift of Discerning of spirits. He keeps us healthy with the gifts of Healing and meets our needs with the gift of Miracles. He supplies our needs through the gifts of Giving and Mercy. He helps our ministry through the gift of Administration and Serving.

Every time we use the gifts of the Holy Spirit, the Holy Spirit is changing us and making us more like Jesus, just as He does when we worship and pray.

In Romans 12:2, Paul directs,"*Do not be conformed to this world but be transformed by the renewal of your mind, that you may prove what is good and acceptable and perfect*". According to him, every time we use a gift of the Holy Spirit, we are not allowing ourselves to be conformed to this world but we are being transformed by the renewing of our minds. In this way, we prove what is the will of God, what is good and acceptable and perfect. Thus, if a Christian has the gift of Prophecy, every time it is used, he or she is being transformed by the renewing of the mind and is not being conformed to this world. More than that, those who hear the prophecy are receiving a convincing demonstration of the Holy Spirit and power. The listeners know they are truly hearing from God.

Thus, if a Christian has the gift of Service (Romans 12:7) by using it, he or she is not being conformed to this world, but is being transformed by the renewal of his or her mind. In the same way, if a believer has the gift of Teaching (Romans 12:7) every time that believer uses it, he or she is not being conformed to this world but is being transformed.

Of course the same is to be said about the use of all of the other gifts of the Holy Spirit. Their use transforms both the users and those who see and hear and experience the gifts in operation.

The opposite is also true. Every time Spirit-filled Christians do not use the gifts of the Holy Spirit when prompted to do so, they are being conformed to this world and are missing out on being transformed by the renewal of their minds. Nor are other people's lives being transformed. Worse yet, they are not presenting their bodies as living sacrifices and are thus not holy and acceptable to God, a condition causing them to miss out on their spiritual worship.

The more cocoon time that we spend with Jesus, enjoying Him, the more we can be changed.

The more cocoon time we spend in an exciting relationship with the Holy Spirit, the more we can be changed.

The more cocoon time we spend basking in the love of the Heavenly Father, the more we are changed and strengthened to break free.

Flying Free

It is by cooperating with the Holy Spirit, and not conforming to the world in the midst of our worship, that He is able to transform Christians to *"Let love be genuine; hate what is evil, hold fast to what is good; love one another with brotherly affection; outdo one another in showing honour"* (Romans 12:9,10). Then they shall *"Never flag in zeal, be aglow with the Spirit, serve the Lord. Rejoice in your hope, be patient in tribulation, be constant in prayer. Contribute to the needs of the saints, practice hospitality"* (Romans 12:11) and do all the other things that Paul encourages Christians to do. Then they will know the *"joy of the Lord"* which nobody can take from them (John 16:22) and *"the peace of God which passes all understanding will keep their hearts and minds in Christ Jesus"* (Philippians 4:7).

Then we shall be *"a chosen race, a royal priesthood, a holy nation, God's own people"* (1 Peter 2:9). We are holy people not because of what we do, but because of the transformation God has wrought in us.

Life as a Butterfly — Understanding True Holiness

"You, therefore, must be perfect, as your heavenly Father is perfect" (Matthew 5:48). To many, this Scripture is almost laughable. Perfection, the way we define "holiness," appears to us to be a totally unattainable state. However,

it's not impossible in the way that God means perfect. It had to be attainable if Jesus said that we needed to be that way.

The Greek word that is translated "perfect" does not mean perfect in the sense of never sinning or doing anything wrong. It means *"to bring to an end, finish, complete something; to carry out, accomplish, perform, fulfill, keep something; the end or goal of something"* ("A Comprehensive Dictionary," W.E.Vine).

This means that to attain perfection in the Greek sense of the word, simply means to accomplish the purpose for which we were born, saved, born again, baptized in the Holy Spirit, and gifted by the Holy Spirit. It means to allow God to make the necessary changes in us that will make it possible for us to accomplish our purpose. It means to allow the Holy Spirit to make us like Jesus.

The mistake most of us make is that we equate holiness with never making any mistakes. We look at moral standards and laws and try to teach people into holiness. We read the Bible and then go out and try to live according to its teachings and think that is how holiness is achieved.

I had a music director in one of my churches who, after reading the Sermon on the Mount, decided that she was going to live that way. A few months later, she suffered a complete emotional breakdown. She thought that all she had to do was read the rules and follow them and she would become healthy and holy.

That is not how it works. We have to learn how to cooperate with the Holy Spirit. He is the one who will make the changes in us. As we yield our hearts, which are the control centers of our lives, He changes our minds and "reprograms" us with God's new life in Christ.

What this means, in terms of practical application, is that where a person has been trying to stop swearing, for instance, but lacks the will-power to be successful, the Holy Spirit can give that person a "spiritual mouth wash" by which he can suddenly stop swearing.

Another common trouble spot is relationships.

Traditionally, the concept of holiness rejected any mention of divorce, in spite of the reality that marriages were breaking up. Biblical holiness, on the other hand, implies the renewal of love as the husband and wife are changed by the Holy Spirit. The sanctity of the marriage is established by cooperating with the Holy Spirit by using his gifts and spending time serving and worshipping God.

Traditional holiness categorically presented the Bible as a rule book, which made it impossible to serve God and be happy. Every time a person tried to live by the commandments, he failed miserably. On the other hand, true holiness gives an added dimension to reading and studying the Bible. Something dynamic happens when we read it. The words direct us to Jesus and encourage our relationship with Him.

"You search the Scripture, because you think that in them you have eternal life; and it is they that bear witness to Me; yet you refuse to come to Me that you may have life" (John 5:39–40). It is the time spent with Jesus that makes a person holy and acceptable. He is the one who changes us. Because the Bible has a dynamic power built into it, Paul tells us that we can experience *"the washing of water with the Word"* (Ephesians 5:26). It is by this washing by the Word (the Scripture), that we are made clean and fit for Holy use. After receiving the baptism in the Holy Spirit, Bible study becomes no longer a chore, but is exciting. Fresh discoveries lead to the recurring question: "Why didn't I ever see that before?"

Flying Grace-fully

Holiness comes through a process of what I call "grace-perfection." It means a life of constant forgiving of sin on our part, just as there is a constant forgiving of sin on God's part.

I am living in grace-perfection when I seek forgiveness every day, accept it, and go about my Heavenly Father's business. It means that whenever we recognize an area of sin, or failure, we confess it, repent of it, and give the Holy Spirit permission to remove it and replace it with the fruit of the Holy Spirit. This grace-perfection gives the credit to God for all of the changes in our lives and not to us, *"lest any man should boast for we are His workmanship, created in Christ Jesus for good works, which God prepared beforehand, that we should walk in them"* (Ephesians 2:8–10). It leaves no room for anyone but Jesus Christ to get the credit.

In the process of holiness, prayer becomes a time to enjoy God's presence and abide or rest in Him. It becomes a time when we share what is on our minds and we listen to Him. Gradually, we grow to the place where spending time in the presence of the Lord, enjoying Him, becomes more important than getting our prayers answered. We look for excuses to be with Him. It becomes a time when *"mysteries"* (1 Corinthians 14: 2) are spoken and a beautiful intimacy with God grows.

Thus, the "new holiness" of the New Testament is not just not sinning. It is spending time with Jesus, in the power of the Holy Spirit. It is living in the presence of the Heavenly Father which takes us through the metamorphosis from an awkward, disobedient, ugly sinner into a born-again, beautiful, grace-full, obedient believer!

Bibliography

Bibles

"Biblia Hebraica", Ed. Rud. Kittel, The American Bible Society, Wurttembergische Bibolanstalt Stuttgart, 1963.

"The Greek New Testament," The United Bible Societies, 1975, West Germany, 1975.

"The Holy Bible," King James Version,
The World Publishing Company, Cleveland, Ohio, 1945.

"The Holy Bible," Harper Study Bible,
Revised Standard Version, Zondervan Bible Publishers, Grand Rapids, Michigan, 1976.

"The New International Study Bible," Zondervan Bible Publishers, Grand Rapids, Michigan, 1985.

Lexicons

"A Greek-English Lexicon of the New Testament and Other Early Christian Literature,"
Wm. F. Arndt and F. Wilbur Gingrich, the University of Chicago, Chicago, Illinois, 1957.

"Hebrew and English Lexicon of the Old Testament,"
F. Brown, S.R. Driver and C.A. Briggs, Oxford University Press, London, 1962.

References

"A Grammatical Analysis of the Greek New Testament," M. Zerwick and Mary Grosvenor, Biblical Institute Press, Rome, 1981.

"Synonyms of the Old Testament," Rev. R.B. Girdlestone, Wm. B. Berdmane Publishing Company, Grand Rapids, Michigan, Reproduction 1897.

"The Acts of the Apostles," The Daily Bible Study, William Barclay, The Saint Andrew Press, Edinburgh,1961.

"The Letters to the Corinthians," The Daily Bible Study, William Barclay, The Saint Andrew Press, Edinburgh, 1961.

"The Letters to the Galatians and the Ephesians," The Daily Bible Study, William Barclay, The Saint Andrew Press, Edinburgh, 1961.

"The Epistle to the Galatians," The International Critical Commentary, E. DeWitt Burton, T. & T. Clark, Edinburgh, 1962.

"The First Epistle of St. Paul to the Corinthians," The International Critical Commentary, E. DeWitt Burton, T.&T. Clark, Edinburgh, 1962.

"The First Epistle of St. Paul to the Corinthians," The International Critical Commentary, A. Robertson & Alfred Plummer, T.& T. Clark, Edinburgh, 1967.

"A Comprehensive Dictionary," W.E.Vine, MacDonald Publishing Company, McLean, Virginia.

"The Screwtape Letters," C.S. Lewis, MacMillan Company, New York, 1976, 1994.

Concordances

Nelson's Complete Concordance of the Revised Standard Bible, Ed. John W Ellison, Thomas Nelson & Sons, New York, 1957.

Concordance to the Greek New Testament, Ed. by W.F. Moulton & A. S. Geden & H.K. Moulton, T.&T. Clark, Edinburgh, 1963.

The Exhaustive Concordance of the Bible, James Strong, Abingdon Press, New York, 1980.

Notes

[1] Note: see more on this phenomenon in Chapter 7 under "The Gift of Miracles."
[2] *George Whitfield* by Arnold Dallimore, "Signs & Wonders," 320-331.
[3] *Brother Against Brother, The War Begins,* Ed. Wm. C. Davis, 21.
[4] *Webster's New World Dictionary,* College Edition, Nelson, Foster & Scott, Ltd., p. 1168.
[5] *The Screwtape Letters,* C.S. Lewis, MacMillan Company, New York, 1976, 1994.
[6] *Vine's Expository Dictionary of Old and New Testament Words.*

Books, Audio Cassettes, and Videos

Like a Rushing Mighty Wind **Prices include shipping and handling.**

by Rev. Gordon Williams with Diane Roblin Lee

Book: $20.00 donation (3 for $50.) Quantity______ Total ________

The Testimony of Gordon Williams

Making Yourself Available to Jesus Christ

Video: $20.00 donation (3 for $50.) Quantity______ Total ________

Audio Cassette: $10.00 donation (3 for $25.) Quantity______ Total ________

The Baptism & Gifts of the Holy Spirit

Using the Spiritual Gifts Skillfully

Video: $20.00 donation (3 for $50.) Quantity______ Total ________

Audio Cassette: $10.00 donation (3 for $25.) Quantity______ Total ________

From Caterpillar to Butterfly

The Key to Christian Maturity

Video: $20.00 donation (3 for $50.) Quantity______ Total ________

Audio Cassette: $10.00 donation (3 for $25.) Quantity______ Total ________

Generational Curses-Gone Forever Quantity______ Total ________

Exciting Praise! Quantity______ Total ________

Booklets: ea. $8.00 donation

The Answer by Lifeline Music Ministry featuring Margaret Williams

Music Cassette: $10.00 donation (3 for $25.) Quantity______ Total ________

Music CD: $15.00 donation (3 for $50.) Quantity______ Total ________

Water and Fire by Lifeline Music Ministry featuring Margaret Williams

Music CD: $15.00 donation (3 for $50.) Quantity______ Total ________

Please send to: **TOTAL** ____________

Gordon Williams Evangelistic Association or G.W.E.A.

11 Bayberry Rd., Orangeville, ON, Canada L9V 1A1

Name	
Address	
City	Prov./State
Country	Postal/ZIP

To book evangelistic meetings and crusades,
please phone or fax

The Gordon Williams Evangelistic Association Office:
519-940-9197

11 Bayberry Road
Orangeville, Ontario
Canada L9V 1A1